"*The Divine Art of Dying* is a magnificent achievement. Beautifully written, it is a moving and inspiring book about taking control of your life as it starts to come to a close."

    — Will Schwalbe, author of the *New York Times* bestselling *The End of Your Life Book Club*

"This book is like wise hands extended to those dealing with death. Speerstra shares the skillful means and open heart necessary to survive the common miracle of death with a grace we might call divine."

    — Stephen and Ondrea Levine, authors of *Who Dies?: An Investigation of Conscious Living and Conscious Dying*

"A profound and practical guide to the art of living well while dying and of helping others do the same. Both authors are compassionate and skillful guides into another country."

    — Mary Pipher, author of *Another Country* and *The Green Boat*

"Fortunately, one can now take life's final exam with an open book and the answer to mortality's question can be found within the pages of *The Divine Art of Dying*. How then shall we live? Fully. Intentionally. Attentively. Lovingly."

    — Ira Byock, MD, bestselling author of *Dying Well: Peace and Possibilities at the End of Life*

"*The Divine Art of Dying*, like the ancient *Tibetan Book of the Dead*, is a wise and compassionate guide to how we may travel the last stage of the human journey with grace. It will be in my knapsack when I traverse that 'unknown country from which no traveler returns.'"

    — Sam Keen, lecturer and author of the classic book *Fire in the Belly* and *In the Absence of God: Dwelling in the Presence of the Sacred*

"This incredibly eyes-wide-open comforting and informative and inspiring guidebook recasts anticipation of imminent death into an awakened celebration of life for the dying person and her or his companions. I feel the wiser for having read it. An important book for everyone in the family of life!"

    — Sylvia Boorstein, author of *Happiness is An Inside Job: Practicing for a Joyful Life*

"This book does a great service by taking us to and through the point at which death is no longer an abstraction. From concrete suggestions for caregivers to the ramifications of mundane decisions, such as getting a chair for the shower, to spiritual questions, the authors give us hope. As Karen Speerstra writes, 'All this is not easy, but it is, at some mysterious level, profound.'"

    — Sheila Himmel, coauthor of *Changing the Way We Die: Compassionate End-of-Life Care and the Hospice Movement*

"Every aspect of life holds the possibility of an experience with the divine: birth, youth, marriage, middle age, and, according to Karen Speerstra and Herbert Anderson, even death. Or to be more precise, particularly death. *The Divine Art of Dying* is a book filled with hope, about an area where we often see no hope."

    — William R. White, author of *In Over Our Heads: Meditations on Grace*

"In this wise, compassionate, and deeply sensitive new work, Karen Speerstra and Herbert Anderson succeed at framing death not as an intruder to be feared but as a natural — even beautiful — part of what it means to be human. To anyone engaged in the end of life, *The Divine Art of Dying* is unforgettable and essential reading."

    — Mark Glubke, LPC, grief counselor, Kalamazoo, Michigan

"In my work in hospice and experience of my own life, I have learned that when we are open to living and dying consciously, more awake and aware, the grace and gifts are astounding. In *The Divine Art of Dying*, Karen and Herbert invite readers into that grace. Blessed be the invitation they are extending."

    — Sarah Johnson, former hospice nurse and chaplain; leadership consultant

"*The Divine Art of Dying* is an amazing project. Filled with powerful, 'transparent' imagery, Ms. Speerstra's journal reflections are remarkably insightful, a testament to an articulate, honest, and spiritual woman. It will touch many, many lives — living and dying — with grace and wisdom, just as it has mine."

    — James Warnock, BCC, palliative care chaplain, Napa Hospital, Napa, California

"This is a book that needed to be written. It is a deep well of spiritual support for those at the end of life as well as the people who love and care for them, filled with compassion and the authentic wisdom that comes from living with the reality of impending death. We can all benefit from this truth-telling about dying gracefully when our time comes."

    — Gretchen Brauer-Rieke, certified Advance Care Planning facilitator, Portland, Oregon

"I was particularly grateful to be reminded of the paradox and ambiguity inherent in preparing for death and think that many people could be greatly comforted by having that articulated."

    — Louise Kaye, retired gerontology physician, Sydney, Australia

"The text, both the scholarly and the anecdotal, reads as a 'buffet' of information for the voracious reader anxious to be fed. This is a rich book that does not try to replicate any of the great texts on death but shows a respect for them."

    — Sally Thomas, former hospice nurse; spiritual director trainee, Denver, Colorado

"Speerstra and Anderson have deftly done what few manage — coauthor a book that integrates personal experience with solid research and sound theological reflection in a cohesive and compassionate guide for others to explore the choices that come with end-of-life decisions. It is neither prescriptive nor capricious; rather, it preserves space for authentic soul-searching. Theirs is a courageous offering to others who find themselves in the crucible of life-limiting illness."

> — The Very Reverend Dr. Steven L. Thomason, MD, Dean and Rector,
> Saint Mark's Episcopal Cathedral, Seattle, Washington

"Karen and Herb's book gives us all both a practical and spiritual guide to the process of living as we are dying. They define the considerations needed as we move into final stages of our lives — considerations that outline our wishes and relieve family members of difficult decisions as our death approaches. *And* as they outline those considerations, they gently explore the emotional and spiritual mysteries that accompany approaching our death."

> — Penny Hauser, psychiatric nurse (ret.), Las Vegas, Nevada

"By flipping the death paradigm from one of failure and loss to one of natural inevitability, Speerstra and Anderson prep the reader to do the necessary and empowering work needed to achieve a good death in America."

> — Dr. Jessica Nutik Zitter, palliative care physician; frequent contributor to
> the *San Francisco Chronicle* and *New York Times*; author of forthcoming book on
> end-of-life issues

"For me, an avid rower and sculler, the cover image of a small boat carrying us on our own particular journey (sometimes journalized) of life and dying is particularly evocative. The combined voices of the coauthors provide a remarkably insightful and touching book, including a final textual glimpse of the symbolic boat at the ending. This book should be welcomed by all of us as we anticipate our own dying — and for those of us as clinicians, clergy, hospice staff, and family members who will be energized by its reading."

> — E. K. Rynearson MD, Clinical Professor of Psychiatry, University of Washington

"Our interfaith hospice choir has been singing music of comfort in hospice settings multiple times each week since 2008. *The Divine Art of Dying* is a grace-filled balance of direct, honest, personal testimony and insightful spiritual observations on the process of living and dying. It will be wonderful accompaniment to our singing for patients and their families in their end-of-life situations."

> — Lynne and Paul Rahmeier, Sounds of Grace (www.soundsofgrace.org),
> Winchester, Massachusetts

"Through soul-baring reflections and thoughtful analysis, this book dives into the sacred depths of the dying experience with subtlety and grace. A widely accessible resource for anyone facing end-of-life issues and the messy, terrible, ambiguous, and wondrous aspects of the dying process. I am deeply grateful for the kind of courage and love it takes to bring a book like this to life."

— Heather Isaacs, M.Div. hospice chaplain, Napa, California

"I too want to live well through it all, and this blessed — even mystical — gift shows me how it can be done with class, peace, and joy."

— Jim Fish, Lutheran pastor, Santa Rosa, California

"When my time comes to die, Karen and Herbert's book will be my guide to conscious dying. The intimacy of her journals interwoven with a wealth of wisdom from many spiritual traditions invites us to the Divine Art of Living as much as the Divine Art of Dying."

— Sharon Bauer, psychotherapist, Waltham, Massachusetts

"*The Divine Art of Dying*, Karen Speerstra's final earthly gift to us, is a how-to in the face of the myriad end-of-life factors all of us eventually confront. This richly moving glimpse into her soul and heart gives us a loving, humanly enriching word-portrait of a remarkable dying woman, and is a true memorial to the vitality of her earthly life in our parish. It is a blessing worthy of our eternal thanksgiving."

— Joanna Gillespie, PhD, independent scholar, Rochester, Vermont

"Like old friends, Karen and Herbert share stories and reflections with the reader that gently guide without imposing answers or solutions. This joyful book uniquely combines memoir, metaphysical insights, facts about palliative care and hospice, and practical tidbits for people living with a life-limiting illness and their caregivers. I will return to this book again and again over the years to draw from its deep well of meaning and authenticity."

— Jennifer Reidy, MD, Co-chief, Division of Palliative Care, UMass Memorial Health Care, Worcester, Massachusetts

"Because I knew her, every word that Karen has written in this book holds something sacred for me. And yet, the true and lasting gift of this book is that every word written by Karen and Herbert will offer the reader something sacred and helpful as they journey toward their own death or that of a loved one. Karen, this is one last beautiful gift you have given me and so many others. Thank you!"

— The Right Reverend Thomas C. Ely, Episcopal Bishop of Vermont

THE DIVINE ART *of* DYING

How to Live Well While Dying

KAREN SPEERSTRA + HERBERT ANDERSON

Foreword by Ira Byock, MD

Published by DIVINE ARTS

DivineArtsMedia.com

An imprint of Michael Wiese Productions

12400 Ventura Blvd. # 1111

Studio City, CA 91604

(818) 379-8799, (818) 986-3408 (Fax)

www.mwp.com

Cover design by Johnny Ink www.johnnyink.com

Cover image "Means of Egress" by Laura Baring-Gould

Copyediting by Gary Sunshine

Book layout by Gina Mansfield Design

Printed by McNaughton & Gunn, Inc., Saline, Michigan

Manufactured in the United States of America

Library of Congress Cataloging-in-Publication Data

Speerstra, Karen.
 The divine art of dying / Karen Speerstra + Herbert Anderson ; foreword by
Ira Byock, MD.
     pages cm
 Includes index.
 ISBN 978-1-61125-023-7
 1. Death--Religious aspects. 2. Death. I. Title.
 BL504.S66 2014
 202'.3--dc23
                                   2013047709

Printed on Recycled Stock

Table of Contents

Foreword

Mortality can teach us a lot about life. If only we'd let it. Of course, most of us don't let it. Our reticence to learn from mortality is understandable. We were raised and live in a death-defying culture. Many of us shudder in recalling the deaths of people we knew, wince at the thought of those we love eventually dying, and keep our own death a distant abstraction.

This deep-seated aversion is natural and, for the most part, healthy. After all, life is precious and finite. We wisely do whatever we can to preserve it. We don't smoke. Avoid excess fats, salt, and preservatives in our diet. Wear seat belts. Check for lumps. Submit to screening and probing of our intimate parts.

I do.

Yet in addition to the preventive value of these health behaviors, they serve as modern rituals that protect our psyches from the anxieties of contemplating death. In distancing us from the ever-present mortal backdrop of life, we miss what death has to teach us.

Mortality is a harsh teacher. The first lesson it delivers is that death is inevitable. It will happen to you. It will happen to me. The final exam it gives entails just one question: How then shall we live?

Remarkably, I read the answer in this book.

The Divine Art of Dying eludes categories contributing to the literatures of memoirs, psychology, philosophy, and spirituality. Karen's unblinking observations and soulful reflections comprise a rare addition to our cultural mosaic: a closely examined life through illness and dying.

While most seriously ill people eschew close inspection and introspection, Karen pushes nothing away. Recognizing that her life was ebbing, something she could not change, Karen courageously turned to face death directly. She did not give up nor give in. Instead she chose to creatively live her mortal life fully. Her stance is at once life-affirming and defiant: Death will not rob her of life, until it does. She accepts the hard realities and is grateful for common pleasures and tender mercies. Her voice carries no hint of anger or admonition, nor is it ever saccharine.

Years ago, a person living with advanced cancer described to me feeling that contemplating death was akin to staring at his brightly lit face in a magnifying mirror. The normally smooth texture of his skin was full of disturbing imperfections. As he kept looking closely the psychic makeup dissolved and his reasonably pleasing face disintegrated into frighteningly motley parts.

The threat of death turns a magnifying mirror on one's "self" — what psychologists would call one's ego — and shines a glaringly surreal light on what we see. The resulting close inspection can dissolve the illusion of stability, security, and any confidence in the future, giving rise to existential terror — like vertigo at the ledge of an abyss — the danger of falling into limitless darkness. No future. No hope.

Karen's experience reveals that the abyss and sense of impending disintegration are as illusory as the stability and security that preceded illness. Instead of shrinking from death, she expands to absorb it. Instead of letting it disintegrate her, she integrates the fact of death within her changing worldview and healthy sense of self.

Her reality evinces the full extent of our shared human potential. It is possible to learn to fall. It is possible for us to grieve the loss of what was, and let go; changing in hitherto unthinkable ways, becoming unrecognizable to our selves, feeling naked and vulnerable, and yet, becoming fully alive in this moment. Each moment.

This is the marvelous paradox of well-being. While some people suffer horribly despite normally functioning organ systems, others express feeling healthy despite the discomforts and disabilities of incurable diseases. Some people express a sense of well-being through the very end of life. *Dying well* is not as oxymoronic as it first sounds. After all, human beings are only partly physical. *Being human* entails core emotional, social, and spiritual dimensions of experience. *Feeling well* as one dies may be the pinnacle of human potential.

The process of living attentively and intentionally through the course of incurable illness entails a succession of "letting go's" as parts of our selves no longer fit. The tasks of completing a life involve turning over responsibilities and relinquishing roles, grieving the loss of habits and pastimes, saying good-bye to friends, relatives, and lovers. As hard and unwanted as it may be, the process of letting go can lighten without destroying a person. A person may become less dense without disintegrating. In growing through a progressive, incurable condition, it is possible for people to remain whole even as they dissolve from life.

Mortality teaches clinicians that there is more to doctoring than diagnosing and treating injuries and diseases, more even than saving lives. Mastery of physiological, pathological, and pharmacological knowledge and expertise is essential, but insufficient. Science only becomes medicine when it is applied with caring intention to promote the well-being of people — mortal people.

Reading *The Divine Art of Dying* as a palliative care physician, I was reminded that beyond skillful alleviation of symptoms and suffering, the highest clinical goal is helping a person to feel well through the very end of life.

Real doctoring involves commitment, loving intention, full attention, and a willingness to listen with one's heart open, despite empathy's emotional toll.

I hope people savor *The Divine Art of Dying*. Like a delectable, patiently simmered bisque from loving chefs, it is rich with wisdom, spiced with morsels from philosophers, theologians, artists, essayists, novelists, playwrights, and poets, and generously sprinkled with insights from ordinary people living through the extraordinary personal experience of dying.

Fortunately, one can take life's final exam with an open book and the answer to mortality's question can be found within the pages of *The Divine Art of Dying*.

How then shall we live?

Fully.

Intentionally.

Attentively.

Lovingly.

Ira Byock, MD
Missoula, Montana
October 2013

xiii

Introduction

The Divine Art of Dying looks at that unique moment when a person turns toward death and acknowledges his or her own mortality. It's the point at which they know that at some time soon they will, as the fourteenth-century Dominican spiritual thinker Meister Eckhart put it, sink into the "naught of the Divine."

We have deliberately chosen not to write another end-of-life book, for there are a plethora of those available. Instead, we seek to address an earlier moment in time that we call *a moment of blessed recognition*. Some call it "the fitting moment." Or "the act of consciously dying." This moment comes at various times for each of us. Whenever it comes, it's usually the point at which death is no longer an abstract concept. This book seeks to rewrite the old cliché "I want to live until I die" and make it "I recognize I can choose to live fully, sometimes sadly, but often joyously and with great gratitude, for as long as I can."

We teamed up to write this book in order to help people who are irreversibly ill (along with their friends and family) navigate the perilous journey to the point at which one decides to discontinue curative treatment and turn toward death. This author team combines Herbert's years of teaching, writing, and lecturing on death and dying and bereavement with Karen's writing and experiential insights.

Physicians have always been called upon to relieve pain. Therefore, the phrase *palliative care* has been around for a long time. However, in our more complex medical world, the term has now taken on a more specialized meaning. It indicates more of a team approach to working with the family doctor in order to improve the quality of life for both the patient and the family. Palliative care focuses on symptoms such as pain, shortness of breath, fatigue, constipation, nausea, loss of appetite, or difficulty sleeping. The team also helps navigate our complex medical scene as well as make informed treatment choices. Palliative care can offer professional support in making earlier medical decisions. It can be desirable socially and spiritually to make earlier decisions about dying. However, just because these decisions come sooner doesn't mean making them is any easier. We hope you'll find within these pages helpful ways to deal and cope with, face, and grow from what will be, without a doubt, very difficult times.

Once the decision has been made by people who are now dealing with death "up close and personal," many, such as Karen has done, will come to the realization that they can still live fully until they die. We might call this the *Divine Art of Understanding*. And we believe each of us has this capacity. We just need to be reminded of it. But it's more than dying well. It's about how we might die in love. Or, playfully putting it another way: how might we love to die. We realize, however, that not everyone has Karen's background and many are angry and fearful, disappointed and anxious. This book speaks to those emotions as well.

By coupling the words *dying* with *divine* and *art*, we imply that dying is not technology driven, but instead holds the possibility of being as God-filled, loving, and as sacred as being born. Dying, just as any other point during our lives, can be an integrative event, rather than a splintering one. We don't negate the fact that it will be lonely, for we all finally do it alone. But by framing death and dying as a divine art, we hope to paint a picture of integrative wholeness that we all very humanly and naturally encounter at the end of our lives. It holds the potential to be both sad and joyous. It's not something to be denied or feared but to be embraced and loved, as all of life can and ought to be.

We believe dying is more about telling stories than going through stages, because these stages, even those so eloquently stated by Elisabeth Kübler-Ross, are not necessarily neatly linear. Dying, like living, is a movable feast of choices and responses to circumstances. The poet T. S. Eliot once observed that there are two possible responses in life to every situation: "What are we going to do about it?" and "How shall we behave toward this situation?"

The generosity of stories interspersed throughout the book offers new ways to hold and frame one's end times and all the various situations that poses. These stories speak to the abundance of insights people have gleaned by being awake and aware as they ponder dying. We call attention to celebrating humor and the ordinariness of life. We enjoy all the little things; the small but very meaningful moments during this time of passage. And we draw attention to how we can trust the grace and gifts of strangers who come to the dying person at this time.

This, then, is a book about making choices, thinking in advance about how we might behave toward this situation of dying and deciding what we're going to do about it. It's about how we live with and care for those we love, including ourselves.

Part I, "Taking the Turn Toward Death," explores how we might responsibly decide to forgo further medical treatment and what that might mean. Because of the promises of medical technology we find ourselves awash in decision-making and trying to figure things out. That moment to turn toward death rather than away can happen at any time and, most certainly, at different times according to how and when people make various responsible decisions.

Part 2, "Orienting Toward Death," presents a discussion of how we move back and forth on this journey, experiencing ambiguity and paradox, chaos and trust, and how we wait for things to happen. The dying person holding the death-compass continues to adjust her course. Anyone who participates in the sport of orienteering knows that it's important to hone one's navigational skills. We may hold some maps, we may have a GPS, or we may devise and chart our own plans. However we decide to travel from point to point, each one of us begins our human life journey at birth and at some stage in our lives, we know, deep down, that there will be an ending to this life. Our job now is to better understand and explore this amazing journey.

In Part 3, "Living Until We Die," we seek to celebrate and uphold everyone participating in this amazing process. After making her decision to stop treatment, Karen discovered she was free to live with more acuity, more vigor, and certainly with more urgency. She, as well as others, can learn to triage energy, time, thoughts, and language. This section gets into the hard work the dying must do. They don't have to do this work, of course, and many may choose not to undertake it, but if they do it is our intention to offer help.

Finally, Part 4, "Dying Into Life," looks more deeply at how we die into life. We discuss the art of letting go and we explore how last moments are marked, measured, and treasured. We look at grief and grieving, but more in the context of the person dying than those who will deal with their own grieving later. We discuss end-of-journey rituals and throughout we take a hard look at what people fear at this time, for we recognize that fear often stems from loss. Or from what we perceive we are losing.

Each chapter opens with an entry *From Karen's Hospice Journal.* Death remains abstract — something that happens to someone else — until, that is, it becomes very personal. These opening words offer the reader Karen's very personal views on what is happening to her and to her family and those around her. Both authors have experienced that moment of blessed recognition. For Karen, it came ten years after her first diagnosis of ovarian cancer. For Herbert, the moment came when he was diagnosed with prostate cancer, now successfully treated.

We've designed this book to address the possibility that facing one's death head-on may also be an opportune time for everyone concerned to explore his or her own spiritual agendas. We've decided to seriously think about what our virtues are now that we're discussing these moments of blessed recognition. Virtues make up our soulfulness — the essence of paradox because they're *in us* as well as *around us*. They're both human and divine. Virtues are both part of us now and part of the larger landscape through which we travel. The Greeks explored these morally excellent portions of who we are and called them the really good parts of us — the things that promote collective as well as individual greatness. Since they are already a part of us, they can't be taught, but they can be nurtured and named.

We tuck these little notes into sidebars and call them *Our Divine Human Virtues*. The first one you'll encounter is "faith." For Paul Tillich, a Lutheran theologian, faith is the experience of surrender to one's ultimate concern. Knowing what is "ultimate" in our lives is a lifelong quest and one certainly not to be abandoned at death. Having faith in ourselves, in our medical teams, in all those caregivers around us, and ultimately, for many, in a power beyond our weakened physical selves, enables us to begin to view death as a divine art.

If you've picked up this book, you may be someone who has already decided or you may need to decide or you may have had it decided for you that nothing more can or should be done to cure a disease. You may realize that further treatment will diminish the possibility of continuing to live fully until you die. Or, you may be a family member or a friend or a medical caregiver for someone who is dying. You, now, must concur with an individual's decision to suspend curative treatment. That's why every chapter ends with very practical suggestions *From the Caregiver's Guidebook*.

We need not fear death even though we do. We need not fear pain even though we do. Ira Byock, the widely recognized physician writing our Foreword, points out that pain can be dealt with more effectively because of new developments in palliative care.

We intend this book to be a spiritual resource supporting people who choose to take the turn toward death in order to live fully until they die. It is for anyone who wishes to know how to walk with someone toward death; how to listen carefully, advocate appropriately, avoid "fixing," and begin to live gracefully with the helplessness.

The support of a dedicated hospice team also makes it possible to live comfortably and peacefully at this juncture of life. There is still hard work to do letting things and dreams and people go. The dying will grieve for all we're leaving behind. Those who are gifted with time for living while dying have an amazing opportunity for quality conversations, joyous gift-giving, and deepening friendships as we love and are loved. We want this to be a book to inspire, to help and to offer courage to others who can intentionally choose, as Karen did, for our final passage to be as rich and as fulfilling as possible. Living while dying is our final human act — it's not a medical craft, but a Divine Art. We offer this book as a gentle and loving gift to you.

Karen Speerstra & Herbert Anderson

PART ONE

TAKING *the* TURN TOWARD DEATH

The Porch Light Is On

"When I thought I was learning to live,
I was also learning to die."

Leonardo da Vinci, *Codex Atlanticus*

ℵ *from* Karen's Hospice Journal ℟

Ever since my 2003 ovarian cancer diagnosis I've known that all the decisions I made going forward would be totally up to me. It has been that way since the beginning of our marriage. My husband, John, has always said that decisions about my body are my own. When I had to face the cancer music, I chose chemotherapy, with his blessing and total understanding. It kept me alive for ten years and we've never been sorry. Unlike so many other cancer patients, I was fortunate. I tolerated the treatment. Even after several remissions and re-entries, I had never been nauseous from the chemicals, but then, at the end of 2012, I noticed I was having a lot of problems. What once kept me alive was now destroying me.

I was not recovering between monthly infusion installments as I used to and one day I looked down and my fingernails were bleeding. A few days later they started to turn black and blue and they felt as if I'd slammed every one of them in some diabolical car door. What is this, some enhanced interrogation technique? Okay, Karen, I said to myself. If chemo is doing this visibly to your hands what's it doing to your insides? It's no wonder your stomach hurts! One day people will look back on this barbaric chemo treatment and ask, "What were we thinking?"

My tipping point came the day after Christmas, when we returned from visiting our old friend Herbert and his family in Connecticut. After a series of mishaps in a pelting snowstorm, we got stuck about fifty yards from our front door. It meant we had to walk the rest of the way uphill to the house. Fatigue piled up, like the snow lining our Vermont driveway. Doggedly following in my husband's tracks, I slowly trudged up the hill. I wanted desperately to curl up in the snow. "Hypothermia — please, just take me!" It was then and there I decided: no more chemo for me. I'm looking for some quality of life now — quantity be damned. "I want to get my snowshoes out again."

But when I told our older son, Joel, about my decision, he said, in a tone I rarely hear from him, "You made the decision to stop chemotherapy just because you couldn't walk through some snow up to the house?"

That question, with the heavy emphasis on the rising inflection of the final word "house?" sums up every family member's angst when the one who knows she is dying makes a decision with purpose rather than how it seems: on purpose. The subtext is: "You're doing this to us! How could you? Why wouldn't you keep on seeing more of those expert 'ologists'? Why not sign up for clinical trials? Surely there's something more that can be done." What is unspoken is: "We love you! We can't let you go!" and "If you really love us, you won't give up. You won't decide to leave!"

But I'm determined. I will consciously trade the treatment not only for more physical stamina, but also for what I hope will be a more wide-awake brain. I want to participate fully in my living until I die. And I want to be conscious enough to grasp some of the finer points of this whole mysterious "dying thing."

Following infusions, I felt as if I were being pulled into chemo-dementia. I found myself editing a piece of writing and suddenly I couldn't see the difference between "breath" and "breathe." Either seemed like a perfectly acceptable word so my brain stopped caring. This was not a happy place for an editorial mind like mine! And the chemicals accumulating in my system increased the neuropathy in all my fingers and toes so that my body seemed to be dying by inches from the outer extremities, in.

As I slogged through deep snow that post-Christmas night, I moved ever so slowly toward the porch light which cast a yellow glow across the snow-covered patio. I am home.

Going home. That's how so many have described dying. That is, at least, for the ones who came back and could later articulate and share with others their near-death experiences. "Why did I return? I liked it there. Why couldn't I stay?" So often the answer was: "It's not your time yet. You have more to do."

Since that snowy night I've often thought about the question we all ask ourselves from time to time: What's the purpose of all this? I seem to be drawn now to living and dying with purpose. Asking my journal that question in the wee hours of the morning, I write:

> *Perhaps your purpose now is to help others to be authentic and real. That's the way you can uphold your friends and loved ones. By encouraging real conversation, real dialogue, and to honor and to express: "This is where I am now and we may be at different spots in this continuum of life. And that's okay. It's a movable feast. Let's enjoy it!" The porch light is on!*

※ ※

A Blessed Recognition

The turn toward death is a decision to choose life, to live as fully as possible until the end, and to be an actor in living while dying. We like to call this moment a *blessed recognition*. Others may call it consciously dying. It's choosing to live until we die — with the emphasis on living. Taking this turn, then, becomes an authentic journey and a movable feast with unexpected detours and surprising opportunities for giving and receiving love and then giving it all away again. A headline in a recent church newspaper said: LIFE ABUNDANT ALL THE WAY TO THE END. Choosing to participate fully in living toward death can become a grace-filled time overflowing with new discoveries and love from unexpected sources.

Each individual comes to the moment when it is right to take this turn in his or her own way. For many, when a treatment no longer works, it's an opportunity to look at bigger and stronger treatments or additional alternatives. But for Karen, this first decision was obvious to her. The treatment was hurting more than helping. Nothing could change the reality that Karen would die from the illness she had successfully put off for ten years.

Sometimes it is less a choice than a startlingly cold realization that death is near. We simply need to decide how to act toward what has happened. Sudden, incapacitating illness like a heart attack or a stroke or rapid-onset cancer often means that some decision about continuing treatment will need to be made. For others, it may be that the medical team has tried one or more experimental procedures without benefit and they finally tell the patient and the family that they have exhausted all options. Or it may be that one family member returns home and encourages the rest of the family to decide to "let Mother die peacefully and without more interventions." That was what Daniel did.

We Have To Learn What Mom Wants
Herbert's acquaintance, Daniel

Dorothy, my mom, was fighting cancer. Despite the surgeon's dire predictions, they scheduled her surgery for November. She was eighty-two. Everyone pretended that she would live to ninety, as planned. So we collected every story we could find of people who had survived what she had — and there were many.

Mom was scared. Who wouldn't be? She hated what her illness was doing to her, but with great bravery she continued to fight cancer. By February she couldn't eat or drink. We were all there, beside ourselves, trying to hang on to our positive attitudes in the face of a very poor prognosis.

When I arrived from Boston (and I admit I hadn't seen Mom regularly as the others had) I knew something was wrong. "You can't do this," I said to my family. "We have to begin talking about the reality of what is happening. We have to learn what Mom wants. We can't continue to live in a dream world. We have to let Mom know that we can and will function without her. We must begin to let her know that when she is ready she can die."

I guess it was a persuasive speech because everybody began to talk with Mom about her death and tried to figure out how she wanted to die. As a result, we got to read piles of letters from women all around the world for whom Mom had been a role model. She lived long enough to hear from so many people. We were able to cry together and we grew stronger as a family because our mother had the courage to allow us to walk with her up to the moment of her death. And the funeral in our synagogue was a celebration of Mom's life, lived fully and openly and graciously up to the end.

Honoring Our Choices

The story of Dorothy's dying is a testimony to the incredibly rich and textured experience that is possible when the person who is gravely ill makes the decision to turn toward death. Dorothy could make that decision because someone in the family was willing to intervene and halt the family's fiction of endless treatment. There is, of course, no guarantee in advance that this journey with a loved dying person will be without pain and disappointment and misunderstanding and heartache. But, as with Dorothy's family, it could be honest and honesty deepens love.

Our Divine Human Virtue

FAITH

Faith is that unseen thing that you hope for; it's your inner companion when you're alone. It's an unearned gift that reminds you the Divine Source will uphold you long enough for you to accomplish what you set out to do. You are supported now by an assurance that in spite of how it may seem at times, the world really is a benevolent place with your best interests at heart. When we act in faith, Dag Hammarskjöld said, "miracles occur."

What is the right moment? How will we know when it is time to decide to terminate treatment? If we are anxious about making a wrong decision, we may never choose. In every moment of our lives, we make choices: to go here or there, to do this or that, or we determine how to hold or frame something. Positively or negatively. Productively or destructively. Do we wish to be filled with love or filled with fear? It's always our choice.

Minutes before Ireland's beloved poet and Nobel laureate Seamus Heaney died at seventy-four, he texted his wife: "*Noli Timere.*" "Don't be afraid."

Like anyone caught in a death-dealing disease, Karen had her moments of doubt and sadness during the ten years she lived with ovarian cancer, but they didn't last long. "I was too busy," she said, "and too focused and too preoccupied with other things. I tried not to let cancer define me. I told myself I was more than the disease. And even now I am still a living person much more than I am a dying person. And I constantly remind myself: 'Don't be afraid!'"

Being free to decide, however, depends in part on the willingness of family and medical practitioners to ascribe to an individual the capacity to be a decider. The dying person is free to exercise his or her autonomy in deciding and living toward death only if she or he is perceived to have the competence to decide, particularly by families and physicians. Whether and how people live until they die is partly determined by how much personal authority caregivers encourage them to take.

Two things are true. Life is irrevocable. We cannot give it back or trade it in for a different size once it is given. And choice is also irrevocable. We cannot *not* decide. And yet the meaning of life and the freedom to choose are shaped by birth and death and therefore limited. Some would say that the intention of the dying person is not the sole or even primary determinant. So autonomy is not an absolute. We live and die and make choices in the midst of meaningful communities and the constraints of insurance companies and government. Our freedom to decide is modified by ethnic customs, the culture we live in, and the families we are a part of. Despite these social factors that form us, we do still have the capacity to make choices. That's what makes us fully human.

Impediments to Deciding

It is not easy to decide to face death head-on. Karen's son Joel initially thought she needed a better reason than not wanting to trudge through any more snow. Her younger son, Nathan, once asked her whether or not she was a fighter. She said, "No. I accepted that my body is hosting errant cells and I don't know why. But I don't fight it. I accept that they are there and I've tried, with the help of my terrific medical team, to embrace what is and I decided to live as long and as comfortably as possible. Two major surgeries later, I'm still alive, still talking to my body, still asking why the tumor cells keep on growing. But I'm not 'fighting' them any more than I am now 'fighting' death. Both cancerous and noncancerous cells are a part of me. Living and dying are a part of me. And you know, Dad has said he'll never allow my obituary to read, 'She valiantly fought cancer for ten years.' Instead, he'll write, "She lived joyously with cancer for ten years.' Do you see the difference?"

This is the way Karen framed her very personal decision to continue or discontinue life-prolonging treatment. Some may choose to do it the way Karen has done it. Others may not. Individuals with life-threatening illnesses and their families may resist making the decision to suspend treatment even when they know that more treatment may diminish the possibility of living fully while dying. They hope for another, more optimistic, medical opinion or a new magic drug or the possibility of another treatment just around the corner.

Physicians are often the first people blamed for the impulse to postpone death. Most nurses believe that they recognize a patient's imminent death sooner than most doctors do. As long as death is perceived to be the enemy, medical practitioners feel that they lose when people die. Although this perspective is changing significantly — particularly with the advent of palliative care — medical practitioners are still reluctant to tell patients and their families that death is not just inevitable but imminent. And families like Dorothy's are reluctant to hear dire predictions from a physician. Instead, they adopt a positive and hopeful attitude, bargaining or negotiating for more time.

The most common impediment to making the decision Karen made is the mistaken perception that if people are told that curative measures are no longer effective, they will give up the hope that humans need to keep living. And so, in order that someone who is irreversibly dying not be told the truth of his or her condition, family and friends and medical practitioners and clergy fabricate a web of deception perpetuating some myth of cure. This actually results in more isolation. The dying person then lives in a lie and loses the capacity for hope that honest relationships provide. Because hoping is born in community, the absence of honest conversation is ironically against hope: it isolates the patient from his or her family as well as from reality.

Similarly, the fear of being abandoned by their medical practitioners if treatment is discontinued, particularly a beloved oncologist, may keep people from making this difficult decision. Patients who fear abandonment may insist on one more medical procedure simply to avoid being cut off from what has grown so familiar. They've grown accustomed to the labs and the tests and they've thrived under the care of good medical teams looking for a cure. In order to avoid abandonment, irreversibly ill patients support the medical quest to solve "The Riddle" of disease and cure, as Sherwin Nuland puts it. In the end, it is a bad bargain because it limits the time for living while dying.

Although we may not say it out loud, there is a belief widely held in American society that we are obligated to do what we can do to prolong life. Along the way, we confuse *is* with *ought*: if we can do it, we ought to do it. Too often, we feel obligated to prolong living beyond what's reasonable. This conviction is wedded to the common American misperception that anything is possible. Although we acknowledge that we cannot be in two places at the same time, we are reluctant to admit that we are finite creatures and not everything is possible.

When Karen decided to stop taking chemo, one of her first thoughts was, "Now Medicare won't have to pay for my hugely expensive infusions. Maybe another younger woman can benefit from what's not spent on me." We spend so much money in trying to extend lives beyond any rational need for them to be extended. We put people through so much suffering in the name of "let's cure this horrible death-thing." And we spend so little energy and money on nurturing health and well-being. Not everything is possible and even if some medical procedures are possible, they may not be prudent or wise.

Finding Out That Purpose Matters

When she had clarity about a purpose for living fully until she died, Karen was at peace about her decision to turn toward death. But her peacefulness did not arrive immediately. When Herbert tentatively invited Karen to reflect together on her experience of dying, her first answer was thanks, but no. She said she was too tired. Moreover, Karen knew she had page proofs to read for a new book, *Color: The Language of Light*, and the thought of launching another project was simply too daunting. But then a month later, she took a trip to the Yucatan, and after talking to her family, she decided undertaking a new book would be the right thing to do. "My good friend, Herbert," she thought, "might help me deal with the many issues I'm already facing. Writing with him could be therapeutic. And I'd have something concrete to focus on."

Launching a new project is a little like both birthing and dying: it requires faith and trust because you don't really know what's coming. Not everybody who is dying will write a book, even though many wish to. But they may have stories to tell that will be forgotten if they are not told. Or debts to settle. Or thank-you notes to write. Or possessions to give away. Or places to visit. Or books to read. Or conversations to have. It is important for everyone to do the work they are drawn or even called to do and keep the focus on living. Even though someone is dying, she or he is still living. She or he still has problems to solve and needs to be met. It may be that the gift of this time of intentional living while dying will make it possible to focus on one last thing from her or his bucket list.

Ernest Becker, the author of the Pulitzer Prize–winning book *The Denial of Death*, was interviewed by Sam Keen for *Psychology Today* just before he died. These two men mutually respected one another. They were both humble in the face of death and they exhibited a sense of wonder at the mystery of God and of life.

Near the end of their conversation, Sam Keen said that his dream was to be alive all the way to the end of his life. "Well," said Becker, "if you are really a live person, you are bound to be more and more interested in experience, more and more things to discover, if you are a growing person." Becker had it right. There are always more things to learn and new adventures to experience. If we keep living and growing while dying, we are less likely to feel that we are finished.

Karen thought this decision to stop treatment would be the most difficult decision she'd make. Little did she know there would be many more.

FROM THE CAREGIVER'S GUIDEBOOK

The turn toward death is a decision to choose life — to live as fully as possible until the end — to be a living actor while dying. Along with the person who is dying, you are on an authentic journey and a movable feast with unexpected detours and surprising opportunities for giving and receiving love and then giving it all away again.

1. Honor the patient's will even if it seems contrary to the wishes of friends and family. When a loved one has made the difficult decision of accepting his or her death, the obligation of family and friends and medical caregivers is to support their loved one in that decision.

2. For many individuals and in some families, the turn toward death is regarded as a personal decision to be made only by the one who is irreversibly ill. For others, it is a corporate choice requiring input from a number of family members. Keep in mind that just because the patient has decided to take the turn toward death, he or she is not choosing death or rejecting family and friends.

3. The person you care for has now admitted that she or he is powerless to impede or stop the process of dying. You, too, are vulnerable at this time because you are now aligned with someone who is powerless.

4. Decisions at the end of life are easier to make if people have already considered their options. Determine what "advance directives" are legally binding in your state and encourage everyone to make decisions about end-of-life care while they are well.

HOSPICE AT THE DOOR

"You matter because you are you,
and you matter to the end of your life."

Dame Cecily Saunders, founder of the Hospice Movement

✎ *from* Karen's Hospice Journal ✎

Like Alice, I feel as if I've fallen through the rabbit hole. The "H" word flashes red neon across the landscape of my brain. It's only two a.m. but who can sleep with all this visible noise going on? I've known hospice *would become a part of my future vocabulary for ten years, but the conversation my husband and I had yesterday with my oncologist, Lloyd West, placed it squarely front and center. Fortunately for me, Lloyd is the kind of doctor who doesn't avoid "The Conversation" as they call it in the medical world. "Now that you've made the decision, which I totally understand and endorse, to stop chemo treatments, you're eligible for hospice care and I'd recommend that you get the paperwork underway as soon as possible, even though you may not need those services for some time."*

"For some time." His echoing words followed us down the hall after he hugged me and told me he'd miss me. Some time. *Did he say it might be five months? Six months? What did John hear? I was in danger of falling into that pleading mode and asking for what most people bargain for — some more time. I felt like a suicide bomber walking out to the parking lot with a heavy device of wires and exploding shrapnel tightly strapped around my waist. I wasn't sure when it would go off, but my body knew it wouldn't be long now.*

I'm reading a wonderful book that Will Schwalbe wrote about his mother's dying. In The End of Your Life Book Club *he puts into words exactly what I'm thinking right now. "Of course, we are all dying and none of us knows the hour, which could be decades away or tomorrow; and we know that we need to live our lives to the fullest every day. But I mean, really — who can play that mental game or live like that? And there's a world of difference between knowing you could die in the next two years and knowing that you almost certainly will."*

A world of difference. *I'm living in that world now but I'm suspecting I'm not talking about two or three years more. Not after the ten I've already had. Am I talking about one?*

For a decade I have totally trusted my team to know the best medical course available through these muddied waters. They didn't pull any punches. "It's treatable but not curable." I remember telling one of my first oncologists, after reading Jerome Groopman's book The Anatomy of Hope, *that tumors don't read medical textbooks, so let's see what plays out. But deep down both John and I knew that I had one of those kinds of cancer little research is being done on because the survival rates are so low. What treatment I engaged in has always been my choice based on my medical team's best judgment and experience. Groopman also convinced me that "[t]reatment is a train that can be stopped at any time. You're in charge." I decided it was time to let my inner conductor know that the train should stop at the next station. Chemo no longer serves any good purpose. I hear screeching brakes.*

Within a day of telling Jonna, my primary and palliative care physician, that I wanted to sign up, the hospice team appears at my front door. "Well, that was fast," I mutter. I know Lloyd said it might be a good idea to get things rolling long before I needed it, but this seems a bit too efficient. Jonna, who also is now my hospice doctor, said I had a couple of choices of which service to engage and with her help, I decided on a national one — Bayada — located close by.

Knock. Knock. Here they are, my case nurse, Sherri, and another nurse in training. They take off their muddy shoes and we sit down in the living room to get acquainted. "So what do you know about hospice?" I tell her what I know. It seems I've learned quite a bit over my decades of living. In fact in the '70s I helped to start a hospice program in a small Wisconsin community, thanks to my friend Mike, a great family practice physician who understands more than most about living and dying. And I've just seen my good friend Jan through her hospice experience. She taught me a lot.

Sherri nods, smiles, and opens up the booklet she brought and goes through it page by page. "I'll leave this with you, but I'm going to ask you to sign the document here saying you understand what I'm explaining." Okay. I'm struck by how real all this is now. It's not some academic exercise. The hospice team's approach to every one of the topics I'm now thinking about is filled with such integrity and purpose.

"You'll be taping a DNR (Do Not Resuscitate) notice on your refrigerator. Jonna will be your hospice doctor and she'll bring you one. Everyone has a refrigerator, so that's where people are trained to look for it. It will alert any emergency personnel, if they're called to your house, not to start lifesaving procedures. You'll never call 911 no matter what. Instead, you'll call our emergency number staffed 24-7. By entering hospice care you are agreeing that no extraordinary measures will be taken to prolong your life."

Right. I don't want to die in a hospital with tubes coming out every conceivable orifice. Or be kept alive far past when I know I want to say good-bye to this physical body. No heroic measures. I know I'm not saying good-bye to the "larger me" inside, so, I'm fine with all of what hospice means.

"Let's do a site visit now. We have to assure our team that when they come here they'll be safe. Smoke alarms? No crazy electrical cords? No ceilings are about to fall down? And of course we want to know the house is safe for you as well. Stairs? Handholds in the bathroom tub and shower?

"We need a copy of your documentation outlining power of attorney for health decisions and for financial decisions. Have you thought about funeral arrangements?" John helps me respond because suddenly I'm out of breath.

As we talk, Sherri types all my responses into her handheld computer notepad so everyone on the team (there are six people listed as My Team, not counting Jonna and her backup palliative care physician-colleague) has the same information. I think, "I suppose before computers, people wrote all this stuff down and stuck the papers in crevices here and there."

I'm learning how to think about a team of strangers coming into my private space. My mother's Scandinavian voice whispers in the background, "Have you dusted? Are there dishes in the sink? Is the floor vacuumed and, most importantly of all, are the bathrooms clean?" And what about going forward? Will I need help to get all that done? How needy am I? How needy will I become?

We say good-bye — until next week.

I sit down to write about my initial hospice visit and the phone rings. It's the hospice spiritual director. She wants to visit. I explain our Vermont road is so muddy my husband, John, would have to ferry her up, as he did for Sherri, about two miles to our house. It's something our Subaru is happy to do — but it's not necessary, I explain. "I have a plethora of spiritual guides right now including my coauthor, Herbert, as well as John, the man I've lived with for almost forty-nine years, who is a Lutheran/Episcopal minister. I think I'm in a good place, but thanks!"

Then the social worker calls to make a connection. I know it's their job. But I'm fine, I say. "I'll let you know if I need you. Or I'll let Sherri know." She's coming every week.

Am I really dying? I feel like such a fraud being in hospice care. But Sherri explained they are coming to establish a relationship more than anything right now. I have no more than hung up when the hospice coordinator calls to make sure we have their emergency number. "Yup. It's on the refrigerator."

It seems I have to schedule my life around my hospice team now. Or, perhaps I'll learn how they can schedule their work around my ongoing life.

ℵ ℷ

Karen's decision after Christmas to discontinue her treatments was personal and private, shared with her family and a few close friends. For many, that decision leads, sometimes urgently, to entering hospice. Karen waited a while, took a vacation, and did some more writing before signing up for hospice. The immediate arrival of her hospice team was a startling reminder to Karen that her dying was no longer private and she was surrounded by compassionate and competent professionals who will accompany her on the journey. She has observed over and over again how fortunate she is to have a quality team. As people decide to enter hospice earlier rather than later, the initial arrival of the hospice team is likely to be much more relaxed and far less urgent.

Hospice: Solace and Refreshment

In ancient times a hospice was a place where anyone could find a bed, a bowl of soup, some bread and wine. Travelers found solace and refreshment in the midst of a journey. For the Hospitalier Knights, hospices were their welfare stations serving people traveling to and from Jerusalem. It was appropriate then in 1960 for Dame Cicely Saunders to borrow the word to describe a new way of caring for dying patients when cure is no longer possible. Saunders opened her hospice on Sydenham Hill with three goals: manage pain, alleviate loneliness, and retain personal autonomy as long as possible. Kids could visit family members. Customary living patterns, like a glass of sherry at five o'clock, were assured without the interference of excessive technology. Florence Wald, Dean of Yale University's School of Nursing, went to visit Saunders at St. Christopher's in 1974 and soon thereafter started the US hospice movement by founding the Connecticut Hospice, the first residential community for the terminally ill. She later set up hospice units in prisons. Wald died in 2008 at ninety-one and was called "the mother of the American hospice movement." The movement Dame Saunders began has transformed end-of-life care and made it possible for people to die surrounded by the warmth of love.

Hospice was not always a necessity. Even within our own lifetimes, we had grandparents who died at home, with no lifesaving measures being taken. Death was understood to be a part of life. Children witnessed it. The concept of *chronic illness* wasn't even in our vocabularies, a hundred years ago. If you had diabetes, you died pretty quickly. If you had a heart attack you were unlikely to survive and most cancers could cause you death within a relatively short period of time. Now we have a medical community that provides a system to keep us alive longer. But, unfortunately, we don't yet have the social system, the caregivers, or the will and understanding to respond humanely to chronic illness. Then,

Our Divine Human Virtue

TRUST

"As soon as you trust yourself, you will know how to live." That's what Goethe said. Did he also mean that once you learn to trust yourself — and those around you — you will also know how to die? Trusting implies hanging on even if you aren't sure how strong the rope is. Trusting means we are centered and strong. To trust means to give up our isolation and be willing to rely and depend on others.

some people like Dame Cicely Saunders began to question and hospice was born.

What can a present-day patient expect from hospice comfort care? Ira Byock lists its key elements this way: to have your pain and other physical symptoms regularly assessed and competently treated; to get adequate information in terms anyone can understand; to have your care coordinated between visits and among all the team members; to know about crisis prevention and emergency plans; to be cared for by quality staff; to have one's family supported throughout, including after their loved one's death. The hospice mantra: *just be there.*

When Goethe was about to die, he cried out, "Light, the world needs more light." Many years later, the philosopher Unamuno reacted to Goethe and said, "No, Goethe was wrong. What he should have said was 'warmth, the world needs more warmth.' We shall not die from the dark but from the cold." Hospice seeks to provide such warmth by creating places of safety and comfort by ensuring easy access to family and friends. Moreover, hospice care urges caregivers to acknowledge the reality of the situation of those approaching death.

End of Life Care: The Challenges

As in Karen's case, the medical system regulates most hospice care and insists that any person receiving the hospice benefits has a life expectancy of six months or less. This could discourage patients from signing up for hospice and support the reluctance of physicians to talk about the end of life. It is possible, however, to "reenlist" in hospice beyond the six-month time frame. A physician's signature can extend coverage, but to avoid Medicare fraud, all cases are scrutinized to make sure hospice care is legitimately needed and lawfully provided. It's a proven fact that with a personal reason to live and good end-of-life care, people often exceed that six-month time frame. While the six-month limit may seem harsh, the interpretation of the rule varies from state to state. Advocates can change the current Medicare system.

This emphasis on life-threatening disease as a problem to be solved still dominates medical practice and often subverts the goals of hospice. Sherwin Nuland has observed in *How We Die* that "the quest of every doctor in approaching serious disease is to make the diagnosis and design and carry out the specific cure." Solving "The Riddle" has its own reward and drives the engines of medicine. The desire to solve a medical problem and the reluctance to admit failure when it can't be solved prevent physicians from acknowledging when the end of a life is near.

In "How Not to Die" in the May 2013 issue of *The Atlantic*, Jonathan Rauch describes the determined efforts of Angelo Volandes, MD, to enhance patient communication and decision-making about end-of-life care using videos providing patient treatment information without evoking intense emotions. The major problem is unwanted, avoidable, and therefore *wrongful* care. "I think that the most urgent issue facing America today is people getting medical interventions that, if they were more informed, they would not want." It happens all the time, said Dr. Volandes.

On one level, it's very understandable. Physicians' training usually doesn't include palliative care. They are programmed to fight, fight, fight to destroy death. Doctors may also fight to prolong life based on their own fears of death. Or they may be reluctant to commit time or energy to someone who is dying because of their own personal fears of the unknown. On the other hand, they may have known someone close to them who has died and they are struggling with their own grief. However they view life and death, most feel their main job is to cure disease or at least to prolong life — at any cost.

Cost. Aye! There's the rub. Doctors and hospitals usually get paid by the services or procedures they do. This is called "fee for service." Many compassionate physicians fight this, but the majority require one more test, one more trial, one more MRI. One more scan. One more attempt to stave off what we all know is inevitable at some point. We know even if this time the patient survives, there will always be another disease they'll have to "conquer." Or not. And, of course, a patient or the family will ask, "Isn't there something else we can try?" When the incentive is to get paid more for ordering yet another "service" or the alternative is to recommend that the patient now move into comfort care, the decision seems pretty obvious to most doctors. Furthermore, our medical community, with fewer and fewer family-oriented physicians, is now hampered by "expert doctors" who perform their work in silos of their wonderful areas of expertise, but without knowing or having the time to learn about the whole patient and her or his needs. Some hospitals attempt to correct this by assigning a person in charge to coordinate care. All of this care is very expensive.

It's good to remember that hospice care operates on a different payment structure. There is a flat fee per day for any care they provide. The care they provide is by no means contingent on cost, but it offers an alternative to the strictly medical option currently based on fees for services provided. That's one reason why certain services (not even CPR) are not provided by hospice professionals. Nor are expensive chemotherapies or radiology services. As Karen has decided, a "Do Not Resuscitate" order hangs on her refrigerator. She knows that when that "resuscitate" word is used, what's really meant is only "an attempt to resuscitate." Without that explicit order to NOT attempt it, an emergency response team is duty-bound to try. But "try" is the operative word. Due to a person's age, severity of injury or illness, or time elapsed, it is never more than "an attempt."

Palliative Care and Compassionate Pain Relief

Palliative care emerged as a medical specialty in 1990 and continues to change end-of-life care. Palliative care extends the principles of hospice care to a broader population that could benefit from receiving it earlier in their illness or disease process. The goal of palliative care is to ease and relieve troubling symptoms that result from various illnesses, rather than the cure of a disease. In the vast majority of cases, appropriate pain relief can be provided in ways that do not place patients at risk of a hastened death. In fact, providing pain relief often has the effect of lengthening a life when the pain is no longer debilitating. The physical and spiritual importance of pain management for living fully cannot be overestimated. The promise of pain relief makes it easier for individuals facing a life-threatening illness to take the turn toward death sooner rather than later. The World Health Organization's definition of palliative care supports the aim of this book with these words: *To better serve individuals who have advanced illness or are terminally ill, and their families, many hospice programs encourage access to care earlier in the illness or disease process.*

We've all cut our fingers, broken bones, had headaches. Some of us have even experienced the pain of childbirth. We're human. We know pain. But with most pain, we know it will be gone soon. However, with end-of-life pain, we think, "Yikes! This may never go away and it will only get worse." So fear creeps in. We fear losing control over pain. We fear that we're never going to feel better. Once fear gets a toehold, it grows.

Fear can be a source of suffering and deep pain. Eric J. Cassell in *The Nature of Healing* writes: "Pain is not only a sensation, it is also an experience embedded in beliefs about causes and diseases and their consequences... Today's pain has a past that contributes to ideas about what is happening and will continue to happen. It may bring to mind an event of yesterday and its emotions. (Maybe anger, or perhaps guilt.)

It occurs in a setting (e.g., home, hospital, or hospice) and in a context that includes a relationship with others (e.g., family, strangers, or doctors). That makes it perhaps lonely and estranged for one patient, or supported, cared about, or loved for another."

In other words, pain is very personal.

And pain needs to be viewed from the whole person's perspective.

A multidisciplinary team is more apt to recognize what pain really is, viewed from this larger perspective. For instance, the pain from the realization that a daughter is not coming home or there is no money for private duty nurses cannot be treated with an analgesic. A long-standing difficult and painful life situation cannot simply be glossed over and treated as isolated physical pain at the end of one's life that morphine can cover. Furthermore, the dying person may now have reached a "new pain normal." It's been said that once the door of mortality has been cracked open, the "good life" will never be the same again. But of course the "good life" is open to many interpretations. But being "pain-free" is the one trusty hand-hold most people will grab.

Cassell goes on to say: "If the patient believes that increasing pain means that the disease is worsening, that worsening disease implies an increasing threat of death, it is little wonder that the pain is resistant." However, pain isn't about death. It's about pain. Pure and simple. And pain at the end of life can be controlled.

The physical pain at the end of life may be managed by medication but fear remains a source of pain and suffering. Karen is quick to point out that although she has experienced pain with her disease and certainly with her treatment, she has never suffered. She uses every practice and technique at her disposal to recognize and dismiss fear. Pain is personal but so is suffering. Because suffering is always in the eyes of the beholder, our expectations of life will in part determine what we perceive as suffering. For instance, when we don't recognize our limits and hold unreasonable expectations, dying itself can be an occasion for suffering.

Human beings share the compassion of God whenever we hold one another in our suffering. Compassion is more than sentiment: it is the capacity to hold life when it is fragile. We call it *womb love*. According to the Hebrew biblical tradition, the compassion of God is like a womb that holds something. We are compassionate when we hold in our womb/heart the pain of another. We mourn with those who mourn; weep with those in tears. John Ruusbroec, the fourteenth-century Dutch mystic, said "compassion is a wounding of the heart which love extends to all without distinction." At the end of life, as at the beginning of life, we need communities of compassion to hold our pain.

In a talk he gave two hours before his death in 1968, the renowned Trappist monk Thomas Merton said, "The whole idea of compassion is based on a keen awareness of the interdependence of all these living beings, which are all part of one another and all involved with one another."

Making Dying Public

The decision to enter hospice care is never done easily or lightly even when it is a necessity. Even though everyone readily admits that the conversation is necessary, few families have it. Entering hospice makes one's dying public, even if that knowledge is limited to one's hospice team. Suddenly, the dying one and his or her family must rely on the kindness of strangers. Some people are embarrassed to realize that people will see them at the end when they are not at their best. Others are not prepared to admit publicly that death is near, even when they have chosen not to continue seeking a cure. Still others have consistently practiced avoidance in life as a mechanism that reduces the risk of confrontation. So, naturally, they will want to avoid confrontation with death as well and the hospice team only serves to remind them that they can't hide now.

Even though people say they want a dignified and peaceable end to life — at home surrounded by family without excessive sustaining technology — very few people put those wishes in writing. For instance, the California HealthCare Foundation recently reported their findings regarding end-of-life care:

- 82% of the Californians polled agreed that it was important to have their end-of-life wishes in writing, but only 23% had done so.

- 80% said they intend to talk to their primary care physicians about their wishes for end-of-life care but only 7% had done so.

- 70% said they preferred to die at home but just 32% of those people had made those arrangements.

Cultural patterns, religious beliefs, previous experience with end-of-life care, and even political affiliation affect our willingness even to consider the conversation leading to decisions about care. Why don't more of us fill out advance directives? Perhaps we don't acknowledge that death is real and coming. Or we're not aware of our options. We're not comfortable discussing it with our loved ones or medical team. We're not sure what will happen if we don't do the advance planning. Or no one is available to help us decide. While there have been remarkable changes in the attitude of physicians toward hospice, death remains the enemy that is fought against. Patients and their families all too often continue to encourage their physicians to keep up the battle against death, regardless of cost.

For many patients and families and their medical professionals, the decision to enter hospice depends on a prior choice to deal honestly and very straightforwardly with difficult situations or complicated choices. Karen's oncologist, along with her good friend and personal physician Jonna, helped her name and face up to the truth about her ovarian cancer.

California HealthCare Foundation website, http://www.chcf.org/publications/2012/02/final-chapter-death-dying, accessed August 30, 2013.

People who choose truth rather than avoidance or flat-out denial have discovered the gift of overwhelming love and affection from surprising places.

FROM THE CAREGIVER'S GUIDEBOOK

Informed consent policies and end-of-life documents are geared toward enhancing patient autonomy and protection rather than protecting medical institutions and practitioners. When caregivers advocate on behalf of patient agency and autonomy, they work toward ensuring that the dying person has sufficient information and adequate support to make knowledgeable decisions (when possible) about appropriate care.

1. This is a vulnerable time for the person who is dying. Sit with your loved one as she or he begins to learn her or his options. Help her or him understand what being in hospice care means by being sure you are clear about the nuances of hospice care. Clarify to make sure everyone in the family understands what's "hanging on the refrigerator." But also know that now everyone wants or needs the same information.

2. Ground yourself in knowing this is the patient's decision. Don't argue or promote your own agenda.

3. Stay close but stay sensitive and respect a dying person's request for periods of time that are less filled with people. The old adage that people die as they live seems especially true for certain introverts who can be overwhelmed by all the activity or people.

4. Ira Byock has suggested loving care includes such simple things as listening attentively, sitting quietly, watching carefully, or simply "showing up" at unexpected times. It's difficult but not complicated.

Decisions, Decisions, Decisions

"Decisions are not made in a vacuum.
They are made in the ambience created by the accumulations of past decisions...
If you ask the right question, it can unloose a secret jam of thoughts."

Paul Lehmberg, *In the Strong Woods*

❧ *from* Karen's Hospice Journal ❧

I've added my signature to a lot of documents over the years, but the one I signed the other day was unlike any other I've ever put my pen to. It's called "DNR/ POLST" for DNR/CPR and "Physician Orders for Life-Sustaining Treatment." I tuck it inside an envelope labeled "For Emergency Personnel" and tape it to the side of our refrigerator. Since everyone has a refrigerator, Sherri, my hospice coordinator, says that's where we put things we want others to find. Anyone coming into your home to help needs to know what you want that help to be. The hanging document clearly states: do not resuscitate. *All the extra meds are kept inside the refrigerator so hospice workers will know where to find them. Sherri carefully explained that once I have died and obviously no longer need any of the meds they will retrieve them, lest they fall into "wrong" hands.*

Without my physician Jonna's expert help, filling out this document and the decisions it carries would have been dreadful. Knowing she's done this with numerous patients before, my hand grows steadier. The decisions, signed 4/2/13, carry a life-and-death finality, outlining my informed consent. I won't be having tubes. I have requested no attempts to revive me. I will not be intubated or transferred to a hospital (unless comfort care cannot be met in our home) and I will limit the use of antibiotics. A trial period of hydration may take place, but it's negotiable. In other words, I have decided not to drink or eat at the end... unless, as Jonna explained it, I want to hold out for a visitor coming in a few days. Or I change my mind. So there are limited interventions written into this document. It's what we decide together, John, Jonna, and I. Lovingly. Carefully. Thoroughly.

In my hospice admission booklet, my rights and responsibilities are clearly stated. I see outlined there ten items alone on my rights regarding decision-making. I jointly participate, for instance, with my hospice team in my care plan. I can choose my own physician. I can refuse services or request changes without fear and I participate in the selection of my caregivers. I won't participate in experimental treatments or research unless my consent is obtained and I (or my designated power of attorney) will make all my health-care decisions. That's empowering in a situation where I no longer seem to wield much power. Or did I ever, come to think of it?

I've read that 40% of those who die in hospitals spend their last days in the ICU where they're likely sedated, have tubes of all kinds poking out of them. Some have their arms tied down so they don't remove those lifelines, and others have to wear mittens so they don't disturb their end-of-life care. Is that really how I'd want to die if I have an alternative?

Now that I'm enrolled in comfort care, I still have decisions to make. I have decided where the hospice bed will go... near my favorite view of the mountains, near the upstairs deck overlooking some flower gardens. I daily decide what to eat and how much. I listen to my body for clues. What am I thirsty for that won't be too acidic? So far, I can decide what to wear. How much to sleep. When to nap. What to read. Which Netflix to watch. And how to spend my time with friends.

Deciding to write this book with Herbert was another decision on the journey. I love that he's not only a competent writer and a brilliant thinker, but his name means "bear" and he gives great bear hugs.

Since I tell everyone that Herbert and I are writing this book about dying, I don't have to worry about who knows what about my current state. It takes a lot of energy to figure out whom you can safely talk to, so I've decided on full disclosure even though it's hard for some of my friends to accept my candor about death. Nevertheless, transparency is what I've chosen.

I've also decided I'll later be deciding how much and which kind of opiates to take. John keeps reminding me I don't have to be a martyr and that I will need to get ahead of the pain. Several drugs are available to me but I have a need to be aware, awake, and clear about this final passage. Conscious dying, they call it. Just as I

·

fought the anesthetist not to drug me up for the birth of our second child, I want to be conscious of this passage — this birth of my own into a new realm. I'm sick of "do not go gentle into that good night. . ." I want to go gentle. Unfearful. And at peace. And I believe that's what my family and friends will help me to do. I choose active dying just as I've chosen active living. I want to die as I have lived — a full participant in all life has to offer.

Of all the decisions Karen has made, her determination to be transparent about dying with others was one of the most important. She wanted to live fully and freely without hiding. She chose to tell and hear stories and harness her increasingly limited energy for quality, creative time right up to the end. But she was surprised by some of the responses she received by making her story known. Old friends reconnected, expressing gratitude for her wisdom. Several people thanked her for gifts she'd given them over the years. Local newspapers interviewed her. She was a guest on several radio shows that elicited even more connection with people she did not know who wanted to thank her for what she was doing. She made a choice for life and it created new networks of care. In fact, deciding for hospice care and choosing transparency redefines the meaning of pro-life. Karen will die with loved ones around her. Secret-keeping and withholding the truth about a diagnosis or a treatment plan isolates. Transparency creates communities of compassionate care.

There are, of course, limits to transparency. Truth-telling is not an absolute. The decisions we make create a context that affects whom to tell and when.

I Have Prostate Cancer
Herbert

I had a paintbrush in my hand on my sixty-third birthday when the urologist called to tell me that the biopsy of my prostate showed a mildly aggressive form of cancer and he recommended surgery. I did not throw the brush. That afternoon, I had a haircut and told a perfect stranger, "I have prostate cancer." He did not seem interested but that did not deter me from speaking openly about the diagnosis of cancer.

A month later I was having a beer with a friend at a conference of pastoral counselors and told her that I was worried about being so peaceable about the diagnosis. "Am I in some kind of denial?" I asked. Her response was helpful then and still is now. "You have been teaching death and grief for twenty-five years," she said. "Don't you think some of it might have rubbed off by now?"

So it had. Despite considerable anxiety about death in my early years, talking openly death in life had changed me. I hope that I will be able to keep this peaceableness when death is near for me personally.

Deciding Again and Again

Living as we all do in complex systems, making decisions is a complex and challenging process. Even sixteenth-century Machiavelli said that things always vary according to circumstances. Decision-making can't be reduced to specific rules. Making decisions requires sufficient information but even with sound research it's difficult to predict unintended consequences. The question is not so much, "What shall we do tomorrow?" but rather, "What shall we do today to prepare for tomorrow?" Ralph Stacey, who writes about chaos and complex systems, says that "by focusing our concern on present issues that have long-term consequences, we are actually dealing with the long term in a more realistic and creative way." We are, in fact, always selecting our future by the choices and decisions we make in this very moment. But for the one who is dying, today is the only significant moment.

The most difficult decisions may actually occur after one has acknowledged her upcoming death and enrolled in hospice. We can't always know the outcomes of our decisions. Nor can we know in advance who will be most affected by what we decide. Moreover, the choices may be influenced by the dying person's social context, values, and beliefs. If making decisions at ordinary times is complicated and stressful, making the many decisions around dying is likely to be even more difficult. The dying person has a single agenda, when all is said and done. And that is to get ready to die. That readiness includes deciding and deciding again and again.

Decisions made at the end of life are often ambiguous and complicated by unexpectedly powerful emotions. Families that have not learned to live with mystery and ambiguity are sometimes torn apart by the complex decisions that must be made when a family member is irreversibly ill or dying. We are more and more aware of the importance of advanced directives as one way of preparing for the end of a life. However, advanced directives do not eliminate ambiguity at the end of life. Our willingness to live with wonder and mystery as dimensions of both living and dying is a spiritual practice that will make it easier to embrace end-of-life decisions already made when one's life situation was less ambiguous.

Our Divine Human Virtue

PEACE

Having to make decisions can cause turmoil. How do we rest easy with all of this? How can we trust that all will be well? Elie Wiesel said that we must remember that peace is not God's gift to his creatures, but our gift to each other. And to ourselves. When we show our faithfulness to one another, stillness unfolds in our hearts. It's then that we can settle down and settle in to truly listen to what is important.

Every choice we make leads to new decisions that cannot be avoided. As long as they can remain conscious and aware, dying people can and should keep taking responsibility to decide things right up to the end. Hospice care ensures patients that everyone is committed to enhancing their ability to choose and to purposefully make decisions assuring their well-being. "Dying is fundamentally a personal experience," Ira Byock observes. "If it is truly your choice, it is also your right to be 'left alone.'" But recognize, he says, that your relatives and friends each have their own personal experience with regard to your dying.

Advance Directives Make End-of-Life Deciding Easier

Advance directives are tools that translate a patient's end-of-life goals in an easy-to-understand, portable way. These signed medical orders, acknowledged as understood by the patient's signature, cover seven specific issues and are binding to emergency and hospital personnel if the person is transferred. They are much more specific than living wills. The documents themselves vary from state to state and can be easily found online and downloaded.

The POLST (Physician Orders for Life-Sustaining Treatment) is a care planning tool that reflects the patient's here-and-now goals for medical decisions that may confront him or her today and converts those goals into specific medical orders. POLSTs were first introduced in Oregon in the early 1990s. At the time of this writing they have been adopted in about a quarter of our states including Karen's home state of Vermont, and are under consideration in many others. The document offers patient choices ranging from aggressive treatment to limited interventions to very simple comfort care. In some states these orders are called MOLST (Medical Orders for Life-Sustaining Treatment) or by other similar acronyms. In Vermont, Karen learned that she signed not only the POLST but also a COLST, which means she has authorized Clinician Orders for Life-Sustaining Treatment. It's best to know precisely what's available where you live.

Karen had to make some decisions regarding whether she wanted comfort measures only, and if she desired limited additional interventions such as antibiotics to treat painful infections if they arose. Her hospice doctor gave her the pros and cons of each decision, making it much easier for her to decide these important things in a stress-free environment. She is also aware that her condition will likely result in her not eating at the end and she made it clear there were to be no feeding tubes. Advance directives do not, however, eliminate the need to decide again and again.

When we procrastinate and don't make firm decisions about end-of-life issues, we are actually deciding to let all the stakeholders who make money from medical procedures dictate how we die. Knowing that, many still ignore the logical choice: to complete our advance directives. Why don't we do it? Perhaps it's because we don't acknowledge that death is real and coming. Or we're not sure of our options. Some people are not comfortable discussing it with their loved ones, their spiritual guides, or their medical team. Many times patients wait for their doctor to tell them what they should do. And, ironically, doctors wait for the patients to ask about what is happening to their body. So people play the waiting game and precious time elapses.

Deciding is what dying people do. Some call this having agency. It's the ability to rationally and responsibly claim one's ability to decide and to act as a person with autonomy. In other words, one develops the skills and capabilities that make it possible to choose and to embrace actions that are fully one's own. When one acts, one is able to turn a static noun into a vibrant verb. We can turn "connection" into "connect"; "building" into "build"; "health" into "healing." "Death" into "dying." When we think about dying, it is particularly important to keep other verbs in mind as well: remembering, praying, thinking, wondering, waiting, loving, forgiving, watching, touching, and even worrying, all of which are part of how we approach the end of a life.

Caregivers Make Deciding and Acting Possible

In order for the dying person to experience the freedom to decide and act, caregivers must help. Physicians need to take enough time to explain medical options so that an individual can make responsible choices. Hospice caregivers regularly know what to do in order that individuals can live fully until they die. Friends and family may need to accommodate. They might have to set aside their own desires or plans in order to make some sacrifices on behalf of their loved one.

In a culture devoted to freedom for self-fulfillment, the need to make sacrifices in ordinary living is easily overlooked. However, in order that the dying person might live as fully as possible, it will be necessary for caregivers to set aside their own convenience and personal preferences or even sacrifice needs and desires at life's end. Sacrifice seems like an antiquated word, but it still means giving up something precious. It means to make holy. It involves unselfish acts that can diminish careers, time, money, even sleep. Herbert's colleague Robert's wish to teach one more class was made possible by the care of others.

Robert taught the class on a Friday and the following Thursday he was dead. The faithful care exhibited by his colleague, his wife, and his medical staff made it possible for Robert to live as fully as he could to the very end of his life.

In the past, even our best ethical reflections about care of the dying focused on piling on more and more interventions and authorizing

A Professor Continued On — with Support

Herbert's colleague Robert

I had breast cancer first and then lymphoma. The treatment for lymphoma was brutal but it gave me a couple extra years. When the lymphoma returned I was clear that I had neither the desire nor the energy to go through the treatment again. My wife, Donna, hated the prospect of my death but she supported my decision. At a Christmas party at the seminary in California where I teach, someone asked me if there was anything I really wanted to do. There was! I said I wanted to teach my course on the Gospels (Matthew, Mark, Luke, and John in the New Testament). Later, I learned that a colleague had volunteered after the party to teach the class with me just in case I could not finish. My oncologist went along with it and concocted the right cocktail to keep me alert. And before each class, Donna would clean every surface I might touch with disinfectant because I had no immune system. I had a wonderful and charitable group of students because I would lose track sometimes of my thought pattern but my faithful colleague and sidekick Gary was always nearby to get me back on the road.

"newer" and "better treatments." As long as death was a problem to be solved, we tried to prolong life or at least postpone death.

When it is determined that cure is not likely to be possible and more aggressive treatments would just be futile, many medical professionals decide "less is now better." So they tend to withdraw everything, including their ongoing emotional support. Naturally, the patient feels totally abandoned. But thanks to palliative caregivers and spokespeople like Ira Byock, many of us now view end-of-life care as *more additive than subtractive*. Karen has often expressed the security that she feels has been added by her being in home hospice care. She knows the people around her are people she can trust. She has "the kit" with pain relievers and other drugs in her refrigerator and she knows how to use them. She has signed a COLST to ensure that if, for some reason she is transferred, her wishes will be honored. She is surrounded by relationships that bring her peace. All these things have been *added* to her life and they bring quality to any dying person's ending times.

It is not always possible to be a full participant to the end. Therefore, the dying must trust that families will interpret the advanced directives as they were intended. That is an act of faithfulness. Given the emergence of complex institutions that support remarkable medical advances, the greatest challenge for the dying may be to trust their well-being to impersonal procedures, anonymous physicians, and serial nursing staff. When a dying person opens her eyes and says to her trusted caregiver, "Are you still here?" she is surprised by faithfulness. But even our most faithful care can be fragile. And the one dying knows it. At her end, one of Karen's friends with brain cancer was confused much of the time. Once she confided to Karen that she thought her husband was wishing she would go because he was getting so tired. Karen admitted he may be tired, but she reminded her friend that she knew him well enough to know he would never abandon her.

The decisions made while dying are shaped by many significant relationships. Because relationships keep changing, the right questions change as well. In trying to answer the complex moral questions that are created by medical technology today, we cannot base our decisions solely on rules. Making responsible decisions is a process that never ends. We need moral conviction and moral wisdom to live fully until death. We also need trustworthy myths that help to make sense of the inevitable discontinuity of death. We may imagine being drawn into the light or setting out on a journey. Or perhaps we imagine death to be a sleep or a voyage to another shore. We don't know. These are simply metaphors that help us through the uncertainty of dying. But what we do know is that Divine love is stronger than death. When we die, we believe, we are held in that all-embracing love. We have a relationship that endures. That is enough for us to know. It is, in the end, all we can know. The rest is mystery.

From the Caregiver's Guidebook

Dying is not a single thing. Decisions will need to be made throughout the process. You may find yourself caught between family members with differing viewpoints about how the decisions are made and why. Or even if they should be made.

I. Remind yourself that the patient is the primary decision-maker in all choices regarding health and treatment. When the dying person is unable to express those decisions, it is desirable for him or her to have signed the earlier directives document regarding any future possible medical actions. Not everyone lives in states with POLST so a living will may provide some of the direction their family will take. Although keep in mind, it's the POLST, not the advance directives or the living wills, *that are the medical orders.* By being the patient's health-care agent, you can legally speak for him or her about medical care when the person is unable to speak for himself or herself.

2. When conversations about patient care occur, it is often useful to have as many of the stakeholders in the room as possible to hear what is said or decided. Because relationships keep changing, the right questions will change as well. Be open to the shifts.

3. Seek other expert help when you're not sure. Your task is to be the problem solver when the patient is not able to think clearly of all the ramifications involved in making particular decisions. Remember, we can't always depend solely on "rules." Use your moral conviction and wisdom.

FACING FINALITY

"Good-bye world!... Good-bye to clocks ticking —
and my butternut tree!... and Mama's sunflowers — and food and coffee
and fresh-ironed dresses and hot baths — and sleeping and waking up! —
Oh earth, you are too wonderful for anyone to realize you!"

Thornton Wilder (Emily) *Our Town*, Act III

⚘ *from* Karen's Hospice Journal ⚘

I believe this world, as Emily Dickinson put it, is not a "conclusion; A sequel
stands beyond"... "Invisible as music, But positive, as sound." While I believe, with
every fiber of my being, that a sequel exists, I also believe that everything that physi-
cally makes me this seventy-three-year-old-body-named-Karen will end. Over.
Finis. Done.

In reading Thomas Moore again — a wise man who spent twelve years as a
monk, and a former psychology professor — I am struck by how he deals with
his own mortality. I concur with him: there is no end to this journey we are on
into eternity. But then, what is eternity if not this little slice of life I am presently
experiencing. "Our job," he says, "is not to look for an end but rather to see the end,
death and the eternal in everything we do."

Herbert is wonderful. He encourages me to view life with a sense of paradox
and awe. Our irises are blossoming right now — purple and yellow, delicate
orchidlike gifts that grace our gardens with very little help from us. Water. A little
mulch. A little plant food. That's all. Irises are gifts. Like grace itself, I don't deserve
them, yet there they are, frilly bobbles in the June sun.

According to Hindu mythology, Krishna's mother looked deep into his mouth
and what did she see there? The universe. I look deeply into my irises, and what do I
see there? I see wilting and decay as some of the slender pods turn crisp right before
my eyes, curl up, and die. I put them in vases and they are beautiful for several
days. They're not as ephemeral as our oriental poppies, but almost. Before my eyes
they fold in on themselves and shrink.

Maybe in "that other place" blossoms won't die. But right now I'm living in a world where death is real. And I am circled in eternity.

My old mentor, the twelfth-century nun Hildegard of Bingen, said "love is at work in the circles of eternity, without reference to time, like heat within a fire." Eternity doesn't run in a linear fashion, but spirals. Like a metal spring, it holds me fast to this life, while at the same time propelling me, Slinky-like, into dimensions yet to come. I live here and there. Another writer whom I admire, Frederick Buechner, said in Wishful Thinking: A Seeker's ABC, *if you spin a pinwheel fast enough, all the colors blend into a single color — white, the essence of the combined spectrum. And if you spin time fast enough it all blends into timelessness or eternity: time past, time present, and time to come all combined.*

Or as T. S. Eliot put it: "The end precedes the beginning / And the end and the beginning were always there / Before the beginning and after the end. / And all is always now."

ℵ ℷ

The complex simple weaving of beginnings and endings, of finality and eternity, is a daily struggle for many as they strive to keep all signs of the end or finality far, far away. But for Karen, as evidenced in a blog she wrote about four months into her hospice care, she thinks more about time now and realizes it may not be as most of us have envisioned: *"Einstein taught us that time doesn't flow in one direction. It spirals. The future and the past exist simultaneously. One of the things people in my condition think about is what am I really afraid of when I face — rather up close and personal — my own death? Pain? That can be controlled. Abandonment? Perhaps. But the larger fear may be that we're most afraid of being free of time. Outside time. When you're outside of time, you're no longer in control. S-C-A-R-Y!"*

Don't Fence Me In

Some of us are old enough to remember a song by Cole Porter made popular by Bing Crosby that included these words:

Oh, give me land, lots of land, under starry skies above,

don't fence me in.

This old pop song captures a common sentiment: we don't like limits of any kind. We long for freedom, lack of constraints, independence, open country. We disdain and even fear anything that might restrict that freedom. And we all share a deeper conviction: we are reluctant to acknowledge that we're human. And finite. How do we know? We wear trifocals. We have gray hair — or no hair. We get senior discounts, have gimpy knees, and have experienced the death of our parents. We've gone through menopause; we've written our wills. We have diminished energy and some memory loss. We're finite beings.

We know we're mortal, but somewhere deep inside, we still think we're going to live forever. Well, if not forever, for a long, long time. Karen's husband has picked 110. Of course people opting for more years would want the mind and body of a twenty- or thirty-year-old. David Ewing Duncan has asked about 30,000 people how long they would like to live: 60% opted for a life span of 80 years; another 30% chose 120 years; almost 10% wanted to live 150 years; less than 1% wanted to live forever.

One day who we are — our physical bodies, minds, psyches, or whatever makes us "us," in this physical humanness — will die. The Germans have a phrase for it: *nichts ewigkeit* (nothing is forever).

Our Divine Human Virtue

LONGSUFFERING

We enter life embracing the pain of being squeezed into this world. We die by being squeezed out. But life is so much more than pain and suffering and we realize that when we allow ourselves to *be*, just as we are. And allow others to be just as they are. Ken Wilbur, who watched his wife die, said, "Suffering smashes to pieces the complacency of our normal fictions about reality." The truth is, we have everything we need within us. The rest is fiction.

However much we might rail against limits in life, we cannot escape the fact that pleasant vacations end, bowls break, students graduate, people retire, and body parts wear out even when they don't become fatally diseased. This blessed recognition we talk about, this turn toward death, is a recognition of our limits. Not everything is possible. We are, after all, finite creatures.

Living with Limits

Malcolm was taking a walk when he saw a frog on the sidewalk. He was startled to hear the frog speak. "Hey, old man, if you kiss me I will turn into a beautiful princess. I will be yours forever and we could make mad passionate love every day." Malcolm put the frog in his jacket pocket and kept walking. "Hey, old man, I don't think you heard me. If you kiss me, I will turn into a beautiful princess and we can make passionate love every day." "I heard you," Malcolm said, "but at my age I'd rather have a talking frog."

Life would be a lot simpler and dying a lot less complicated if, like Malcolm, we were all a little more accepting of our limits and our human finitude.

For the most part, we take for granted that we are finite in space. We know we cannot be in more than one place at a time. Nor can we fly. But we are also finite as we relate to time. Let's call that *temporal finitude*. It offers us the opportunity to round off time and evaluate relationships or life events. Still, we fight our time limitations and when we approach death, we feel our dreams have been disrupted. James Baldwin called this gap between what we thought we would become and what we have become "baffling geography."

Instead of being Malcolm and peacefully passing up the frog's limitless promises, end times can overflow with sadness and disappointment. Through life, we've thought the sky's the limit. So we buffer death by building bunkers of toys. We live in a society that measures human worth by how much we possess. Put simply, living with limits is more about learning to live with the awareness that not everything is possible. And less truly can be more.

A few years ago, Karen's friend Anne Gilman wrote a book called *Doing Work You Love*. Anne says it's a myth to believe that you have unlimited potential. You don't. But you do have potential. And you have limitations. "If you weren't born rich, safe, supported, loved, in great health and shape, white, male, tall, handsome (with hair), smart, outgoing, and from a social nondysfunctional family, you have different limitations." But, she points out, everyone has talents, dreams, and potential within their limitations. Sometimes, as in end-of-life decisions, we are limited by the choices we make.

Understanding that we are limited creatures makes that blessed recognition more likely when our own death is near. This high recognition comes to us without our asking for it or even wanting it. And it's blessed because, like the old Scandinavian concept of rune-blessings, it is, indeed, hallowed work. The word *blessed* is linked to the old Germanic *blothisojan*, which means "to hallow with blood." But instead of viewing this end time as a hallowed blessing, it can, for many, be more of a despicable curse. People easily fall into feelings of abandonment and separation. What we're suggesting is that people take another look. Finitude can be a good thing. And even if it isn't acceptable, being limited is very human. Josie, Karen's granddaughter, seems to have this clearly in mind already at age five.

Check the Box
Karen

I call it a *Josie-koan*. When our kindergartner granddaughter visited us, I was taking naps in the afternoon pretty regularly. But then later I would have plenty of energy to play and cook and read with her. One afternoon I lay in bed with the door shut. She opened it very quietly and tiptoed in and placed a sheet of typing paper where I couldn't miss it. On it was very carefully printed "**How M e n y?**" with three boxes under the question.

Josie had quietly shut the door behind her. When I woke up and pondered her little note to me, I wondered what she meant when she had painstakingly drawn three boxes with her little pencil. Her parents subscribe to *Highlights for Children* so I've seen similar boxes to check off. Perhaps in her head, she had been asking me:

How many more minutes/hours are you going to sleep, Grandma? How many more naps are you going to take? How many more days before I have to go back to Colorado with Daddy?

Or maybe even without knowing my condition (although we believe children know much more about death and dying than we give them credit for), she may have been verbalizing the unspoken question most people have now that I'm in a home hospice care program: How many more weeks or months will you be around?"

Who knows, Josie, I thought. I live from moment to moment. We all do.

Our Human Challenge

In *The Denial of Death*, Ernest Becker regarded the struggle we have with being finite as the human problem. Like Cole Porter, Becker maintained that there is a natural and inevitable urge to resist being fenced in; we deny death and rail against our limits. "The prison of one's character," Becker observed, "is painstakingly built to deny one thing and one thing alone: one's creatureliness." Avoiding signs of an illness, resisting a trip to the doctor when one does not feel well, seeking to make ourselves seem powerful even at the expense of others, or engaging in heroic efforts to prolong life when we are irreversibly or gravely ill are all signs of our anxiety in the face of our human finitude. Sometimes the negative behavior that comes from the inability to tolerate finitude exaggerates our suffering. Beginnings and endings shape us and give us character. Even so, it takes courage to face finality.

Family members may continue to insist on extreme medical procedures because they don't want to lose the battle against cancer or because they are reluctant to let the patient go lest they be accused of abandonment. Physicians may be attentive and faithful as long as there is some possibility of defeating death. At least for now. But once finitude is acknowledged both in our living toward death and in the practice of medicine, and once no more heroic medical procedures are considered to be beneficial, then faithful care is necessary. The desire to avoid someone "dying on my watch" that often propels medical professionals to transfer an irreversibly ill patient to someone else's specialty unwittingly diminishes hope through abandonment.

Change in medical care is not likely to occur until there is a shared acceptance of finitude by patients, their families, and physicians. The good news is that recent studies suggest that more Medicare patients now are choosing to spend their final days in hospice care rather than die in a hospital. A new report from the Dartmouth Atlas Project, which analyzes Medicare data, shows that there was an 11% decrease in deaths at the hospital while those enrolled in hospice care rose nationally from 42% in 2007 to 48% in 2010. While there is still a long way to go, more and more hospitals are improving their end-of-life care and, as a result, they save end-of-life costs from high ICU bills. Thankfully, physicians, it appears, are beginning to catch up to their patients' wishes. When medical professionals are able to acknowledge the limits of cure, then the focus will shift to easing the patient's suffering, the patient's end-of-life wishes will be respected, and the patient will be given freedom to die. Death is real. To continue to struggle against this fact is not only irrational, it's impossible.

Someday You Are Going to Die
Karen's friend Jonna

When my daughter was seven, we were canoeing and camping in the Quetico, west of Thunder Bay, Ontario. Low blueberry bushes crept out of crevices in the long sloping rock where we had pitched our tent. The water lapped against the shore. As the sun set, I sat on my sleeping bag in the dusk. Our two older daughters were lying in their sleeping bags across from me. As I nursed our baby son, I sang to him — most likely nonsense words. Maybe about the loons; maybe a lullaby about Lake Superior.

Our older daughter sat up and began to cry, loudly, deeply. "What is it, dear one?" I asked. "What is wrong?" And she replied in a torrent, "Your voice is so sweet and you are singing to Sam and holding him and feeding him and someday you are going to die."

How do you respond to that recognition of death coming out of this den of warmth on an island of calm? I'm sure I said something like, "Sweetheart, my love, I love you and will be here for you." I may have told her, "I will not leave one day before my time, and I will hold you in my heart wherever I am." I'm sure I thought, *This is my job, little one, to prepare you for this.* I know I thought, *Jonna, you just don't know how to soften this hurt.* As J. M. Barrie, the author of *Peter Pan*, wrote: "I'm not young enough to know everything." But my wise daughter seemed to know.

We forget how much we know, or if we ever knew it. The sweet, frightening sadness of that summer night on the lake, the humid tent, the heat rising from the rock warmed by August sun. It all came together with the sharpness of a knife, that said, "Your singing is so sweet, and someday, you will be gone from me. You will be gone."

And knowing that life is not limitless, that the sweet song holds in it the seed of ending and loss, is the wound and the blessing every wise child carries.

The Wound and the Blessing

Jonna Goulding, Karen's hospice doctor, poignantly recalls her child's wisdom that beginnings and endings, love and loss, wounds and blessings live together from the beginning of life. It is a truth that frees. We find meaning at the end of life by living in the truth. Wounds and blessings commingle through all of life. When we are able to acknowledge that death is immanent as well as inevitable, it should be easier to set aside our character armor in order to live freely and creatively until we die. When our faithful companions who accompany us are willing to tell us the truth about dying, we are able to face the end of our lives with less anxiety.

In his interview with Ernest Becker on his deathbed, Sam Keen asked him how he thought about himself as he was dying. Becker said this: "Well, I suppose the most immediate thing I feel is relieved of the burden of responsibility for my own life, putting it back where it belongs, to whoever, whatever hatched me. I think this is the most immediate thing I feel, a great sense of relief and trust that eggs are not hatched in vain." All the unavoidable anxiety we have felt throughout life about being responsible or making things happen or caring for the ones we love is let go — given over to God or whomever we regard as the source of being. We have our life as a gift. We are able to let go of that gift — put our life back where it came from — if we trust that our life has not been in vain — that it had meaning.

Life *is* finite but in the end so is our anxiety. We can let go of life's gift more easily if we recognize that we have lived with a purpose. But we can do this only if we trust that our life has not been in vain and that it had meaning. The Dalai Lama said, "If you are mindful of death, it will not come as a surprise — you will not be anxious. You will feel that death is merely like changing your clothes." Finally we can let go of all responsibility for making things happen and acknowledge that we lived life as a gift. It has meaning.

FROM THE CAREGIVER'S GUIDEBOOK

For many people who are dying consciously, the finality of death on the horizon is sometimes less difficult than other signs of "ending" they now face. Faithful care for someone who is dying consciously means facing that this is, indeed, final! That's not easy, but it means that you need to consent to everything "the end" means. You need to face it for yourself and for the person who is dying. For the person who is dying, losing abilities, physical and mental, can be more difficult than the finality of death itself. It is not easy for the caregiver, as well, to see all these losses along the way.

1. You are all facing the finality of dying now. You have every reason to be tired. It's so common, there is actually a phrase for this state you're in. It's called *compassion fatigue*. Pay attention to your own needs as well as to those of the people around you.

2. Recognize your limits and the limits of the person who is dying. Embrace them. It won't be easy, but with other people's help, you'll be able to do it. Don't think you have to do everything! Others may want to give as well.

3. Remember that not everything is possible — for you or for the dying person. And that's okay.

4. When we accept that cure is no longer possible and only care is called for, we need an extra measure of commitment to stay present with someone whose life circumstances cannot be reversed. Resist the impulse and often unspoken desire to flee from helplessness or futility.

PEERING INTO THE DARK

"Death isn't the problem. Fear is. And fear is something we create."

Julia Assante,
The Last Frontier: Exploring the Afterlife and Transforming Our Fear

❈ *from* Karen's Hospice Journal ❈

I think a lot about light these days. And dark. I guess you can't have one without the other. I'm not sure how the Hopi people view the dark, but I've read that they don't say that the light *flashed. They simply say "flash." No subject. No time. No space. Just* flash.

If dying is actually moving into the light — flash! — in an instant, as so many think it might be (and some have actually "come back" and reported that), then maybe living is more like continuous stumbling around in shadows and squinting in the dark, waiting for "flash."

When I researched light for Color: The Language of Light *I was astounded to learn that physicists (we can trust them, can't we?) believe that every atom inside us, around us, and inside everything on earth once came from the stars. Every breath I take is a star-breath. A science writer named Kenneth Weaver said, "It may come as a shock to learn that nearly all the atoms in our body and in the earth were once part of a star that exploded and disintegrated, and that probably those same atoms were once the debris of still an earlier star." And that of still an earlier star and that of an earlier star and. . . I believe that the light within me goes so far back, just thinking about it all makes my brain hurt!*

As a reader of Genesis, I am in awe of a world created from the simple words: Let there be light! And there was. Long before the sun. Or the moon. Or even the stars. So, how could there be light before there was light? And what was that primordial light, anyway?

I've read that nothing is ever destroyed — it just changes shape according to the ways we view it. Am I living in some kind of semi-light illusion? A magic show? A movie, flashing onto a screen through some giant projector?

Maybe everything I'm seeing now is really negative space — you know, those different shapes that morph out of the object we thought we were seeing. The lady or the vase? The old woman or the young woman? Maybe life is one big tricky Rorschach test after all. We just peer into the dark and we see what we expect to see. Maybe it's eternity we're trying to see, when in fact all of time-eternity is right around and within us. Eternity is nowhere. Now put a space between those words and you get "now here." I'm living in it. Now. I'm dying in it. Now. Flash!

> *Seeing into darkness is clarity...*
> *This is called practicing eternity.*
>
> *Lao Tzu*

𐤀   𐤊

Once again, Karen's fertile and courageous imagination invites us to embrace light and darkness, hope and despair, joy and sorrow as expressions of the mystery of authentic living while dying. Eternity is nowhere and "now here." Fleeting fear of the unknown and unknowable need not prevent us from embracing the richness of mystery. Here is a promise to live by: wonders lie ahead.

Developing Night Vision

When Karen's boys were young, Madeleine L'Engle was, for a time, a constant nighttime companion. In *A Swiftly Tilting Planet,* they heard about the dark: "Light and darkness dancing together, born together, born of each other, neither preceding, neither following, both fully being in joyful rhythm." L'Engle's story goes on to describe how this dazzling light was swallowed up by a star and the glory of the harmony was broken by "screeching, by hissing, by laughter which held no merriment but was hideous, horrendous cacophony." Who wants that? Is it our job, too, to help bring the light back? Yes! We believe it is. Perhaps the most important thing we can do is to make the dark more conscious, as Carl Jung put it. It's our job to call things by their right and real names and to acknowledge the shadows along with our own finitude.

Nights can hold terrors, no doubt about it. We often lie there with our eyes wide open like Job, who said, "In the night my mouth is pierced with sorrows and they that feed upon me sleep not." Dark often seems negative. Hidden. Confining. Secretive. Dangerous. Nights can be scary and uncomfortable, as opposed to day, which always seems friendlier.

When the sun disappeared in an eclipse, people once thought it was eaten by dragons. We're prone to equate darkness with death, with dying stars and dark skeletons and monsters. But what if out of primal darkness, new life emerges?

All creation comes out of nothing, the theologian Matthew Fox reminds us in *Original Blessing*. "There is a necessary link between darkness, nothingness and creativity. All creation is birthing something where previously there was nothing. Darkness is the origin of everything that is born — stars born in the darkness of space, our ideas and images born in the darkness of the brain, children born from the darkness of their mothers' wombs, movements of liberation born from the darkness of slavery and pain." We're born into light from our mothers' womb-dark. All our organs function quite nicely in the dark — even our brains.

What would we learn of the dark if we listened and touched it more? Many mystics over the years have discovered how to embrace the dark and learn from it, as Juan de Yepes or St. John of the Cross did back in the sixteenth century. He was jailed for nine months and there in his

Our Divine Human Virtue

HOPE

Jerome Groopman says hope is the path to a better future. What is a "better future" when one faces one's own death? Is it a pathway to a pain-free existence? A path leading to a place we have only dreamed of? A dark walkway in search of some starlight? Or a time when everyone can say good-bye? Hope was the only thing left in Pandora's box after she set all the scary things free. Hope flutters in our breast, offering a soft and tiny bit of something to cling to.

cold, dark cell, he was visited by angels. One night he escaped with his poetry under his arm. In *Dark Night of the Soul*, he described how the soul must empty itself in order to be filled with God. He called this "soul-purging." We emerge from the dark, he said, and are filled with flaming light and love. He died at forty-nine after writing the words, "In the happy night. In secret, when none saw me, nor I beheld aught, without light or guide, save that which burned in my heart."

That dark contemplation can be quite painful. But at some point we realize that we need the dark in order to see the light.

Living and Dying in Darkness and Light

Peering into the dark is like looking through the mist. In order to help clear our vision at this time, which can be filled with tricky shadows, it might be helpful to turn to Celtic wisdom, the kind about which Frank MacEowen writes so eloquently. In *The Mist-Filled Path*, he asks us to reclaim our holy senses. By that, he means we have many more than the five we think we have. Approaching death, we enter a thin place, a threshold place, where the natural world as we think we know it and other worlds intersect. Ancients thought of this as a crossroads-place. A Lakota medicine man named Buck Ghosthorse said, "Sometimes we have to travel to the edge of ourselves to find our center." It's where we wait in darkness. We wait in the unknowing for that moment of holy knowing.

Douglas John Hall, a Canadian theologian, makes darkness particular. He has no interest in false lights or various religions and world-views. He has no interest in courting general darkness except when it is already our condition. "Only light is final," he says. We won't know that light until we stand, honestly and knowingly, exactly where we are. He calls for "specific light." Without it, we delude ourselves with artificial light. What matters, he points out, is one's own darkness and one's own particular dying. It takes courage, he says, to stay in the dark until the light comes... the light that is always for a particular darkness. Then we have hope. It's from this courage to stay in the darkness that hope is born.

At the time of this writing, Margaret Rothschild, a friend of Herbert, is near death and she chose to spend her last days living as fully and consciously as possible. And to share all this with her friends. "I am trying to witness to others," she wrote in an email to her friends, "as much as possible that this can be a grace-filled time if one is conscious and aware of the constant presence of light and love." It does not take special talent or paranormal abilities to live fully while dying, Margaret noted, "just a little courage and the willingness to go into the unknown without a preconceived outcome." She acknowledged moments of fear of the unknown that pass quickly. "I guess it's natural to be afraid of the completely unknown and unknowable but it seems also natural to embrace it, to embrace the richness and promise of mystery."

In *Natural Grace*, Matthew Fox recounts a visit with a friend who was dying of AIDS. He describes saying good-bye and looking into the blackest eyes he had ever seen. Like a black whirlpool, even though when this person was well, his eyes were blue. Fox thinks his friend's eyes had already made the journey into the dark before the rest of his body did. "Loss and grief are another journey into the darkness or into suffering. But... light and darkness are moving along together." Death, he goes on to say, "is an emptying, but it may also represent the polar opposite: a filling with the deepest light and beauty of the one who undergoes it."

Suffering Is Optional, Sadness Is Not

Profound sadness accompanies us in the darkness and through the mist. Rather than being something to try to avoid, for we can't avoid it, we can only welcome it and let it do its work. In sadness, we often carry the weight of our lives — and of the world. Thomas Moore in *Original Self* writes: "Generally our moods don't exactly come and go; they appear and subject us to a particular alchemy that transforms us, helps us deepen and develop." By peering into the darkness, we deepen — and that can be a very good thing.

The poet John Keats called our world "the vale of soul-making." He wrote that pain and suffering were necessary because earth is a place "where the heart must feel and suffer in a thousand diverse ways." The Russian, Rasputin, often described as a holy fool, like other monks at other times, agreed to endure suffering as part of his calling. But as the holy people of the Ute nation taught us, "Do not murmur when you suffer in doing what the spirits have commanded, for a cup of water is provided." Christian theologian Paul Tillich makes a similar connection between sadness and suffering and authentic living: "Christianity demands that one accept suffering with courage as an element of finitude and affirm finitude in spite of the suffering that accompanies it."

Karen has said she believes that while she has experienced pain, she is reluctant to say she has suffered. She has read theories of pain and how, as explained by Jerome Groopman in *The Anatomy of Hope*, belief, expectation, and desire activate our brain circuits where we experience pain. Recent brain studies indicate that we actually have pain "centers" in the cerebral cortex that activate neuropathic pain. We've all stubbed our toes or cut ourselves and then "waited" without pain for the brain to say, "This must hurt!" And then the pain comes. Or people with phantom limbs can sometimes feel pain in a limb that no longer exists. Scientists tell us that there is an overlap between these brain-pain centers and the emotional-processing centers of our brain that explain this. Daily, Karen reminds herself that sadness and pain are inevitable but suffering is optional.

Tibetan Buddhism teaches that suffering is a feeling that our wishes are not being fulfilled. Or that no one is listening to us or does what we expect them to do. We say we suffer the loss of a job. We suffer emptiness in our relationships when we can't find the right partner. At the time of death we may feel our ground shifting or even disappearing. Our thoughts become muddled. We're exhausted. Habitual patterns, or a need for drama, can keep us stuck in a suffering mode. But we are each responsible for being awake and recognizing how we may have been suffering long before facing our death. And we learn to accept it. And allow it to be transformed, like a seed, long buried in the dark moist earth, rising to become a radiant flower.

We all live with this mystery. We can't use our usual senses on this journey, so we enter the darkness carrying a backpack of unknowing.

I Just Feel Good

Herbert's friend, a hospital chaplain

Deacon Bates was eighty years old. He had worked as a custodian for the Pennsylvania Railroad all his life. Although we had not spoken of dying, Deacon's doctors had told me he was near death. One day I commented on the fresh flowers "that brighten up a room on a cloudy day."

He said, "I was feeling lonesome sitting here looking at my flowers. I don't like to be left alone." It's an empty feeling, I observed. Deacon responded, "I remember feeling this way twenty or thirty years ago when I worked the night shift at the train station. Along about three a.m. it was so quiet waiting for the next train."

Later in the conversation, Deacon said, "You know what, Reverend, I think about heaven now... what's it going to be like when I die."

"What do you see?" I asked. "Oh, I don't see anything. I just feel good. And worry a little bit. I'm kinda looking forward to seeing what God has in store." I left assuring Deacon that whatever happens after death will be fulfilling.

Deacon Bates, it would seem, was more willing to live with the uncertainty of not knowing than his chaplain. Elisabeth Kubler-Ross suggested that the dying use three languages: *plain speech* ("I have only a short time left"); *symbolic nonverbal language*, particularly used by children to convey an awareness of death that adults cannot speak of; and *symbolic verbal language* ("waiting for a train") which the dying use to communicate what they are experiencing through richly symbolic images that do not always make sense to the logical mind. If we listen carefully to what they say in nonliteral ways, the dying will tell us what they know.

Continuity and Mystery in Living and Dying

The belief that the soul or spirit or essence of an individual will survive the death of the body is commonly held with considerable certainty. Even when the speech about life after death is explicitly religious, people's expectations vary. Whatever images we hold, they will provide continuity for the individual at death. Meister Eckhart believed that physical life dies but "being goes on." It seems, there is more — more life, more love, a greater Self after death, more work to do, more understanding after death.

Whatever our views of life after death, our longing for continuity remains. Sometimes people seek to ensure continuity with habits. Cultural traditions have the effect of maintaining a connection between who we are and who we have been, between where we are and where we have been. At other times, people will make choices about where they live and where they work to make sure that a life has continuity. One aim of hospice is to preserve personal continuity in the face of death. Karen has explained to people that being in hospice care offers her security. "I know who is coming to care for me. I know they're competent. They give me a heads-up (when I ask) and help me anticipate what's coming. The paperwork's done. I don't need to worry about anything." Continuity of care is like a safely net that makes it possible to live fully without unnecessary anxiety until we die.

There is great diversity about what is required at the moment of death to make sure one's future life is assured. How one dies, many believe, has eternal implications. For Christian believers, we are not saved by doing good — as desirable as that might be in itself. In Buddhism, the goal at death is for the mind to be as unattached, as calm, hopeful, and as clear as possible. Hence there is a great reluctance to use medication that would diminish the mind's clarity. Islamic believers prepare themselves for existence beyond death by confession of faith. Those at the bedside moisten the mouth and will repeat the words over the dying patient who, if unable to speak, will lift an index finger. For Hindus, it is important that last thoughts or words be of God to ensure rebirth to a higher realm. If possible, the person near death is lifted from the bed to lie on the floor close to the earth. In Jewish practice, the body should not be left unattended from death until burial.

Taking the turn toward death sooner rather than later makes it possible for everyone — patient, family, and friends, medical professionals, and hospice caregivers — to work toward preserving continuity for someone who is living toward death. Death is a mystery because it is the end and not the end. There is finality to death. But there is life hidden in God, which is beyond death. Our continuity is in God's love from which we cannot be separated. The rest is mystery that cannot be domesticated either by medical technology or by end-of-life strategies.

FROM THE CAREGIVER'S GUIDEBOOK

Embracing both light and darkness, seeing clearly and seeing dimly, living toward eternity and abiding in eternity characterize conscious dying. All are true. In order to walk alongside the dying, as we shall see in "The Blessed Ambiguity of Dying" (p. 71), when we learn more about the ambiguity of dying, caregivers need to move into an unknown process without a preconceived outcome.

1. There is no formula for dying. No anticipated path. We remain open to surprises. Caregivers honor the uniqueness of each individual by paying careful attention to the particular darkness and the particular light of the loved one dying. Things change at night. The distance to the bathroom gets longer but less so when the sun comes up. Make sure the way to the bathroom is clear, there are handholds, and they ask for help to avoid falling.

2. While there are dependable caring strategies at the end, family and friends need to listen carefully — especially when the language or images seem strange to the logical mind — to hear how dying persons describe their own journey to death. The patient may talk about different ways of traveling and they "want to go home." One hospice professional said that following this is "like dancing, but about a half a beat behind."

3. Set a timer to go on at dusk so there is a dependable light. A clock within sight will also assure the dying one, who may nap a lot, when real night has come.

4. You will witness what is coming, and it will come when it will come. You can't always anticipate it, so remember that there may be surprises and that the end is always shrouded in mystery.

About the Cover Image
Means of Egress
by Laura Baring-Gould

The cover of this book shows a temporary sculptural installation that I created, with the help of many others (including Karen and her son Joel) in 1995. Titled "Means of Egress," the exhibition featured five illuminated boats, fifteen to eighteen feet in length, soaring in the wooden arched ceiling of a chapel that had recently been converted into a cooperative gallery outside Boston, Massachusetts.

Visitors entered the one-month exhibition by walking through January snow into the darkened gallery interior where eleven tons of coarse rock salt covered the entire floor. The glowing boats, built from plans of Viking funerary vessels, traveled overhead.

It was a powerful exhibition — one that received many awards, but also broke attendance records as people flocked to the gallery to sit and stand quietly on the salt and watch the boats' passage across the arched chapel ceiling. Two of the vessels were filled with reflections from light moving on water, while a sound piece by Caleb Sampson of low tonal melodic calls echoed through the space.

Historical research had led me to make the connection between navies of ships and the overturned boat-shaped naves of churches, and the ancient use by many cultures of boats to bury their dead and send them into the afterlife. For some, the piece was a connection to ancestry, for others a liminal moment of beauty and formal or archetypal juxtaposition of a boat hull and a chapel ceiling. For most, however, it was a time to pause and connect with those greater questions of human fragility and departure.

The story I rarely tell about "Means of Egress" is that my father died at sea, having left his overturned Alaskan fishing boat to swim to shore in frigid water. This happened when I was in college, years before I became a sculptor. It must have been obvious to many as I built the boats and busily arranged for the generous loan of the rock salt that this work was about my father and his death. For me, however, it was not until a quiet moment in a frantic day of raising the boats in the church ceiling that I realized this piece was about witnessing and being present to my father's passing.

These questions about death and dying have remained at the core of my work ever since. With each opportunity, I am drawn to combine materials of mythological consequence (honey, beeswax, salt, copper) with universal forms (boats, kivas/temples, horns, trees, objects of bounty) to fill a buoyant need to connect what has come before to who we are now.

Ancient cultures knew, and practiced, many ways to integrate death and dying into life and living. In our own culture we are very far away from this. My artwork, spawned from my own experiences with loss, remains a vital means of forging resonance between our internal and collective experience. Within all of it I hope to offer, and echo, possibilities for connection and egress.

an essay

ꝏ ON TRANSPARENCY ꝏ

What if God were a verb? A dynamic verb such as *becoming, unfolding,* or even something more provacative like *exploding*? And what if everything and everyone were safely, firmly, and lovingly lodged inside this verb? We would be energy in motion. We'd be alive — through and through. We'd be able to adapt and sustain life because we were a part of this amazing "verbness." And we'd also be transparent to one another.

Dolphins have been around for millions of years. They are deep breathers and speak in clicks with long- and short-range sonar systems. The anthropologist and humanist Ashley Montagu once said that because their brains are so large, perhaps one day they will teach us what our brains are for. Jacques Cousteau claimed dolphins have a language of two thousand words, making their active vocabulary larger than that of many humans. If a dolphin is no longer hungry she can project an image of a belly full of fish. And unlike humans who bluff and exaggerate about eighty times a day, dolphins can't lie because they so easily see into each other. It is said of dolphins that they know, as do whales, where all their peers are, what they're doing and maybe even thinking. They know if one of their family is in trouble or hungry. Or dying.

If we were more like them, we wouldn't be able lie to each other. Deception would not be a part of our inherent makeup. We'd see inside others because we'd remember that we were all created of the same nonjudgmental verb-stuff, and we'd know the truth of everyone. We'd observe with crystalline clarity. And we'd be transparent to each other.

"I can't imagine that," you might reply, "because I'm just human and humans learn early on how to deceive, lie, cover up, and explain away. People pretend and suppress. We learn, early on, to guard our vulnerable selves in whatever ways keep us alive."

That's true. We do. But perhaps humans could practice a more dolphin way of being. Maybe we just haven't learned to access a deeper humanity within us — one more resilient and more open to honest exchanges. What if we didn't hide and, instead, we shared our stories? We'd have meaningful conversations. We would risk honestly describing how we're feeling about everything and allow others to join us in meaningful conversations about all the ramifications that create this amazing verb-filled process we call life.

At the end of one's life it would likely mean we could finally be more conscious about what we want to happen next. We could decide rather than slip into a protocol-world where established medical practices will automatically kick in and the decisions are made for us. The majority of humans now believe that a life should be prolonged — no matter what. But a new transparent stance would admit that we will die one day. Of something.

And what if, like those playful dolphins, we practiced valuing every single present moment and did not fear the future. The word "dolphin" is closely connected to Delphi in Greece — *delphys*: the Womb of Creation. What if we midwifed each other into a new consciousness about dying? What if we chose transparency as our guide so we could help to birth a different and better way of being — up to our very last breath? We'd become amazing swimmers!

PART TWO

ORIENTING *toward* DEATH

The Blessed Ambiguity of Dying

"God has placed the deepest and most fundamental contradictions in human life not to be resolved but to be lived in the full consciousness of their contradictions."

Jacob Needleman, philosopher

ℵ *from* Karen's Hospice Journal ℣

Lately, I've been thinking a lot about caterpillars. And how they become but-terflies. I chuckle at the New Yorker cartoon of two caterpillars looking up at an airborne butterfly and one says, *"They'll never get me up in one of those!"* There's a mystery about this fuzzy worm inside a chrysalis that holds the potential of flying. What a paradox! I've read that the caterpillar completely disappears, except for a few cells that are called imaginal cells. Imagine!

A paradox refers to two statements that apparently contradict each other but are ultimately true. I'm living on such a teeter-totter now. Sometimes I go up, sometimes I go down. Back and forth. I remember how G. K. Chesterton painted paradox: a truth standing on its head waving its legs to attract attention. I'm living now in layers of multiple meanings. Time is everything; time is nothing. Sometimes I feel as if I'm connected to everyone on this planet. At other times I feel all alone. I know that para means "beside" and dox means "opinion." I am of the opinion that things are right next to me, yet far away. Paradox knows every side of my story. All those waving feet make me dizzy.

Death / birth. Ending / beginning. Alone / together. Strength / weakness. Power-less / empowered. Active / passive. Tears / laughter. Anger / acceptance. Blindness / in-sight. Sweet / sour. Both / and. Or what if I'm suspended in threeness? Black, white, and gray? Or fourness? Denial, acceptance, avoidance, assent?

I echo Alice in Through the Looking Glass. *"I can't believe that,"* she said to the Queen. In a pitying tone, the Queen replied, *"Try again: draw a long breath and shut your eyes." Alice laughed. "There's no use trying," Alice replied. "One can scarcely believe impossible things." "I daresay, you haven't had much practice," said the Queen.*

I daresay I haven't had much practice at any of this!

ℵ ℌ

Most of us have little practice at living with ambiguity and paradox. We would rather say things are this way or that way and be done with it. We presume that one of those ways — usually the way we choose — is right. In order to flee from the anxiety that ambiguity generates, we divide and polarize the world so we will have enemies to fear or hate. We live with duality. But we need to practice exploring beyond it.

Can It All Be True?

Aristotle originally taught us about duality. He said, it's either yes or no. True or false. Either, or. Black or white. But in a world teeming with diversity, twoness is no longer enough.

In the second century, a Buddhist philosopher named Nagarjuna came along and suggested we consider a different way of thinking — one based on a four-valued logic. What happens if besides a right and a wrong way of looking at something, instead both are right and both are wrong? Or neither are right or wrong? Or, take light. Light is a wave. Light is a particle. That means light must be both a wave and a particle. But it can't be both at the same time so is light neither a wave nor a particle? All four compass points are true. If we apply this to our own dying, then, we might say: death is final; death is not final; death is both final and not final; therefore death can also be neither final nor not final. Can all be true?

"Ambiguity is the warp of life, not something to be eliminated," as Catherine Bateson described it in *Peripheral Visions*. "Learning to savor the vertigo of doing without answers or making shifts and making do with fragmentary ones opens up the pleasures of recognizing and playing with pattern, finding coherence within complexity, sharing within multiplicity." We experience this vertigo, this multiplicity of meanings and interpretations of life's decisions, moment by moment. We are not likely to embrace many meanings or multiple truths if we have had little practice in "believing impossible things" or recognizing that most of life is full of ambiguity and paradox.

We exist in a relational web. There is a world that I construct and there is a world that you construct and I must contend willy-nilly over that which I have no control. As a result, ambiguity is not just about uncertainty: it is about the inevitability of twoness or threeness or even fourness in human life and the consequent possibility of alternative meanings. We might even say that paradox is a form of systematic ambiguity at a very deep level. And it's everywhere.

Consider, for instance, a family's capacity to be together. It really depends on its ability to be separate. Solitude and community are paradoxically connected. Consolation is found where our wounds hurt most. We get over loss by dwelling on it. As humans, we are soul and body or soul-bodies; we are no longer what God intended us to be and not yet what we shall become. Autonomy and community are always paradoxically connected. We say death is friend and enemy, an act of completion and a thief, a moment and a process. In the midst of ambiguity and situations full of paradox, we still must make choices about how we live and die. And we can.

The Blessed Paradox of Dying

We love to think of things coming in neat and definable stages. But as humans, we are not that easily boxed. Later, we will consider how we die more according to stories than stages. But, the stage-specific approach to dying introduced by Elisabeth Kübler-Ross quickly became the way to think about dying and even grieving. The movement from denial through anger, bargaining and depression to acceptance does identify attitudes and emotions commonly experienced by people who are dying, but the framework does not reflect the ambivalent character of living and dying. Being grateful does not keep people from bargaining for more life; hope and depression are not mutually exclusive; acceptance of death includes the commitment to keep living. Dying people who are ambivalent are not confused. Quite the contrary, they are deeply and intensely aware of the contradictory nature of living and dying. This morning is a good day. This afternoon may not be so good. Emotions can change suddenly and unexpectedly. It is like living on a teeter-totter, as Karen observed.

In *How Could I Not Be Among You*, Ted Rosenthal says there is something about dying that separates you from all other people. Once you have nothing, he said, you can be anything and that offers a feeling of freedom. Rosenthal understood the blessedness of living in paradox and ambiguity. If you have nothing, he wrote, if the future is visible just ahead, if you live in the moment with nothing, then you have everything. Ambiguity is blessed because the appreciation of ambiguity fosters humility in life and wonder at the mystery in each unique self. It presents us with a gift and is blessed because it diminishes the divisions that our fear creates. It challenges us to behold mystery in everyday moments. Of course, not everyone regards ambiguity as blessed or of God. In its extreme form, ambiguity threatens our certainty about what is real or what is true. It shakes our foundations. But when one is dying, there is only one certainty, and that is love, even when our experience of God's love or other people's love is ambiguous.

Defining the moment of death presents a challenge. Is it when the heart stops? When the brain dies? When breath ceases and bodily systems shut down? Solving medical riddles keeps physicians busy, hospitals full, and the cost of health care rising. Even though medical examiners can determine with some precision the actual time and cause of death, why someone dies when she dies remains a mystery.

Our cells die and get replaced all the while we are living. Sherwin Nuland writes in *How We Die*: "[T]he experience of dying does not belong to the heart alone. It is a process in which every tissue of the body partakes, each by its own means and by its own pace." The dying process parallels the living process. Some people believe that at birth each one inherits a limited supply of the "stuff" for living that cannot be replenished indefinitely. Eventually we run out of gas — so to speak — and we die. If one holds such a deterministic view of the process of dying then living toward death may become a more passive waiting than an active participation. One thing is certain, however. While we are living, *we are dying*. Even if we don't develop a life-threatening illness, our body parts wear out. But the moment of death in the midst of that process still remains unpredictable.

The Many Faces of Death

As we have already suggested, the shift from death as a problem to be solved to a mystery to be experienced is pivotal for end-of-life care. Yet, it's a complicated transition to make. Everyone likes to be a problem solver. And not everyone lives easily with mystery. But the mysterious remains mysterious. What matters is how we behave toward it.

E. M. Forster, in *Howards End*, has Helen trying to explain to Leonard that

Our Divine Human Virtue

HUMILITY

Rudolph Steiner said, "The heights of the spirit can only be climbed by passing through the portals of humility." What do those doorways demand of us? The knowledge of our own limitations? Giving up our pride? Truly acknowledging what we lack? Being willing to ask for help? All of the above? All we can ask is to see ourselves clearly. And to thank those around us for helping us to do that.

we are all in a mist and the people who build empires and amass money can't deal with Death. It offends them. But the poet, the musician, and the tramp — they know. She goes on to tell him the difference between Death and the idea of Death. "Death destroys a man: the idea of Death saves him." "Men of the world," she says, "may recoil from the charnel-house that they will one day enter, but Love knows better."

Death is at once a friend to those for whom life has become too much and an enemy when an individual dies with her dreams left unfulfilled. Sometimes, when people outlive friends and relatives, death becomes the best friend they have. Herbert's mother-in-law, Alice, viewed death like that at age ninety-three. She had lived alone for fifty-five years, fiercely independent, riding the buses of San Francisco. When she was being encouraged to take more cabs, she said with uncharacteristic clarity, "Don't you take my buses from me!" Her card-playing friends were all gone and she prayed daily that she would die. For Alice at the end, death was mostly her friend and life was mostly the enemy.

The Roman Catholic theologian Karl Rahner adds yet another paradox to our understanding of death. It is both fate and act, he says. The end of a human life may be a rupture or accident that seems to strike from without, suddenly and tragically. When that happens, we may say that "death took" or "cancer took" my husband, as if death or cancer had control or power to act on us from the outside. At the same time, the end of a life may be an active fulfillment from within, an act of self-completion. Her husband died. It is something he did. We can all tell stories of individuals who waited until a sister arrived at the bedside from New Jersey or the last child married. In those instances, dying happened because a human acted.

It Will Be All Right

Herbert on his mother's death

My mother, Clara, had been in the coronary care unit of a hospital in Jamestown, New York, for several weeks. She was seventy-five and in fragile health because of a heart condition. It was not, however, a life-threatening condition. Her heart was not so good but her hearing was excellent. One day Clara overheard the nurses talking about how she would be transferred the next morning at nine a.m. She was to go to a nursing facility in the same complex and only 300 yards from where she lived with my father. She became distraught. Sometime that night or early in the morning, she woke up the person in the other bed and declared, "It will be all right." At five a.m. my mother died. She *would not be transferred* from what she perceived to be the safety of coronary care. So she wasn't.

In His Lawn Chair and In Her Bed

Karen on her parents' deaths

My father, Juel, feared dying in a hospital from his emphysema. He hated hospitals. But he loved helping people, so after a particularly busy day of lawn care, he came home, sat down in his chair, popped open a can of soda, and died. Mom heard the can drop onto the patio and she knew he was gone.

He had earlier told me about how he had found my uncle Ray, one of his favorite brothers-in-law. "There he was in his rutabaga patch." Apparently, my uncle had laid down, taken off and folded his glasses, removed his hat and there he was — stretched out in his garden, palms together under his cheek as if peacefully sleeping. My dad stretched on the floor to show me how he had found him. From the look on my Dad's face, I knew that's how he wanted to go. Purposefully and as easily as Ray. And he did.

They say couples who have lived together happily for a long time will often die within two years of each other. My mother, Ellen, died exactly two years after my dad died in his lawn chair. Like him, she also spent her days caring for others. My dad's older brother Bill needed help with a move so she enlisted several of her sisters to help clean out his house. She went to bed early that night, according to her last diary entry. "A very busy day. I did a big wash. Dried fast... we worked real hard... Got everything to the garage. Many trips. Cleared everything. I have some things left to do myself. Very tired and sore. Hot day. The temp is now 56." That is the last diary entry she ever made because that night she died in her sleep. And those things she had "left to do herself" never got done. Unless, of course, the "left to do herself" was to die. Death, I realized, is a last entry on a page followed by blank pages.

For Karl Rahner, death is both "actively achieved and passively suffered, of full self-possession and of being completely dispossessed of self." Herbert believes that his mother died rather than be transferred to a nursing home. Karen believes that at some level, her parents did not want to linger. And she, herself, has made the decision not to prolong her death. Those who regard death as something outside of life or alien to living will find that choice difficult to understand. If, however, one holds that death is the important fact about us because it is the end of every other fact about us, then choosing to enter the process before the fact is a bold commitment to living while dying. Dying then becomes the final fact about a life.

Embracing Contradictions

The idea that death is morally neutral — a natural fact of life, given in creation and declared to be good — has been challenged by Robert A. Burt, who writes about the intersection between medicine, law, and culture. The provocative title of his book, *Death Is That Man Taking Names*, comes from an old song that includes these lines: "He has taken my father's name and he's left my heart in pain." Try as we might, we cannot negotiate or control the end of a life. We may deny our ambivalence about death, but it cannot be suppressed indefinitely. Like some powerful surging river, ambivalence is unavoidable. It floods over us in living and most certainly in dying. Our names are taken.

If we embrace contradiction and learn to live paradoxically, then there is always another side that needs to be heard. Activity and passivity are both essential qualities of being human. We are both subject and object, both actor and one being acted upon. If we believe we are created in the image of God, then to be human encompasses creating, producing, initiating, and making things happen. But it also means we are fully human when we are passive, incapacitated, ill, waiting, needing, dependent, suffering, receiving, and submitting. This is hard to embrace because we live in a culture that prizes autonomy, idolizes independence, and values self-sufficiency. We prefer self-reliance. Who, in their right mind, would relish helplessness, dependence, and neediness? It takes courage to admit one's helplessness. When we know what our needs are, we are empowered — empowered enough to move into our ultimate passivity and to die with neither resistance nor fear.

We are, after all, helpless at birth. We come from the earth and we return to it. A feminist theologian named Penelope Washburn said, "The acceptance of death is the recognition of our ability to surrender our struggle for conscious articulated existence, to surrender ourselves to the bodily memory of the dark and the warmth."

Those who visited St. Christopher's Hospice in London in the early years observed the positive connection between the emphasis on the acceptance of death and the feminine atmosphere of the hospital. The womb and the tomb are one. Dying is a surrender to the earth and God's embrace, according to Roman Catholic theologian Teilhard de Chardin:

"At the last moment when I feel I am losing hold of myself and am absolutely passive within the hands of the great unknown forces that formed me; in all those dark moments, O God, grant that I may understand that it is you... who are painfully parting the fibers of my being in order to penetrate to the very marrow of my substance and bear me away within yourself."

Sometimes we die as we have lived and sometimes not. Sometimes a short life may be full and a long life may be empty. And sometimes how we die is the best thing we do in a life. Even when we feel empowered to make choices, death will remain an ambivalent guest.

FROM THE CAREGIVER'S GUIDEBOOK

Because dying intensifies ordinary emotions, be prepared for both ratio-nal and irrational thinking to the end. Today death is a friend; tomor-row it might be an enemy. Choosing among several appropriate options for sustaining care depends on the same willingness to consider several possibilities simultaneously. The meaning of death and the concerns about dying vary from group to group, from religion to religion, and from individual to individual. Respect for those differences is an essen-tial part of care for the dying.

1. When the dying person is overwhelmed by too many treatment options, you may be called on to help sort out the choices in a non-anxious and calm way. Provide favorite books, tapes, remote controls, and writing materials within easy reach. Use extended reaching tools for easy grasping.

2. Human life is never a life wholly to itself. Dying is no different. Dying is a team sport, Timothy Leary once observed. Let them lean on you when they can no longer lean on themselves for support. But always allow them to try to "do it" and "decide it" for themselves when they can. A bed trapeze can offer a patient the opportunity to move more easily. A dying person often gains confidence and a sense of control and competence when she is supported in making single decisions at a time.

3. When the dying person lives comfortably with paradoxical mys-teries that accompany dying, medical professionals and family and friends should set aside problem-solving impulses in order to embrace the wonderful and complex mystery of simultaneously living and dying.

4. Maintaining a continuity of presence in the face of discontinuity of thought and feeling is what will turn your presence into loving care.

How Do We Talk About Death?

*"Death is the side of life which is turned
away from us and upon which we shed no light."*

Rainer Maria Rilke

ℵ *from* Karen's Hospice Journal ✒

On New Year's Eve after I had already made my decision to stop chemotherapy, we had dinner with friends. After dessert, one of them said, "So, what does this coming year look like for you?"

I felt the question deserved a direct, transparent, and real answer. Taking a sip of water, I replied, "Well, since I decided to stop taking further treatment, I'll be entering hospice care soon. So I think it's likely I may not see this year through to the end." Silence. I've experienced such thundering silence with others since that New Year's Eve conversation when I tell people I'm now in hospice care. You can see their eyes click up into their heads as they begin to calculate the weeks and months I might have left. Some actually ask me, "How long will you have?" Language leaves them, just as language leaves me, too, with only a wide swath of confusion behind.

Word sounds come from our breath and the vibrations we create. Regardless of where they're born, babies blow milky breath-bubbles, and they all begin by saying "ahh." Soon, like little Buddhas, they add mystical consonants: "Ohmmmm" and, of course, "Mamamamama." Words carry our stories and key up our songs. Old words, such as logos, scratched onto parchments tell of creation, the first and most sacred utterance. Words can be wonderful tools, as are symbols, to express and clarify what we're thinking. They can also be thin, weak, and useless. Like the question: "How long do you have?" Which words shall I use now to talk about what's happening to me?

When I say "death" it's harder to come up with a concrete image than if I say "car," for instance. With "car," my mind immediately goes to "red Subaru." But

"death"? What's that color? What form does it take? When I check my Roget's
Thesaurus *for help, I find words such as:* Decrease. Terminal. Deteriora-
tion. Extinguishing. Unhealthy. Receding. *I want to spend what time I have
left writing a new* Hospice Thesaurus *filled with words for dying that sound
more like:* Hope. Joy. Increase. Vitality. Fulfilling. Ongoing. Paradoxical.
Powerful. Eager. Energetic. Whole. *All feelings are true.*

*In talking to my husband, now I find myself using "you" more than "we" in
conversations about the future. "You'll enjoy visiting Herbert and Phyllis in Sonoma." "You should think about getting a lawn service and help with the gardening."
"You might take another cruise." I leave "me" out of those plans. I continue to search
for the "right" words, the most "helpful" words. Sometimes I hit a wall.*

*As long as I can remember, I've wrapped myself in the flesh of language. Now I
wallow in an alphabet of ambiguity. I don't know what I'm thinking until I speak
it. And even then, I'm not sure. Language is just too finite to describe the infinite,
and that's what death seems like to me now. Infinitely indescribable.*

༄   ༄

Three themes from Karen's reflection about language at death merit
careful attention. Authenticity is transformational. Secondly, grammar
matters. If we are alert to the pronouns and verbs they use, we will
learn from the dying. And third, silence is appropriate when words are
not enough. Karen's decision to speak openly about dying, as we noted
before, not only eliminated her anxiety about determining how much
people can handle or what language can they bear to hear, but it also
invited liberating and life-affirming conversations with many people. In
all conversations at life's end, paradox prevails. If you want to be my
friend in my dying, I want you to forget I am dying. Second, you must
never forget I am dying.

What Language Shall We Borrow?

Whether you're the one dying or you're someone who now spends your time with the one who is dying, it's not easy to know how to talk about it. We sometimes think even mentioning the "D" word is too morbid. Too discouraging. Too stressful. Julia Assante in *The Last Frontier: Exploring the Afterlife and Transforming Our Fear of Death* writes: "Discussing death with the dying is practically taboo. We collude in the belief that it is too stressful for them. What is disguised as good bedside manners is really rather a ploy for dodging awkwardness, confusion, and powerful emotions on everyone's part. We are too uncomfortable to tread on religious beliefs or to encourage the ill to confront their ambivalence."

So we tiptoe around and talk about everything but death. The fact is, however, we may create more stress by avoiding talking about it. The one who is dying may not want to talk about what's happening because she doesn't want to add further burdens on her family. She is always trying to judge how much to say, to determine how much people can handle, and what language they can bear to hear. But then again, she may just be waiting for the opening to freely talk about everything.

Karen first spoke of writing this book to Bridget, a young friend, who said, "I hope your book will help us know what to say, because I just don't know what to say to you right now. I love you and I don't know what to say."

Karen met with a group of hospice and chaplaincy volunteers at her local hospital after being about three months into hospice care. They wanted to know more about dying from the dying person's perspective. But more importantly, they wished to learn better ways to help family members deal with their emotions.

Karen offered this: "Listen carefully. Hold their feelings as best you can. Be empathic. Let them know concretely that you have heard their pain. But remember, the emotions of family and friends are not the responsibility of the dying person." She emphasized how important transparency is at this time and how authentic conversation can't take place without it. "Once you get over the 'oh, I can't stand the thought of losing you and it hurts so much' phase, you'll return to your normal way of talking to each other. Laugh! Use humor. It's your friend!" Then she told them about the dying woman whose husband was having such a difficult time at her bedside. The woman looked at him and her last words to him were: "Buck up!"

The Dive

Karen's son Nathan

How many other children (and I still am a child when it comes to my relationship with my parents) have their mom ask them to write about this kind of transition? Mom actually talked about a "deadline"! I have taken a gulp and dived into writing this so many times and floundered so many times that I can hardly unclamp my toes from the diving board anymore. It doesn't really matter if the dive is swan or belly flop or drunken sailor. That's the dive. Let's be clear, I'm fine with her dying. Hell, she's excited. Excited but scared. She's giggling like a schoolgirl wading water-dress deep into the Atlantic Ocean. So, she's going and you know it, I know it. I'm dealing with it and dealing with it fine I guess. Mostly now I find myself worried about Dad out there caught somehow underneath his lawn mower or snow blower, depending on the season, but I really just don't want to write about her dying.

Because I had such problems getting a handle on this, Mom wondered aloud as to what my daughter thought about Grandma Karen dying. Josie knows that Grandma Karen is very sick. She knows that sometimes she has lots of hair and sometimes none at all depending on if she gets her wig on in time. She knows that Grandma needs lots of naps.

I know what Josie thinks about death. It's a place where her first dog, Loki, is currently playing fetch with the angels and that's all well and good. As to our former fish — "all drains lead to the ocean" which is fine as well. "Tony," the ant that she feeds on the front sidewalk, has died numerous times (sometimes daily; mostly accidentally).

Josie's current phone habits tend to frustrate everyone. You'll be lucky to get anything out of her on the phone other than an enthusiastic "I love you Grandma! Bye-Bye!!" Maybe that's all any of us needs to know about dying.

Drawing Rings

When the clinical psychologist Susan Silk was diagnosed with breast cancer, a friend said to her, "This isn't just about you." Susan digested that for a bit and thought, "This isn't about me? Are you telling me it's actually about you?" In thinking about what we say to people — appropriate or not (such as "I wasn't prepared for this. I don't know if I can handle this") — she came up with what she calls "Ring Theory."

Draw a circle, Susan instructed in a blog dated April 7, 2013. It works for any sort of crisis, but for the purposes of this book, let's imagine a dying person. Write the dying person's name in that circle. Now draw a larger circle around it. In that circle write the names of the people closest to the dying person — family members, best — very best — friends. Now draw a larger circle around that and write the names of less intimate friends. Now draw a circle around that for everyone else — community members, email buddies, etc.

Here's how it works. The person in the center ring can say anything she wants to anyone, in any ring. She can kvetch and complain and whine and moan and curse the heavens and say, "Life is unfair" and "Why me?" That's the one payoff for being in the center ring.

Everyone else can say those things too, but only to people in larger rings. When you are talking to a person in a ring smaller than yours, someone closer to the center of the crisis, the goal is to take your cues from him. Listening is often more helpful than talking. But if you're going to open your mouth, ask yourself if what you are about to say is likely to provide understanding and comfort. If it isn't, don't say it. Don't, for example, give advice. People who are suffering from trauma don't need advice. They need support. So say, "I'm sorry" or "This must really be hard for you" or "Can I bring you a pot roast?" Don't say, "Well, let me tell you about what happened to me!" Or "Here's what I would do if I were you."

Our Divine Human Virtue

HONESTY

Being transparent opens you up to being vulnerable — not always a happy place to be. We like strength better. We fall into duplicity when we feel unsure of ourselves. Lying to ourselves and to others can become a habit. "I feel fine." Oh, really? To be candid, we have to release our fears and come out from under the shadows. We then find joy in becoming real. No more fibs. No more hiding. No more covering up. We are what we are. Thank goodness!

If you want to scream or cry or complain, if you want to tell someone how shocked you are or how icky you feel, or whine about how it reminds you of all the terrible things that have happened to you lately, that's fine. It's a perfectly normal response to dying. Just do it to someone in a bigger ring. In other words, "comfort in, dump out." Complaining to someone in a smaller ring than yours doesn't do either of you any good. On the other hand, being supportive to her principal caregiver may be the best thing you can do for the patient. That caregiver also needs to feel grief and together you can express your common sadness.

The Complexity of Talking about Death

When we don't know what to say about death, we tend to fall back onto platitudes and clichés that sound hollow as soon as they leave our mouths. "God works in mysterious ways." (Are you saying God *wants* me to die? But we all die! What's so mysterious about that?) "I understand how you feel." (No, you don't. One day you will, but right now, you don't. No one else can really understand how I feel. And maybe you should read "How Are You Feeling?" p. 189). "Let me know if I can do anything to help." (Would you please carry out the garbage? Or do my laundry?) "You're not dying, you're just ill." (No, I'm really dying). "My cousin had cancer and she's completely recovered. I'm sure you will be cured soon." (Each person's cancer is unique. When my doctor told me this was treatable but not curable, I believed him. So should you.) "I don't want to lose you." (Oh, for heaven's sakes. You'll be fine.) "You look great!" (Really?)

We are on a first-name basis with death from all our TV crime scenes, autopsies, reality shows, and our up-close news coverage. But it's always someone else's death. We kid about death, tell jokes about death, and think up clichés to describe death: we kick the bucket, croak, sing our swan song, and go belly up. It's curtains for us. We buy the farm, give up the ghost, cash in our chips. Even public references to someone's death often use "passed away" rather to say a person has died. In the medical world, people expire much like a credit card. When we say "death took," we imply that death has power over us and is not a part of us. However, when someone is dying, we are not likely to say he or she "is in the process of passing away." We overlook positive descriptive words about death such as peaceful, blessed, quiet, calm, pain-free, rest, coming home. And we all too often lack the impetus to create meaningful and authentic conversations around what death means.

As hard as it may seem, we need to be frank. Sigmund Freud was pretty forthright about his tongue cancer, which he lived with for sixteen years. He even once said, "I'm not sick; I just have cancer." In his essay called "Thoughts for the Times on War and Death" he wrote: "To deal frankly with the psychology of death has the merit of taking more into account the true state of affairs and in making life more endurable for us."

Not everyone is willing to hear the truth about death or their own condition. Susan Partovi, an instructor at UCLA's David Geffen School of Medicine and the medical director for Homeless Health Care, Los Angeles, wrote a *Los Angeles Times* article about one of her patients for whom she found that not telling him about his cancer was the right prescription. Pedro's wife asked her not to tell him that his stomach had been removed instead of what he thought was part of his esophagus. "He'll lose his will to live if he knows that his stomach was removed… and I don't want him to know he has cancer." She consulted with a colleague about this course of action, and her colleague suggested she consider the patient's cultural background and what death means to this family. Just to confirm, they asked Pedro, "Do you want to know the details of your illness? For instance, if you were dying or had cancer, would you want to know?" Pedro said, without missing a beat, "No!" The family wanted "everything done" for Pedro and Partovi kept her promise. She didn't tell him he was dying — just that his lungs were "filling with fluid and she was giving him medicine to help him breathe." Pedro died without knowing he had cancer, even though that went against everything Partovi believed should be transparent for the patient as well as the family. But the patient's wishes prevailed.

Real Comforting Conversations

The word *comfort*, derived from the Old French, means "to be strong with." We are called, at this point in our lives, to be strong with each other. Val Walker in *The Art of Comforting* emphasizes being strong with, not for. "Being strong with someone means creating a sanctuary for someone in pain, a respite from the busy, indifferent world around us, just sitting down, listening, and allowing the person to acknowledge his or her pain."

Our tendency is to want to fix things and to get over hard stuff fast. But dealing with dying takes more comforting conversation — even if it is slower than most other ways of talking. It demands deeper listening and the recognition that all of this is often very confusing and unpredictable. Consolation and comfort, in dying as in grieving, are often found where our pain is the deepest or our where our grief about leaving everything behind hurts the most.

One of our latest approaches to enable people to speak about death comes in the form of city-based "Death Cafés." They're not grief or end-of-life support group discussions as much as confidential philosophical discussions styled after European salons. The café sessions are usually facilitated by someone willing to ask questions such as "What is your biggest fear about death?" They are intended for people who may have someone in their family who is dying or for people who are simply interested in exploring generally all ideas around death and dying, knowing they will face it one day themselves. They want to discuss these important topics in ways that are not taboo, trivialized, or morbid.

The poet W. H. Auden acknowledges it's impossible to figure it out. "Death is not understood by death; nor You, nor I." It's simply beyond our understanding so naturally we're loath to talk about it. It's a moment and a process. It's natural and unnatural. Friend and enemy. Continuity and discontinuity. Buddha called it a temporary end to a temporary phenomenon.

We should be aware that religious, gender, and ethical factors determine how we think (and talk) about death. How we're framing dying and death may not be how others think and talk about it. Much depends on

our own personal perspectives as to how we view ourselves as finite beings. Ira Byock reminds us to be careful not to push our own agendas at
a time like this. He encourages us to trust our instincts. We may have to
let go of our expectations. Karen's friend's question on New Year's Eve
"What does this new year bring for you?" opened up the conversation
she wanted and needed to have with them.

Talking about death is a challenge. As Karen said, "Language is just
too finite to describe the infinite, and that's what death seems like to me
now. Infinitely indescribable." Yet we must try. And our best efforts will
be, in the long run, valued and appreciated.

From the Caregiver's Guidebook

"I don't want to talk about it" are seven words that often negatively impact marriage, friendship, and most certainly the experience of dying. Sometimes, words are not enough and song or touch or sighing is required when the pain is too deep. Listen carefully to the dying person and you will discover ways to convey your empathy. Words are windows both to the divine and to the deeply human.

1. Not talking with a dying person about his or her experience isolates. Even so, you will need to honor reluctance to talk about death. Remember to ask another day, however, when he or she may be eager to talk.

2. Be direct. It's okay. But also be calm. Listen to the dying person's complete thoughts. It's important for him or her to "think out loud." Pause. Clarify. Use "I" statements: "This is what I notice..." At the same time, be willing to be corrected when you miss what he or she feels. Avoid "why" questions or comments that carry a subtext of any sort of judgment or require explanation. Help the dying person to feel free to talk. If there is a time when you are concerned about what to say or afraid you are going to say something "wrong," the best thing is to just not say anything and to simply listen.

3. Make sure you understand, as best you can, the medical language so you can use ordinary day-to-day language to describe what is happening. Using language the patient will understand will reduce the dying person's isolation and allow her or him to be the actor in the process of dying.

4. Even though the dying one has made some difficult decisions, it may still be hard for you, the caregiver, to initiate a conversation around those decisions if she or he doesn't seem to want to talk

about them. Watching a movie together might prompt a discussion that otherwise would be hard to get started. Let the dying person lead the conversation. She or he may say something like: "Do you think (so and so) knew they were going to die?" "Do you ever wonder (as the actor did, perhaps) when and how this was going to happen?" "Did he make the decision you would have made?" The conversation will go where it will, but you will have opened the door.

Taking Charge in the Midst of Chaos

"The hope lies in the unknown...
The world is up for reinvention in so many ways.
Creativity was born in chaos."

Charles Handy, *The Age of Paradox*

ℵ *from* Karen's Hospice Journal ℣

I know, deep down, that there is a hidden order even though things look chaotic on the surface. I read Thomas Merton's words: "Beneath the broken surface of life there is a hidden wholeness," and think Yes! I've read books about chaos theory so I know that patterns I thought were set — aren't. When new energy is introduced, matter gets reorganized. Open systems have something called strange attractors *pulling nonlinear systems into new and different visible shapes. It stirs up turbulence. And change. The science writer James Gleick has said, "The greater the turbulence, the more complex the solution, the greater the jump to a higher state." I'm jumping! But to what level of reality? Death is my strange attractor now.*

Living with the unknown is tough. The old Sufi prayer is my ready companion: Lord, help me in my knowing; Lord, help me in my unknowing. *I squint to see these new complex patterns. So I ask myself: What fractals now filigree my edges? I'm in the midst of beautiful, clustered and ever-swirling patterns, some predictable, and some holding surprises.*

Ten years ago I spent about five hours every three weeks at Dartmouth's infusion center for six treatments. Glory be to God, we thought, when my cancer went into remission. It's gone. But of course the cancer wasn't gone. *I just thought it was. People diagnosed with cancer learn to live with words such as* remission *and* tests *and* scans *and* reevaluate.

Over this past decade, I have been determined not to allow cancer to define who I was. I believe I was and still am so much more than these errant cells growing inside me. My friends have pointed out to me that writing a book about dying is my way of taking charge of my last days. And while I won't be able to alter the outcome, I do feel "more in control." Writing this book with Herbert focuses me, provides me with creative energy, and at times makes me smile. Furthermore, it gives me the chance to ask people for their stories, to give and receive gifts, and to have wonderful conversations I most likely would not have had had I just slipped into quiet seclusion.

Still, the prospect of facing so many things I cannot control can be overwhelming at times. The prospect of pain is the big one. Anyone who has had surgery or spent any time around the medical community will know about the pain continuum: "From one to ten what are you feeling now, ten being the worst." I call it "From one to childbirth." Whenever I'm asked about my pain number, I search around thinking, "Whose pain do I compare this to? Is it a six? Or a four? Am I just being a baby and it's really only about one and a half?"

In surveys, people are apt to say, "It's the pain at the end of life I fear, not the actual dying." Since I believe all fears are based on loss, I ask myself, "Karen, what are you afraid of losing? Comfort? Control? Predictability?" But then, I remind myself that losing myself to find myself seems to be the journey I'm taking on now. Pain/pleasure. Control/uncontrollable. Lost/found. Predictable/unpredictable. It's all a construct of my mind and I'll come, eventually, to the point where I probably won't know the difference. And it won't matter. So, deep down, I know any pain I'm experiencing right now does not define me. My hospice team is on top of every aspect of my pain and when I spot those dark pain-clouds coming in, I know they no longer threaten my horizon.

Ira Byock uses the phrase "dying well" to mean one has a sense of living up to the very end. As time has gone on, increased dosages of morphine have become a trustworthy companion to dull the pain and make sleep possible. But I continue to want to be more awake during those precious last moments. Of course, I may still change my mind. But I hold on to his notion that no one need die in pain. That includes me.

ℵ ⁊

In Control or In Charge?

If someone who is dying is asked "How is it going?" she is likely to reply in an equally vague way by saying "Well, it's complicated." Karen often responds, "Some days are better than others. Right now my energy level's great. But I'm really living hour by hour."

Bodies do strange things, evoke equally unknown emotions, and prompt statements like the following:

> Even if you are in hospice care, you can still get shingles.
> The remission you trusted turns out, on further review, to be a false rumor.
> Losing control of body functions is embarrassing.
> My body is changing and I can't stop it.
> The diminishment of body functioning from diseases such as ALS is relentless.
> I feel good today. Tomorrow could be a lousy day.

Barbara Sigmund wrote an "Ode to My Cancer-Ridden Body" that is included in *An Unfinished Life* in which she describes the unpredictable body changes she experienced with ocular melanoma like alienation or losing a friend:

> Hey, old buddy,
> When did you decide
> That you and I aren't
> Best friends?

Body unpredictability and diminishment of functioning often lead to a feeling that things are out of control and chaotic. There are some people who thrive on trying to bring order out of chaos. They may even generate complexity just for the challenge of fixing it. They find strange attractors stimulating. But what they may not realize is that because everything is connected to everything else, a change in one part of their lives changes everything so control is impossible. For the person dying, the body is a chaos barometer that might herald stormy weather.

Today, I Almost Feel Like Living
Herbert's friend Jane

Ten days from the start of radiation (to help control pain), Richard awoke unable to walk, and the oncologist said he had to get to the hospital without delay. A magnetic resonance imaging test of the spine and brain revealed no tumor to explain this handicap and so began a two-week hospital stay marked by increasing pain (and increasing doses of narcotics to control it), extreme weakness and constipation caused by the narcotics. Richard thought there was no point in continuing treatment. His doctors thought otherwise and urged him to continue the radiation, along with medications to counter the swelling and constipation.

My goal, my hope, was that he would live just three more weeks and be well enough on March 26 to attend a musical celebration of his life's work as a lyricist, at which friends and family from far and wide could say good-bye.

On the sixth morning of his hospitalization, his bowel congestion finally relieved, he awoke pain-free and cheerful and announced, half-joking, "Today, I almost feel like living." I began to breathe normally again. But this was only a brief reprieve. A few days later, it became obvious that the treatments were only adding to his misery, not relieving it. Every touch, every movement seemed to hurt him and he was no longer able to get out of bed. I reluctantly abandoned my March 26 goal and arranged for hospice care. There were no more decisions to make. Richard died on March 18.

Richard died when he was seventy-seven. Herbert knew him from their hometown in Minnesota. Jane's memories of Richard's death illustrate one dimension of the chaotic unpredictability of dying. Richard went from living cheerfully to living miserably in no time at all. Mathematician-architect Christopher Alexander said, "You think you see chaos? It's really a rich, roiling, swelling, lilting, singing, laughing, shouting, crying, sleeping order." People who relish surprise and the delight of discovering something new about themselves or life in general will live more peaceably with the chaos of dying. People who don't like surprises won't.

Dying defies carefully ordered plans. It is much too messy and unpredictable. To add to the complexity, the dying one never knows how others will respond. But she can learn to be in charge even though she can't control what happens. Control presumes mastery of people and events that makes it possible to rule or command or simply have the upper hand. To be in charge means she realizes she still has the capacity for action. She still has choices. Control is an illusion. But, while being in charge is elusive, it is still possible.

She Died the Way She Lived
Karen's friend Deadra

My father, a very private man who never wanted to bother anyone with his problems, lay down for a nap after a restless night, fell asleep, and never woke up. My extroverted mother, on the other hand, held court in her hospital room, waiting for all of her friends and family to stop in and say good-bye. Though she was in a very fragile state, she waited for me to fly in from the East Coast to baptize her before she died.

Her closing act featured making sure that both of her children were in the room when she drew her final breath. My brother was adamant about not being there. He was able to stand by her side as the hospital staff disengaged the life support systems, then he left me in the room for what would surely be no more than a few minutes until she died.

But to everyone's amazement, minutes turned into hours. Around lunchtime my brother ventured into Mom's room to see if I wanted anything to eat. I gave him my order and he returned with lunch for the two of us and sat down to eat with me. How Mom must have loved that.

As the afternoon wore on my brother nervously turned on the TV to catch the news. As he surfed the channels he landed on one of Mom's soap operas. I was mortified thinking that Mom's story would end with, "Time of death: half past *Days of Our Lives.*"

At some point my brother settled in and turned off the television. As he became a little more comfortable he held Mom's hand. Mom died late in the afternoon with both of her children beside her... as if she had orchestrated the whole thing.

A thin membrane separates being in charge from controlling. In a way, we might say that Deadra's mother couldn't control her dying, but she was still in charge of it. Her dying was for her an act of completion and she preferred that her children be there at the end to bear witness. It seems that once Deadra's brother was willing to be present with his mother, she could die. From the perspective of her surviving children, their mother seemed to be as controlling in death as she had been in life. Both may be accurate. Dying, however, will not be commanded or controlled. Nor is it possible to have mastery of the process of dying. In a paradoxical way, relinquishing all efforts to control the process of dying is a liberating act. It becomes our way of choosing how to live until death. Letting go or relinquishing is one act; purposefully handing over is yet another. It is important to distinguish between these simultaneous actions if we are to better understand dying.

Handing Over

It seems oxymoronic to say that we can be in charge by handing over. But, while the act of handing over includes letting go and grieving, it assumes a different direction. It moves toward rather than away from what we value. In handing over, we are entrusting what we value (and so entrusting ourselves) to whomever or whatever "hatched him," as Ernest Becker put it when he was dying. It is an act that depends on trusting the divine purpose or creative energy of the cosmos. At the end of life, one can only relinquish a life or hand over one's life to divine purpose and in that action, we find meaning.

Letting go of all we love is painful beyond words. How we "hand over" our life can be our way of transforming death. The acceptance of our own finitude need not doom us to despair. Imagining our end, insofar as it is humanly possible, may evoke massive anxiety. But we can cultivate virtues in those upper reaches of faith and personality development. We will be sad and even forlorn in handing over a life,

Our Divine Human Virtue

JUSTICE

When chaos reigns, it's hard to find anything that feels just or compassionate. Injustices occur when we feel we have the right to judge — one over another, one idea better than another, one way more prudent than another. Justice all too often becomes trampled by power. When we feel separated from Our Source, from God, we are apt to forget that we were created in that image. That *just* image. How can we be less? St. Basil the Great said, "The acts of charity you do not perform are so many injustices you commit."

and at the same time we can experience joy and hope by trusting enough not only to let go but to hand over for safekeeping the life we love to the Divine as we know it.

It is difficult for people who know they are dying to understand that the truth about their situation will set them free. Or that they will find new energy and hope beyond illusion. When we are able to hand over a life at the end, there is great relief. We do not have to be responsible anymore. This is what a dying person has to teach. We do not own our life as a possession. Instead, we can view our life as a gift and we're just giving that gift back to the Source of Life from whence it came.

Taking Charge of Dying Incrementally

Unless an accident takes us quickly, we're apt to die in increments. Slowly. Death is a process and we're not sure where on that spectrum we should get serious. Many of us suffering from heart, lung, or kidney diseases go from crisis to crisis. "Chronic diseases are often predictably fatal," Gretchen Brauer-Rieke, RN, MSN, says, "but on a completely unpredictable timeline, making it difficult to know prospectively when one is actually near the end of life." Moreover, the increments do not follow an even, linear trajectory. There is back and forth as well as up and down.

As in Karen's case, cancer can be held at bay for years but there comes a time when treatment no longer helps. Or, in fact, it's often the treatment that actually causes the death. Most cancer patients who de-cide to stop treatment may have a heads-up time of around six months and hospice treatment can be a blessing for that person as well as for his or her family. It could be longer. It could be shorter.

Brauer-Rieke speaks of another common pathway to death that she calls "prolonged dwindling," which is more common with Alzheimer's and stroke patients. The inevitable limitations of aging or the tragic saga of diminishing for persons with Lou Gehrig's disease are other instances of incremental dying. Death would occur naturally to many people, but modern medicine adds to the increments of dying by seeming to rescue them from death. But we know no one is ever rescued from death! It comes with being born.

Taking Charge by Counting the Cost

As we keep prolonging life, often artificially, health-care costs continue to escalate. Maybe that's good news in disguise. Perhaps, if the costs increase outrageously, we'll begin to realize that there are other ways to live toward death than with an expensive cudgel. We may reach a tipping point about the cost of dying that will encourage us to approach death with caring dignity. Making decisions as medical professionals, family, and the dying patient consider the cost of treatment is another way to take charge of one's dying. This is easier said than done, however. As long as we maintain a "whatever-the-cost attitude" in deciding for ourselves or caring for our loved ones, it's difficult for us to get our heads around cost as an end-of-life factor.

We need to ask ourselves, what are we willing to spend just to postpone the inevitable? In Karen's case, Medicare is covering her hospice care, as it is for many in her situation. Even so, choosing hospice care is a decision to limit cost because expensive chemotherapies or radiology services are no longer possible. These are very personal decisions with public, social consequences. We may, as a matter of justice, decide to have only those medical procedures that are available to everyone in this society. Karen's turn toward death and her subsequent treatment decisions were motivated in part by a desire to support greater medical accessibility for everyone.

Taking Charge by Continuing Advance Planning

Most of us (around 80%) say that if we had our druthers we want to die at home. But the reality is that most of us — again about 80% — wind up dying in hospitals or care facilities. When we don't make end-of-life decisions in advance, others may make decisions for us that may not be in our best interests.

Even when all advance directives are in place, there are more decisions to make along the way about treatment strategies or adjustments to medication to manage pain and enhance living. These changes have consequences. When medications change, because of shifting circumstances, for example, or when pain medication is increased, the dying person may sleep more than usual for one to three days partly because she will be able to catch up on sleep. Family and friends, as well as the dying person, need to be reminded that changes in functioning may be normal, even if they heard about them before. Other changes may be necessary or possible later in the dying process. For instance, Karen's hospice doctor has told her there is a procedure she can do right at home, if necessary, to help alleviate gastric discomfort closer to the end, and it will in no way violate the advance directives. Karen finds comfort in that.

For people with dementia or Alzheimer's, decision-making needs to happen earlier rather than later, while decision-making capacities are still strong.

Taking Charge by Practicing Passivity

As we described in "The Blessed Ambiguity of Dying," if we embrace contradiction, if we learn to live paradoxically, then we will also discover that we constantly need to be "saying the other side." The other side of activity is passivity, waiting and not having or possessing while we wait. This has significance for our consideration of fostering agency and autonomy at the end of life. In our dying as well as our living, we are both subject and object, both actor and acted upon. Taking charge at the end of life may sometimes be more about passivity and waiting than choosing and controlling. Activity and passivity are both essential qualities of being human. In our waiting, our passivity, our *being done to* by countless medical caregivers or medical professionals, we are no less human than in our acting.

In this cultural context, passivity is linked with dependency and has negative connotations. We don't like to be around needy people who are overly dependent. Taking care of sick or handicapped people is a challenge. We are self-reliant people who prefer not to be reminded that we are fragile, finite creatures who get sick and grow old! For some, neediness is more problematic than dying. In a culture that idealizes independence, the neediness, dependence, and passivity that underlie our dying are difficult to deal with. But acknowledging dependence at the end of life is something we can do: we can choose to be cared for. And we will be transformed by making that choice.

Phil Had Clear Opinions
Karen's friend Deadra

I've long observed that people die in the same way they live. It's easy to wear any number of masks in our daily lives, but when we die all of that is stripped away until nothing is left but our essential selves.

My first experience of companioning someone who was dying was as a young hospice volunteer. The man I was assigned to visit, whom I'll call Phil, had very clear opinions on almost any subject, particularly those involving his wallet. For his entire life he had fought for every penny and I could see immediately that it had been his life's mission to protect his hard-won assets.

When Phil entered hospice care he was also engaged in a hot dispute with his city over a property boundary that affected his tax bill. I remember that I could tell what sort of news Phil had received about the dispute just by looking at him. Phil was actually energized when he received bad news about his property. His eyes blazed as he hoisted himself up in bed, all the while recounting the tale of the blow that had been dealt him and what he intended to do about it.

On days when there had been no news Phil was listless and depressed. I could see the energy draining from every fiber of his being. He didn't want to talk and he often fell asleep in the middle of my visit. On those occasions I always left convinced that this would be the last time I would ever see him. And I was always wrong.

One day I went to see him and he was sitting up in bed, grinning. He was so calm and peaceful that I almost wondered if this was the same person I had visited in the past! As I sat down beside him he waved a piece of paper in the air. It was a letter from the city. He had won his property dispute.

He died the next morning.

Phil's story reminds us that the dying person's capacity for action remains important to the end of one's life. To be human is to be an actor, to choose freely.

Human beings are made, many believe, in the image of God. We bear that Divine image whether we are active or passive. We are as fully human when we are incapacitated, ill, waiting, needing, dependent, suffering, receiving, and submitting as we are when we are busy creating, producing, initiating, and making things happen. We can move into the ultimate passive state of dying knowing that we are still fully human, and still bearing God's image. Phil chose to be active to the end. For others, the end of life is stillness and quiet waiting.

From the Caregiver's Guidebook

Dying will not be commanded or controlled. Nor is it possible to have mastery of the process of dying. In a paradoxical way, relinquishing all efforts to control the process of dying is a liberating act. It becomes our way of choosing how to live until death. Nonetheless, there will be surprises. The unpredictability of dying is almost as certain as death itself.

1. Remember to breathe. Stay calm. Caregivers should not overreact in the midst of chaos and varying shades of gray. Those who care for the dying need to be prepared to be surprised and live in chaos. We can't control death any more than we can control the weather.

2. For some people, being dependent on others is as problematic as the dying itself because it embodies their loss of control. If you can respond firmly and graciously to the resistance to being cared for, it will help the dying person take charge of "handing over" care to others. Without being patronizing, offer the dying person choices: Do you want to drink in the chair or stay in bed? Do you want the red blanket or the quilt? Making choices as long as we can make them helps a dying person be in charge of a process she cannot control.

3. Keep the focus on what the dying person needs rather than your own pain and anguish. This is especially important when the dying person makes choices about treatment on financial grounds.

4. Caregivers play a critical advocacy role in support of patient agency and activity away from unilateral medical authority and patient passivity. Increased autonomy does not guarantee, however, that the dying person will choose living rather than dying. Even when patients can easily reach favorite snacks, thermal drinks, etc., they may not always want to eat. They have the option.

Trusting the Capacity of Others

"Trust cannot be given carelessly...
and yet there are people of honor and places of refuge.
One might well ask: What is the alternative to trust?
Have we not had isolation enough?"

Marilyn Swell, *Cries of the Spirit*

⋈ *from* Karen's Hospice Journal ⋈

Ten years ago, when I learned that extensive surgery at Dartmouth-Hitchcock Medical Center would take place within a week, I sensed the urgency around my condition like a sledgehammer coming down. A late Stage III. Big bad numbers. Who knows what's been invaded already.

I began making a "thankful" list of my angels and the gifts they brought. Some I knew; many I didn't know at all until they showed up. Dawna with Reiki. Diane with prayer. Margaret with harp music. Jenny's chakra healing. Sherry's biofeedback balancing, Barbara's healing stones, Julia's watercolors, Mary Ann's stories, Karen's star-filled lap quilt, Callie's star card, Sharon's rituals, Joe's e-jokes — they all held me.

"How can we support you?" my Sophia women's circle wondered. We've meditated and visualized together enough that I felt confident in saying, "Just visualize the Milky Way wrapping me in star-power."

I wasn't even sure what I meant by that request. But standing under the Milky Way that night, with it whirling like big platters in the sky, so misty and reassuring, I knew I wanted to keep that safely held image in my mind as I was wheeled into surgery. There is nothing that tests your trust like lying helpless on a gurney. My new oncologist was on vacation. Covering for him was Dr. Barik, a Jordanian I'd never met before. Like many people at what could easily be my end of life, I had to trust the competence of a stranger. He was obviously a pinch hitter who had just dropped in to New Hampshire from points beyond, and I had no choice but to trust that he knew what he was doing. Before the surgery, he explained to John that if he was back in an hour or so, it would mean they decided to not tackle the task. After over five hours, he returned saying, "I got everything I could see." As it turns out, he certainly knew what he was doing. Residents later told me that they had learned so much from working with him. "Karen, he's read absolutely everything *that's ever been written about ovarian cancer." A stranger-angel who flew in to my rescue. I never saw him again.*

When I returned home, a fingernail moon floated overhead and I thought, "New beginnings." I was bloated. I felt about ten months pregnant. I had to wear some of John's underwear because nothing of my own fit. I wrote in my journal: "Cross-dressing at 2 a.m."

Trust is a funny thing. To define it, I have to look at its shadow and try to see the opposite. To not *trust is to feel very alone. Adrift. Awash. Without a tether to anything. To* not *trust means I have nothing to lean on when I can't stand alone. When I trust professionals, systems, others' experience, I am confident that I can rely on them to see me through experiences I haven't had yet. In one of my first conversations with my first oncologist, he said, "Karen, you can research ovarian cancer all you want on the Internet and you can learn a great deal. Or you can trust us — your team here at DHMC. You've had your surgery. Now we suggest that we do vigorous chemotherapy treatment." I trusted him and all of them to know what they were doing. And to this day I have not researched anything online. And that's not like me, because I love to do research. But I trusted them to know what was in my best interests. They kept me alive for ten years! I harnessed my energy for healing rather than second-guessing my judgment or the competence of medical professionals. But then, when it came time for me to make the hard decision to stop treatment, I trusted my inner gut to know what to do next.*

When I ponder big words like trust *and* faith *I think about how the Hopi people don't seem to worry about concepts like time and space. They experience in life what is manifest, what is manifesting, and what is still unmanifest. They trust the world to operate that way. They don't seem too concerned about the whereness or whenness or whyness of it all. To me, that's pure trust.*

Every time I create something (new to me) I trust that it will work. When I write, I trust that the words will flow, and that, if it's a book, a publisher will step up to make it happen. And I trust that readers will actually turn the pages or access the electronic data. I trust that my friends won't abandon me. I trust that the sun will rise tomorrow. I trust that the robins will find their way back to our snowy yard each spring. I trust that my Sophia-God and my sturdy understanding of the Christ Essence will sustain me through every last breath I take. I trust that the people who drop in to my life have dropped in for a reason and they know what they're doing. I wrote in Sophia: The Feminine Face of God: *"I will guide your feet... you're pillowed and quilted and held... my well goes deep and holds water for a very long time."*

I trust that deep well.

৯ ৶

Trust is an essential dimension of human living but for the dying person it has sacred significance. Karen discovered that truth shortly after she was diagnosed with ovarian cancer. For her, ten years later, trust is still sacred. The necessity of trusting is like breathing. Most of us take trust for granted until it is violated. At the beginning of life, the infant learns to trust the world because the mothering one is trustworthy. Erik Erikson called trust the basic human virtue because the infant learns that the world is a trustworthy place in which to live. It is a sacred matter. Throughout life, we live back and forth between trust and mistrust, between skepticism and believing. At the end of life, we return to the vulnerability and helplessness common to life's beginning and trust is essential again.

Establishing Ties

In *The Little Prince* by Antoine de Saint-Exupéry, the little prince meets the fox, who says he can't play with the prince because he hasn't been tamed. "Tamed, an act too often neglected. It means to establish ties." The fox explains that this is a very long process and you must wait patiently and say nothing because words are a source of misunderstanding. The fox tells the prince he should come at the same time every day — one must observe the proper rites, he explains. When they part, the fox says, "It is with the heart that one can see rightly; what is essential is invisible to the eye."

The fox argues that establishing ties is a very long process, and he is right of course. When one faces one's death, there isn't time. The dying one must now rely on what is invisible to the eye. The heart-stuff.

The need to trust begins with the diagnosis of a life-threatening illness. The impulse to seek a second opinion may be a prudent act. It's sometimes motivated by denial and sometimes by appropriate skepticism, but it may also reflect a reluctance to trust medical judgment. In order to live fully until we die, it is beneficial sooner rather than later to suspend disbelief. Moreover, accepting a diagnosis is only the beginning of countless situations of increasing vulnerability and dependency that require the dying person to trust the capacity of others — some of whom may be strangers. The first surgery after Karen's initial diagnosis was performed by someone whom she had never met and would not meet again. Given the complex institutions that support medical advances, the greatest challenge for the dying may be to trust their well-being to impersonal procedures and anonymous physicians. And they must believe that the drugs prescribed have been adequately tested and will, in the long run, make them better even when they initially may make them sicker.

Trust and Loving the Unusual

Thomas Moore in *Original Self* talks about how we're all vulnerable on our journey and we need the hospitality and understanding of others. Many of those "others" will be unknown to us. It takes an awakened heart to know what it is we truly need. And we need to be brave enough to seek it in uncomfortable places or accept help from unexpected people. "When a society loses its soul," Moore writes, "it develops many neurotic behaviors, among them paranoia and xenophobia… the anxiety in the presence of strangers or simply whatever is strange and unusual." Like death! So how do we develop the willingness to trust strangers and embrace the unusual? It takes courage to enter into the unknown. The more we practice this, the more trusting we will become.

Moore goes on to say that if we are unwilling to engage in this risky practice, we will begin to view everything not connected to our ego as suspect. For many people hospice and palliative care is not a continuation or extension of an active life so naturally they don't easily trust it. But through education and honest conversations, people learn to value competent care at life's end and trust it. For people who are still able to make treatment decisions, it is important to trust that one's own impulses continue to be consistent with long-standing personal values. When one can no longer make decisions for oneself, the dying must trust that families will understand the advanced directives as they were intended.

Trusting Your Choices
Herbert

Shortly after I had made the decision for my treatment plan for prostate cancer, the father of our daughter-in-law, a wise Dutch country doctor, gave me advice that was very beneficial. "Once you have settled on a treatment plan," he said, "don't second-guess your decision. Trust that you have made a good decision and stay with it." I followed his advice and have been very grateful. It is possible that progress of an illness will necessitate reconsidering a strategy but until such necessity, trust the wisdom of your first choice.

Our Divine Human Virtue

SERVICE

The old grail question those armored knights stumbled over was: *Whom does this serve?* When we trust others to serve us, we accept the grail-gift. We are served. When we choose to serve others, we offer the grail to others and are good stewards of all the gifts we have received. To serve, Martin Luther King Jr. said, all you need is a soul generated by love. We are "God-in-action" through our smiles, our willing hands, our busy feet, our gentle voices, and all the other ways we find to show our love.

Ira Byock calls all who love and care about the dying person "family." For Karen, that family is extended through her many Internet connections, her Sophia Sister circle, her farming neighbors, her church community. She calls it honest caring. And the experience of honest, dependable care makes it easier to trust.

What Makes Trust Possible?

It will be easier for dying patients to trust if they are assured that all caregivers, including their physicians, regard *care* rather than *cure* as the basic and indispensable priority in medicine. It will also be easier for patients to trust the treatment process if everyone agrees that death is not the enemy but the necessary endpoint of medical care. Those facing imminent death should be able to trust medical professionals in three distinct ways.

The dying need to lead because they are on a journey caregivers can only follow closely. That is first. And foremost. This can be accomplished only by listening carefully, by knowing the dying person and responding to his or her needs and timetable, and by allowing the one dying to shape the ways the caregiver is present. The will of the dying patient should be, if possible, the primary consideration in all end-of-life decision-making.

Secondly, the dying need freedom to mourn. They yearn to be surrounded by caregivers who will listen empathically to their grief. Grieving seldom ends with one outpouring. The willingness of caregivers to take seriously the pain of losing everything will enable the dying to find enough relief to live the present moment.

Thirdly, those who care for the dying need to acknowledge and be comfortable with their own helplessness. Few things in life evoke an awareness of powerlessness like being in the presence of someone who is terminally ill. More often than not, it is the caregivers' discomfort with being helpless that prompts them to abandon the dying.

Unfortunately, family and medical practitioners often withhold honest information from irreversibly ill persons so "they don't lose hope." One physician supported that practice this way: "It is very difficult to provide open, honest information that includes prognostic information without at the same time destroying the patient's hope." Ironically, hope is eroded when the patient feels isolated and cut off from the honest transparency they long for.

Providing open and honest information about a patient's condition is fundamentally necessary for the dying person's spiritual well-being. Truth about one's situation is what makes possible communities of affection and trust in which hope is sustained. Nonetheless, family and medical practitioners often withhold honest information from a seriously ill person so "they do not lose hope." Unfortunately, the opposite occurs. Of the many ways men and women die alone, Sherwin Nuland observes, "the most comfortless and solitary must surely take place where the knowledge of death's certainty is withheld." If we understand hope only as a future reality, we may miss the sustaining power of hoping with others. If the reality of impending death is denied, hope is impaired rather than preserved for those who are near death. And when hope is impaired, trust is diminished as well. Trusting and hoping are unavoidably bound together.

Trustworthy Caregivers

An astounding number of family members engage in caring for the sick and dying. Some estimate that number to be around forty-two million caregivers. These are the people who juggle other family tasks, work full time, and still spend on average eighteen hours a week (some fifty to one hundred!) helping others cook, use the toilet, manage ostomies, bathe, manage finances, drive to appointments, and on and on. And now our demographics assure us that even more baby boomers will be entering this arena of needing unpaid care. These over-extended caregivers need the support of others who understand what they're up against. They need to lean in to another's pain, but they also need to recognize that they must stay whole and grounded and be open to receiving help themselves. Water does not come from an empty well.

My Hospice Nurse Sherri Is My Hero
Karen

A hero/heroine is a central person who takes an admirable part in any remarkable action or event. She makes special sacrifices for others as well as in her own life. Heroes resolve challenges. In my judgment, my hospice nurse Sherri Lorette is a true hero. She has learned to balance her "feminine qualities" of sensitivity and nurturance with her "masculine qualities" of assertiveness and strength. She practices detached involvement: an essential quality for any hospice caregiver. Sherri has shown how hostility, fear, and conflict can be explored and changed into growth, creativity, and love.

During one of her weekly visits, she explained to me how she uses gentle truths with people. She said she recently cared for a ninety-nine-year-old whose heart was giving out. "I can't make your heart better," Sherri had told her, "but I can keep you as comfortable now as possible." Sherri always brought her a lemon pie for her birthday. Knowing she would not likely reach this next birthday, she brought her a lemon pie several weeks early. They laughed and ate pie together. They were family right up until she died.

Her sense of timing is amazing. As is her gift-giving sense. One of Sherri's home-canned jars of zucchini relish recently made it into our refrigerator. And she has shared just enough of her own bio and family stories that we now feel that we also know and love them.

Her prompt response to pain alleviation has been stellar. She's "on top of" every situation. She knows the system well enough to understand exactly how to get additional meds, etc., in a very timely fashion if and when they are needed. I am grateful that Sherri is my hospice nurse and primary caregiver. She is my hero.

Not everyone is competent at everything. One of the gifts of Nurse Sherri is her willingness to collaborate. At its best, caregiving is a cooperative venture. Some people can do things like waiting and watching and washing. Others need to do the more complex caregiving that may involve managing medication or monitoring body changes. All caregivers, however, whether professional or personal, must be trustworthy. Because people are fragile and easily distracted by pain or discouraged by helplessness, being and remaining trustworthy requires disciplined intention.

In order to stay present and remain faithful, those who care for the dying need to recognize that they too are dying. The dying person's vulnerability is his or her own vulnerability; the powerlessness of the dying is everyone's powerlessness. Beyond understanding the dynamics of dying and beyond effective strategies for care, caregivers need to remember most of all that *we are all dying.*

Surrender, we have already suggested, is not giving up but handing over in trust. Being able to trust our caregivers is crucial. Dying people need to trust that their caregivers allow them every opportunity to continue to act and make responsible choices. As we grow more dependent, the need to trust intensifies. Eventually, however, insisting on being independent begins to make us look foolish and obstinate. In order to live as fully as possible until we die, there will come a time when it will be necessary to trust the assistance and accommodation of others, some of whom may be strangers.

From the Caregiver's Guidebook

Medical technology has increased rather than diminished the need for caregivers one can trust and simultaneously multiplied the need to trust the competency and compassion of strangers. Building trust by being honest is important for every caregiver.

1. Do not promise what you cannot deliver. It is tempting for caregivers to promise that pain will go away or that tomorrow will be a better day or "everything will work out for the best." Trust is built from caregiver honesty. Promise to show up — and if you do, show up. It builds trust.

2. Helping should not diminish a feeling of competence. Trusting others when you can't do something yourself includes the freedom to attempt to do it yourself. Assist when needed, but let the dying one call the shots.

3. Trustworthy caring begins with your willingness to stand in helplessness and hopelessness with the one who is dying. Let the dying person be alone if that is what he or she chooses. He or she can always call you with a bell. Or you might use a baby monitor. Or intercom on your phone.

4. You're helping to create a community of trust. We cannot *command* trust or hope. Nor can we *give* it to another. It can only be embodied as all the caregivers create communities of dependable presence in which hope is sustained and dying persons find wisdom enough to choose their own unique way to death. Let the dying person know when you will be back — post your schedule so the patient will know when to expect to see you again. Place calling numbers within easy reach — and make sure the phone is accessible. Make copies of keys for trusted caregivers in the event no one can answer the door.

HURRY UP AND WAIT

"We are quite naturally,
impatient in everything to reach the end
without delay.
We are impatient of being
on the way to something unknown,
something new,
and yet it is the law of all progress
that it is made by passing through some stages of instability —
and that it may take a very long time."

Pierre Teilhard de Chardin,
"Patient Trust in Ourselves and the Slow Work of God"

☙ *from* Karen's Hospice Journal ☙

Waiting for Godot *(spoiler alert: Godot never comes)* portrays waiting as a time when we care and tend each other. So, waiting, I tell myself, is caring. Be patient, Karen! That's helpful to remember as I wait for lab results, for hospital appointments, for the right people to show up.

My mother, no doubt thanks to her elementary school experience with the *McGuffey Reader,* used to pepper her conversations with phrases like, "All good things come to those who wait." She taught me how important incubation and waiting times are.

All hospice patients wait to die. In a conversation with our Colorado son, my husband John and I discussed when might be the best time to visit. "This is so hard, Nathan, I just don't know what to tell you. Maybe you'll come more than once. Perhaps once with Josie so she can see her grandmother before she's confined to the bed." I'd wanted to plant flowers with her. Michel de Montaigne is supposed to have said, "I want death to find me planting my cabbages." I don't plant cabbages, but I'd like death to find me tending the flowers. And I'd love to have little hands helping.

As it turns out, they did. We had five glorious days of getting her little dinosaur garden gloves dirty. She named the moss roses after her kindergarten friends.

We stirred up pancakes and planned picnics. We drew pictures, read together, and organized Grandma's treasure drawers. She took home one of my fossil rocks to remember those treasures by.

Fossils know how to wait. So do trees. I look at the forest around our house and think, "Take a cue from them, Karen. They know, deep down in their roots, how to transition. What can you learn from them?"

We're all transitioning. We're all leaving behind one story while waiting to figure out how to write the next new story. I tap my feet and drum my fingers trying to make sense of it all. "Life is pleasant. Death is peaceful. It's the transition that's troublesome," Isaac Asimov once said.

Writing about my own transition while so intimately engaged in the process is a bit like trying to write a mountain-climbing guide while hanging off the North Face with cold wind clawing my face. I keep saying, "This dying 'stuff' is truly weird! Yet on another level, it's the most natural thing I can do now." My husband says, "I know. I have to remind myself this is really happening because everything seems so normal." But then suddenly it's Wednesday again and Sherri knocks on the door, stethoscope in hand, asking me how my stomach feels. "Are your ankles swelling? Do you feel dizzy?" And I know I've wandered into some sort of new normal. I sometimes use a walking stick when I'm on uneven ground. And I bought one of those little folding cane-stools you sometimes see people using in museums. I wish I'd had it when we were hiking around Mayan sites in February. I resorted to sitting on a foundation rock wall but not until after the guide inspected it for fire ants. Sitting is good. When I'm in a store, I look around for a chair or an empty shelf or someplace to park my fatigue if only for a few moments. Hospice experts describe waning energy as energy in a box. You can conserve it and save it for tomorrow if you want, but it gradually gets used up. And you'll want to sleep more.

Waiting for dying is in many respects a lot like waiting for birthing and trusting everything will be okay. My son Nate's birth is firmly lodged in my mind since he waited until the last moment before heading down the birth canal. I return to what Neale Donald Walsch says in Home with God: In a Life That Never Ends: the words birth and death could just as well be eliminated from our vocabularies *and we could substitute* creation *for both of them. Believing that in dying we are creating a new existence takes the sting out! Others find comfort in the belief that the new life we are given at death is God's doing. In any event, something new is being born. It's been said that we come into this world on an inhale and we leave on an exhale. All of life, then, is one big breathing exercise. One huge transition. Those shoulders narrow enough to pass through the birth canal are very much like my ever-weakening shoulders that will soon pass through this next canal.*

※ ※

"We'll have the test results back in three days." Those words often evoke terror when there is already some suspicion that the results will indicate a life-threatening illness. And three days can be an awfully long time. These first waiting experiences set the stage for a medical journey riddled with waiting in and out of waiting rooms. Then we wait for the results of even more scans or for surgery to be scheduled or some expert's medical prognosis. When the pain is too bad, we wait for the medication to take effect or the doctor to change the prescription. We wait to have someone tell us whether or not we can go home or if we can drive the car again. We wait for visitors to come and for visitors to leave when we are tired and we're reluctant to tell them to go. We wait for an estranged friend to call back or for morning to come. We wait for the daughter in Brazil to return or for the pastor who has promised to come but has not yet. We wait for sleep to come. And then we wait for death.

Waiting and Dependence

Eventually, dependence and waiting become synonymous. Waiting challenges our desire to be self-sufficient or at least clean up after ourselves. We have to admit we need it, and then wait for help. Anyone who has had an incapacitating or limiting illness knows that the emotions evoked by waiting may be harder to bear than the illness itself. And when the dependence becomes intolerable, we are tempted to bite the hand that feeds us. We might lash out or fall into a depression. Some, like the author and transpersonal psychologist Ken Wilbur, who wrote in *Grace and Grit* about his caring for his wife who was diagnosed with breast cancer shortly after their marriage, turned to alcohol for a time because waiting for her to die became too difficult, even for someone steeped as he is in coping techniques. And the longer the illness lasts, the harder it is for the one dying even to maintain faith in the good will of helpers. The one dying easily imagines her loved ones are becoming impatient with her because it takes longer, now, to walk. And a longer time to eat. And even longer to actually die. Healthy people who are free to come and go with ease have difficulty imagining being limited or confined because of illness.

Wendy Lustbader wrote about being tethered to oxygen in *Counting on Kindness: The Dilemmas of Dependency.* "In order to survive, I have someone take me outside where people come and go. I look at the people going by and they stare at my oxygen tank and the tubing in my nose. I start talking to them to get a conversation going. People like to talk about themselves and they tell me many things. Sometimes I get their whole life story. It's really interesting. I do wish they would ask about my life as easily as they talk about their own. But I am glad not to be staring into empty space waiting for the day to pass."

Waiting to act or waiting for help emphasizes lost freedom. And sometimes with the loss of freedom there is the loss of dignity. Anger and disappointment come easily. It may be helpful, however, to remember that in Hebrew, *waiting* and *hoping* are the same word. So waiting can be so much more than the empty space in between times. If we are able to practice hopeful waiting, we can turn the insults of illness into the privileges of being. Lustbader suggests that people who live well in spite of their illness and increasing limitations are those who allow what she called "divine leisure" to crowd out physical hardship. Howard Nemerov calls that waiting space in *Waiting Rooms* "a cube sequestered in space filled with time. Pure time, refined, distilled, denatured time without qualities, without even dust." Waiting is pure time.

Learning to Wait Is Learning to Die

Waiting is something we've been doing all our lives. We wait for the school bus. We submit a job application and wait for the phone to ring. We wait for a loved one to call. We wait for new glasses when our eyesight fails. Even though waiting is a common life experience, we don't like it. It feels too much like powerlessness and helplessness. But like it or not, even ordinary waiting in the grocery line or for tickets to a rock concert or for test results is preparation for dying.

Our Divine Human Virtue

SELF-CONTROL

When we exhibit self-control, we practice choosing. We choose between despair or hope, depression or joy, denial or acceptance, being greedy or being willing to give, being alone or being with others. We can choose to open up or to close down. It's always our own choice. Self-discipline can be thought of as self-mastery. We practice waiting. We practice managing our time and triaging our energy. In doing so, we find freedom. And peace.

If we have been able to learn patience and how to wait, then we will be prepared for the reality of human passivity and dependence that will manifest itself most fully in waiting to die. If we have lived in this truth throughout a life, we will not find passivity so shocking at the end of life. If, however, we have practiced waiting in ordinary living, we will learn from suffering and waiting what we might not otherwise discover when we are busy making and achieving and possessing. And we will already know how to die because we understand that we are never stronger than when we wait.

What About You?

John, Karen's husband

Nice people, concerned people, ask me, "How is Karen doing?" and then comes the follow-up question: "But what about *you?*"

What does the questioner expect to hear in reply? Usually, some platitude on the order of, "I'm doing okay," suffices. To say anything less would be rude. They feel as if they have to ask, and I feel as if I have to supply an answer, so we can call it "transaction completed."

And that's fine. Most folks don't want to know the whole story, nor could they take it in. I barely let on to myself how I'm feeling most times. The love of my life, my constant friend and companion of nearly a half century, moves a little closer to death every minute of every day. I have been living with this fact for ten years now under several names and playing several roles. And, truly, I am doing okay. But I am still waiting.

When we were very new to this reality, I accepted the role of patient Gatekeeper. I heard all kinds of stories about cancer and cures. "My brother-in-law's sister's husband had cancer and he's okay." Right, so maybe he had a precancerous mole removed. Karen and I were dealing with Stage III ovarian cancer and we knew there was no cure. One can only control it for a time until one can't control it. Our oncologist said as much. We don't need false hope.

Statistically, less than half of those diagnosed with this type of cancer survive more than five years. That's all we need to know. Part of Gatekeeper's job is to damp down the stories and to deal with those who insist we try some alternative medicine. And my Gatekeeper job has been, and still is, to fend off politely any and all who would sap Karen's energy. She has better uses for it.

Caregiver is another of my names. Caregiving takes many forms. Sometimes it's Driver. I can't begin to number the doctor, hospital, and infusion room visits Karen and I have shared. I have not missed even one. It's good to have another pair of eyes and ears in the treatment room.

In 2009, Karen's surgical incision became infected and for six weeks my name was Wound Nurse. At first, Karen worried that seeing the long, deep, messy wound would be too much for me to bear. How could it? When we married, didn't we two become one flesh? The saying "love is blind" extends to all kinds of ugliness. We joked about which nurse would appear each day: Nurse Ratchet or Nurse Jane Fuzzy-Wuzzy. Apparently, I did a passable job with all those dressings. Dr. West offered to certify me and send me out to a wider clientele. On a more ordinary plane, caregiving means foot rubs and back rubs without being asked, and the occasional full body massage. Our code word for a massage: "Can you pencil me in for a four o'clock?"

Before Karen got her first "cranial prosthesis," insurance company jargon meaning a "wig," I gave her the first of several buzz cuts. She even appeared bald-headed on the organ bench at church one morning. Small children were not frightened. Adults were relieved, I think, because no one had to pretend. To live in denial takes too much energy. Finally, enrolling in hospice care announces to the wider world that death is imminent and we can meet it.

When we write her obituary, she knows it won't say anything about "battling cancer" as so many do. Beyond taking regular treatments she never spent much energy worrying about the disease. It would be more accurate to say that she lived pretty successfully in spite of it. Proving that there is a "Divine Art" to dying.

Waiting as a Spiritual Discipline in Living and Dying

Stephen J. Rossetti in *When the Lion Roars: A Primer for the Unsuspecting Mystic* said that waiting is like "standing in the breach." John's story about being a caregiver to Karen over ten years embodies the meaning of "standing in the breach." Family and friends who journey with the irreversibly ill learn well that waiting is "keeping constant vigil." Keeping vigil is being attentive enough to know when a foot needs rubbing without being asked. And as we learn to wait, we become, in the words of Rossetti, "alive to God." He reminds us that sweetness and pain are often intertwined. Neither state is better than the other — just different, and we can learn to accept both with a sense of peace. And we can learn to wait, as John has, for over ten years.

Waiting is a posture of faith and an appropriate spiritual discipline because waiting can portray an accurate description of the human condition before God. It's a state of not having, not seeing, not knowing, not grasping or possessing. We wait for God because we do not possess God. Ironically, the only way we have God is by not having. And surprise, surprise! When we wait for what we do not have, what we eventually discover is that we had it within us all along.

The theologian Paul Tillich once wrote: "Whoever waits in absolute seriousness has already received the power of that for which she waits.

Therefore, we are stronger when we wait than when we possess." This perspective is linked to an earlier theme in this book: life is not a possession. This is yet another paradox: when we wait, we do not possess that for which we wait. This may help us understand why waiting is so difficult for a people who measure worth by possessions. Waiting should not be the occasion for despair. It is the acceptance of not having. Waiting is a spiritual discipline because it reminds us that we do not possess either God or our lives. But even if we agree about the importance of waiting, it is never easy.

Waiting has the potential to be a response to a greater calling. It might be helpful to remember how Jesus waited for the authorities to make their decisions about his future. Before his crucifixion, he waited for others to act. It is not that he went from success to failure, from gain to loss or from pleasure to pain. Rather, he passed from doing to receiving what others did. He moved from working to waiting, from the role of subject to that of object.

Passive Activity: Active Passivity

We are no less human when we are waiting than when we are actively working. The picture of Jesus choosing to be actively passive at the end of his life is one illustration of this deeper truth. We are as fully human when we are incapacitated, ill, still, needy, and dependent as when we actively produce, initiate, and make things happen. The passive states of suffering, receiving, and submitting are not inferior or necessary evils. We can embrace this contradiction and live paradoxically. There is always another side to everything. Waiting can lead to awareness. It's one of the keys to living fully until we die. The other paradox to keep in mind is that each of us dies our own death in our own time... and yet death comes in its own time.

In our culture where independence and self-reliance are not just valued, but idolized, embracing our dependence and passivity is a countercultural challenge of considerable magnitude. But when we recognize our need and acknowledge our helplessness, we are empowered to move into our ultimate passivity, and to die with neither resistance nor fear.

Waiting for what we do not have or do not know and cannot imagine is finally an act of trust. We trust our loved ones. We trust our caretakers. We trust our own bodies to know when it's time to just stop. We trust people to stay present. To be faithful to the end. It doesn't really matter what is said. What matters is that people are present and willing to wait with us. It's then we are connected to that all-encompassing love. Then we can wait and we can die with grace.

From the Caregiver's Guidebook

The movement from being active to being passive, from being in control to being dependent, from taking initiatives to waiting, happens for caregivers as well as the dying. But it is more difficult for caregivers who are still able and mobile, free to come and go. Embracing the helplessness of dying is a choice for caregivers. To care for the dying, as Henri Nouwen writes in *Our Greatest Gift*, is "to help the dying make that hard move from action to passion, from success to fruitfulness, from wondering how much they can still accomplish to making their very lives a gift for others."

1. Care that fosters realistic hope at the end of life demands willingness to stand in helplessness and hopelessness with the one who is dying.

2. When we care for those who are dying, it is important to remember that we are as strong when we wait as when we act. Both are done with intention.

3. More often than not, it is the caregivers' discomfort with being helpless that prompts them to abandon the dying. Caregivers are not helpless. Hospice workers can help you think up easy things to do. Simple acts such as making sure the bedsheets are wrinkle free to help prevent bedsores. Warm blankets or heated beanbags to soften the pain. Warm socks help when circulation slows. Crushed ice and lollipop sponges with water offer moisture when swallowing is a problem. Peppermint-flavored swabs may be welcome. They even come in "coffee" flavor. And there are other ways to alleviate dry mouth.

4. Waiting intensifies vulnerability for the person who is dying, as well as for you. You likely will feel powerless. But remember that hope begins by your being willing to stand with another in his or her hopelessness, without despairing or disappearing.

an essay
⟆ ON STEWARDING OUR RESOURCES ⟆

Adam and Eve, Genesis tells us, were invited to name, care for, and tend all of earth's gifts. Our Creator apparently knows that when we honor our gifts and when we share them with others, our own lives will be enhanced. When we don't, we fall into the fear that our "gifted garden of possibilities" appears to shrink. We begin to think we need to grab it while we can because there's not enough to go around. We call them "limited resources," so we hoard them.

On the other hand, if we approach everyone we meet and truly believe that they are worthy of abundance, just as we are, then we'll find ourselves surrounded by riches of all kinds. The adage "the more we give, the more we receive" is literally and spiritually true. Lao Tzu, the father of Taoism, said in the sixth century B.C.E. that when you realize there is nothing lacking, then the whole world is yours. "If you realize that all things change, there is nothing you will try to hold on to. If you aren't afraid of dying, there is nothing you can't achieve."

Assessing our entrusted gifts, especially at life's end-stages, allows us to develop deeper relationships with everything around us.

We might roughly divide our earth-gifts in this four-fold way: *Gifts of grace* — the loving assurance that we live lives of wholeness and are cared for, even when we mess things up. *Gifts of life* — our well-being. It's true that not everyone lives a life of well-being but each lives with the possibility of deep relationships with all that is living and inanimate, seen and unseen. Our capacity, then, for friendship, community, empathy, and compassion increases. Thirdly, our *Gifts of treasure* — everything we earn, inherit, and are given from the natural world. Using these gifts with care and gratitude and to honor the Creator and passing them on to others when we leave this earth is called good stewardship. And finally, our *Gifts of learning and teaching*, for we are both teachers and students through-out our lifetimes. When a dying person is conscious and calm he or she holds the potential for change. When that person's friends, family, and even medical professionals see this happening, they may begin to consider their own work, their own abundance in the context of living well right up through their own inevitable deaths.

When families have reached that precious recognition and turning point that enables them to know for a fact the person they love is dying, they have the option of surrounding themselves with more laughter, joy, and peace. When they choose more compassion, love, caring, and sharing, over more fear and guilt, alienation, and disharmony, life is enriched for everyone.

When there is a plan for palliative comfort care and when there are trained medical people to implement that plan, *living* until one dies is not only preferable, possible, and practical — it is good stewardship. Time can be attended to. Further suffering can be avoided. Visits and conversations can be treasured. Favorite foods can be savored. Stories can be told, memories can be made and shared, gifts can be thought-fully given and received. Legacies can be assured; relationships can be mended. Instead of clawing and clinging to what was, including more therapies, more treatments, more interventions, the dying person is released. Free. At peace. Everyone benefits; and everyone can join in the celebration of life and be more effective stewards of life and death.

PART THREE

LIVING *until* **WE DIE**

CELEBRATING THE ORDINARY

*"Everybody knows they're going to die,
but nobody believes it.
If we did, we'd do things differently."*

Mitch Albom, *Tuesdays with Morrie*

❧ *from* Karen's Hospice Journal ❧

I have always been a good eater, as my chubby Scandinavian relatives were quick to point out. After putting on the usual middle-age spread, I realized about a year ago that I was losing weight without really trying. I got wonderful smaller-size clothing from a good friend who Weight Watched and I suddenly had new reasons to shop. I marveled at being down to my 1964 wedding weight. At Joel's prompting, I squeezed into my wedding dress again and donned my "pillbox" headpiece and veil as John easily fit into his wedding suit. Joel played wedding photographer and took pictures for our forty-ninth wedding anniversary, which we had the fun of sharing with our friends and family.

All the while I posed on our patio and in our gardens, I thought: you know, this is fun, but it isn't really important anymore. Body image, regardless of how "cute" I looked, is far less important than it ever was before. Oh, sometimes I lament the loss of hair, eyebrows, and eyelashes. And I notice that it's increasingly difficult to sit for long periods of time or even find a comfortable sleeping position because I have bones in places I didn't know existed under my former fat. But I'm at ease with how things are. Well, except for food.

I confess, I'm a foodie. But now I can taste very little beyond salt and sugar and other spices. I tend to order chili a lot in restaurants, chancing stomach upsets in exchange for a few moments of "happy tongue." Hospice Nurse Sherri says it's natural. As we near dying, our body begins to say, "Food isn't so important now." But my husband still enjoys food as much as ever so I valiantly try to keep up with the cooking. There are times, however, when I've said, "Sorry, hon. You're going to have to do this." Nausea hovers close around certain foods — fish, acidic foods, wine — and I keep asking my body, "Do you really want to eat this? Drink this? Won't it be too hard to digest? How about this? Or this?" That's why friends who bring a variety of small containers with good things to eat are greeted with big smiles. Small meals more often seem to be the ticket for me now.

Sherri is apt to say, "Ice cream three times a day works for me if it works for you!" Or, "Oh, so you don't care for apples. How about applesauce?" Or, "Tell me what's your usual breakfast now?"

I avoid watching cooking shows. But surprisingly some days I'm hungry enough to eat most anything. And I love going out to eat with friends — more for the conversation than the food. I often order a milkshake. Or clear soups. Food has become, like some houseguests, an interesting, challenging, beautiful presence in our kitchen. But sometimes I take a nap to avoid food, if I so choose. And now I eat what I choose to eat, when and how much, since I'm not concerned about gaining weight or driving up my cholesterol. How freeing! Bring on the chocolate!

℥ ℈

If we take our cue from Karen's palate, elegant, spicy food may make the tongue happy for a while until ordinary milkshakes must become the new *haute cuisine*. The ordinary and extraordinary exchange places. As death nears, being content with the ordinary is a delightful gift.

Seeing the Ordinary with Eyes of Wonder

In the previous section, we focused on attitudes or soul stuff that orients our living while dying. Trusting, waiting, and embracing ambiguity. People who are dying need to trust the faithfulness, competence, and kindness of caregivers who themselves need to be trustworthy companions. And our willingness to wait patiently is both a difficult and an unavoidable dimension of living and dying. If we have difficulty waiting in grocery lines or for the college acceptance letter or the long-awaited promotion, waiting at the end of life will also be challenging. Embracing ambiguity invites humility and wonder deepens our appreciation of mystery and fosters an appreciation for seeing the ordinary gifts of life. And now, we take a look at the practice of celebrating the ordinary. It all begins by seeing with eyes of wonder.

The author and church historian Karen Armstrong believes the purpose of religion is to hold us in a state of wonder. Perhaps that's also the purpose of our dying.

Awe and wonder move us forward. It's that overwhelming feeling of seeing something in a completely new and numinous way. Life overflows when we're full of this wonderful and extravagant dazzle. The early twentieth-century German philosopher and comparative religions scholar Rudolf Otto suggested that wonder provides an encounter with the holy. We are filled with curiosity and wonder pushes us into what is novel and totally unexpected. C. S. Lewis said when we're in awe we think "every bush is a Burning Bush and the world is crowded with God."

In his book *Wonder: From Emotion to Spirituality*, Robert C. Fuller points out that a third-century B.C.E. Sanskrit text called *Natyashastra* connects wonder to eight other human emotions, which together compose a way to see into divinity. (The others are sexual passion, amusement, sorrow, anger, fear, perseverance, disgust, and serenity, in case you were wondering.)

When these moments of wonder break in they surprise us. We marvel at the ordinary mysteries of everyday living. The nearness of death heightens our awareness of ordinary moments as bearers of grace. Planting flowers with a granddaughter. Late-night conversations about things that matter. Bathing in a sunrise seldom seen. The unexpected beauty of a familiar crystal saltshaker in the sun. An email from a long-lost college friend. Suddenly we shiver. Life is grander than we thought.

Our Divine Human Virtue

JOY

C. S. Lewis once said, "Joy is the serious business of heaven." But we don't have to wait to enjoy life. Joy is deeper than happiness, which is a more on-the-surface emotion. Joy digs down to soul-level and makes our eyes shine. We are vital when we are bathed in joy. More clear. And certainly stronger. The act of dying can become sacred play, filled with joy as well as sorrow. When we celebrate all that is ordinary, joy seeps in. All we need do is embrace it.

When wonder mixes astonishment with curiosity toward the unexpected or the inexplicable, celebrating the ordinary becomes a daily practice. As Albert Einstein said, "He who can no longer pause to wonder and stand rapt in awe, is as good as dead: his eyes are closed."

The Gate of Heaven

Herbert's friend Margaret

The spring blooming days are incredibly beautiful here and I marvel at the constantly changing beauty of light and dark and clouds outside my window. The sublime and the ridiculous intertwine as light pours in and I contemplate love and mystery. On Tuesday I spent some delicious time in a friend's very beautiful garden, a real labor of love and prayer. In the garden is a wonderful area dedicated to Mary. As I sat there, I thought of my journey from cradle atheist to awareness of something much bigger than the individual self and I felt conscious of being called into the experience of something for which I have no other name than love. May we all grow in consciousness and love and gratitude for the many gifts that are available to any and all who see them. As Thomas Merton said, "The gate of heaven is everywhere."

Margaret Rothschild's emails often highlighted the connection between wonder and celebrating the ordinary as she viewed everything with spiritually attuned eyes. At the end of her life, Margaret found stillness and light in the smell of a rose, the voice of a far-away friend, the touch of a daughter, and the gift of seeing more in everything. Here is what she wrote just before she died: "Do not be afraid of the imagination. Use it, dance with it and know that your truth and light will emanate from it."

The clergyman and writer William Sloane Coffin said that spirituality to him meant "living the ordinary life extraordinarily well." We wake up to an ordinary day. The sky is blue. Trees sway in the breeze and birds twitter. Everything is as usual. Our hearts beat; our lungs take in air. We talk to friends. We eat dinner. We brush our teeth. And finally, when we put our heads down on our favorite pillows, we think, "This was a good, very ordinary day."

People who believe, for whatever reason, that their future is bleak or even hopeless, may miss the extraordinary ordinariness available moment by moment. It takes courage to be awake and open to whatever might happen without fearing the consequences. When people are anxious about the future, they have difficulty appreciating every single ordinary and surprising moment. The recognition that death is near allows us to experience heightened states of consciousness. Everyday experiences can, indeed, become holy encounters.

Celebrating the Ordinary: The Practice of Paying Attention

Most of us are so busy, so preoccupied, that we miss a lot of what happens in us and to us and around us. We do a lot of looking, but not much seeing. Long-range planning sets our sights on the future at the expense of the present moment. Obsessions about work or past mistakes or the next appointment are the excuses we often give for not paying attention. We're just too busy to bother. By contrast, paying attention is noticing and becoming aware of blessings we normally take for granted.

Reading is another very ordinary pastime that can take on a whole new meaning at the end of life. When he was with her for the summer, Karen's son Joel and she read aloud Madeleine L'Engle's books just as they had when her sons were in grade school. *A Wrinkle in Time. A Wind in the Door. A Swiftly Tilting Planet.* Extraordinary stories for our ordinary lives. Reading together can turn any words into a shared sacrament.

Focusing techniques that enhance attentiveness (such as mindfulness meditation) help to increase appreciation for the simple blessings of life and banish incompatible thoughts from consciousness. For that reason, celebrating the ordinary is a practice that requires paying attention.

Embrace the temporary.

Live in the moment.

Be grateful for all the little things.

Let your eyes linger on what's right in front of you.

Meister Eckhart said it this way: "The eye with which I see God is the same eye with which God sees me." Some call this the Buddha Eye. If we haven't celebrated the ordinary before dying, paying attention at life's end may require a seismic shift in consciousness that only comes from intentional practice. When we acknowledge the nearness of death and when we have the courage to embrace living fully while dying, then it will be easier to celebrate every ordinary event, discovery, conversation, or gift as a window into the Divine.

Some people describe such an extraordinary ordinary occasion as a God-moment. We discover these wonderful moments when we are willing to be surprised. Wes Avram, a Presbyterian minister, has suggested in *Where the Light Shines Through: Discerning God in Everyday Life* that God subverts any attempt to control these moments. God breaks down distinctions between the meaningful and the unfamiliar. "Traces of God can be irreconcilable with our more thoughtful orderings of life." We cannot locate God in a particular place or time nor is there any benefit in reducing the contingency of life in order to manufacture normalcy.

Longing for the absence of pain or hoping for the touch of a lover or waiting for death all teach us the habits of attentiveness that shape our awareness of God in the ordinary. And in paying attention we discover that God is bigger than our experiences of living and dying. And what at first seems like an ordinary event can turn out to be a miracle.

Our Daily Sacraments of Unnecessary Goodness

And of course, eating is one of those ordinary events that take on extraordinary significance for people who are dying. Karen has always loved ice cream but now eating her husband John's homemade peach ice cream is a transcending moment. Or savoring her son's hot fudge sauce with spicy pecans. Getting all the food groups every day seems irrelevant. As one nears death, the choices narrow and the need for a proper diet diminishes. Moreover, food becomes less important than the conversations that go with eating. People who sit down to share a pizza or a salad can't do it without sharing something of themselves as they pass the salt and pepper. Ordinary meals go way beyond smudged napkins and greasy plates. Because they're shared, they can take on a sacramental aspect. Robert Farrar Capon calls food "the daily sacrament of unnecessary goodness ordained for a continual remembrance that the world will always be more delicious than it is useful." Food had this kind of significance for Jim in his living and in his dying, as Sara Page Watts, Karen's high school friend puts it.

F-O-O-D!
Sara, Karen's friend

To the cancer patient, what a wonderful, terrible, necessary thing F-O-O-D is! It was also a big thing for my Jim during his cancer fight!

Eating had always been a source of pleasure for us. In fact, we centered our days around food. He just couldn't get enough and whatever he made was excellent. So I lost control and joined his food adventure. By the time I dated Jim I had already seen several loved ones unable to eat, so I was thankful to meet a man who could cook and enjoy food. A thing as simple as making Neiman Marcus cookies was pure pleasure for him.

Later, pencil thin, starting to lose the cancer fight, he wanted food, but stared at it as if it were a stranger! I struggled to find something to bring him that would make him say, "Oh, this tastes so good!" After depleting my own recipe ideas, I searched the hot deli section of my local grocery store, bringing him the soup of the day — the spicier the better. Or a couple pieces of breaded shrimp. A small piece of roast beef? No! Yogurt with fruit? Yes! Then, eggnog. That did it. He was thrilled to have eggnog. I was so proud to have found a store that stocked eggnog in the spring. Another great store had barbeque chicken with thin crust flat bread. That hit the spot. For a day!

But always, through all of this — asparagus! Jim had read that asparagus would cure cancer. He ate it every day. We had to blend it with salt, pepper, and lemon juice. He totally believed it would help him fight the cancer. And why not? The oncologist thought it was a good idea too.

Toward the end, there was *no* F-O-O-D in Jim's day. Just a head shake back and forth in response to asking if he wanted anything to eat. Not even Ensure would pass his lips. His food palate was gone; his thoughts of F-O-O-D seemed nonexistent.

Jim had gone full circle with F-O-O-D, just as with life. His desire was gone! No need to struggle with either any longer. Just move on to the next course, please. My table partner was ready to become a spiritual soul not needing such things as F-O-O-D. Spirit life was awaiting him and he was ready — tired of the lack of normalcy here. Our sweet, delicious time together would end.

For Jim, ordinary celebrations of eating became occasions for sadness. Eating is one of those painful paradoxes as one nears death. On the one hand, the nearness of death intensifies the importance of ordinary activities that may have always given pleasure like eating or walking or reading. On the other hand, these activities become increasingly less important as the dying person transcends what is strictly physical and material. Many things we thought were so very important or that bothered us may no longer matter. That is the gift of living while dying. And yet, we are saddened by our inability to do what once brought such pleasure and joy.

The Unpredictable Moments of Grace

In the end, every ordinary moment is an occasion for transformation. Wonder toward the unpredictable surprises in living and dying begins with the willingness to be moved and even changed. Grace is real and unpredictable. No matter how strong or accomplished we are, life-threatening illness or debilitating accidents occur. But even though we have no control over these things, we can still face them with honest courage. We may even discover an incomprehensible mercy that transforms dying into living more fully than ever before. There is always more to discover — more beauty, more hope, more wonder, more joy than we might imagine.

Karen's friend Dan often inspires people with his own cancer-journey stories and how difficult it is at times to find hope in the midst of pain or when confronted with an illness that seems to have a life of its own. It is then that Dan remembers that it is from these very dark and ordinary stable-places that hope is born.

Celebrating the ordinary in living and in dying makes it possible to experience a rich life even under the circumstances over which we have no control.

Karen's friend Mary Ann Garrity wonders about life's ordinary wonders — and if we really notice them.

Does Anyone Really Appreciate Life? Some Do.
Karen's friend Mary Ann

In *Our Town*, Emily asks, "Does anyone really appreciate life?" The Stage Manager answers, "Some do. Poets maybe."

When John called to tell Mike and me that Karen had been diagnosed with Stage III ovarian cancer, I knew the prognosis but still I thought, "If anyone can beat a death sentence, it's Karen."

And she has. For ten years I've observed Karen not dying from cancer but living with cancer. I have never heard her express fear or complain of the chemo side effects no doubt she was experiencing. Anyone who knows her is well aware of her extraordinary gifts and accomplishments — she wrote eight new books during a time many would have spent wondering "Why me, why now?" She traveled from France to Sweden to the Mayan ruins, and organized emergency services for the people in Vermont following the ravages of Hurricane Irene, managing the distribution of needed items like appliances and clothing, as well as information.

And at a time most people would turn inward and just become more introspective, Karen is devoting the precious span of the last segment of her life's journey to a project that might be of benefit to others in their own inevitable transition.

Yes, all those things give testament to the expansiveness of her spirit. But those of us who love Karen know that it's her capacity to see the grandness of an ordinary day: nurturing seedlings in her garden, making hats from repurposed knits, baking hot-crossed buns. Simple endeavors she enjoys for the mere sake of it. Like a poet, Karen knows how to delight in the time she has been given. She relishes her feasts. Most people exist; Karen makes living an art form. She is at peace.

"Being at peace," Karen tells those who ask, means that she's growing into her new (but as old as Julian of Norwich) mantra: "All is well with my soul." Not *will be* well. Not *has been* well. But in this very moment, she *is* well. And by well, she doesn't mean cured. She knows her cancer cells are not likely to go into remission again, although she's quick to point out that miracles do happen. But well, as Julian of Norwich meant well. This old anchorite held a hazelnut in the palm of her hand and saw the earth and knew the earth is well — the people are well. No matter what. No matter how many bombs go off. No matter how many guns are fired. No matter how many oil spills seep into our groundwater. We are well. Earth is primed to support life. Not destroy it. We are loved and unconditionally held fast. Every one of us. But, as Karen puts it, she has the honor and privilege of experiencing this wellness at a level deeper than she may have experienced it before. With eyes of wonder. And that gives her peace. She has a well-qualified hospice team, a hospice doctor she loves and trusts, a family who is privy to her every thought, and friends who genuinely want to support her. We can all choose to believe: all is well with my soul in... this moment. It's simply a new way to hold life.

When people see life this way, they are also aware that wellness is not a solitary thing. "I am well if you are well" is an African proverb that reflects the intimate connection between my wellness and the well-being of others. What affects one, affects all. My well-being is both personal and communal. And the ordinary again becomes extraordinary and the mundane becomes a remarkable sign of grace.

FROM THE CAREGIVER'S GUIDEBOOK

Living on an increasingly smaller stage allows the dying person to find delight in ordinary and sometimes unexpected moments or things. You may find this annoying since it seems the dying person is preoccupied with insignificant things. But remind yourself that it's important to him or her.

1. Friends and family and other caregivers have the privilege of learning from the dying person how to pay attention to the ordinary. Dying is full of surprises. If you can also be open to surprise, there is a greater chance of seeing signs of Divine wonder in the ordinary. Keep favorite foods and objects close and available.

2. If you begin to feel overwhelmed, it is not because you are weak or lacking the courage to cope with all the complexities of modern living or human suffering. Rather, it's because caring for the dying is a daily reminder of our fragility as human creatures. Moreover, medical technology has made dying more complex. Take some time out, relax, and allow others to do the caring for a while.

3. It may not be easy for you to take in all this clarity the dying one may display. And the dying one may have a sense of urgency you do not feel. For the dying, this urgency will likely translate into a lack of patience with those around them. It's your job to honor the truth they may feel compelled to speak now.

4. Celebrating the gift of knowing there are limits is liberating for the one dying but often it is the occasion for sadness for caregivers. Caregivers need to celebrate all the gifts that the dying teach, including how liberating death can be.

TELLING STORIES; SHARING MEMORIES

*"The stories about the end of life that we share
become a significant part of our efforts to make
the loss manageable. No one who has been through such
an event ever forgets it... The processing and
sharing of these experiences enables us to better understand
death, to accept the changes it brings, and to cope
with the inevitable grief."*

Margorie Ryerson, *Companions for the Passage*

⋈ *from* Karen's Hospice Journal ⋈

Stories create sanctuaries. When people tell them, both the teller and listener enter a place that's safe and ringed with magic. I suspect that some stories people tell within their family settings can be painful as well. And as Herbert has explained to me, "often a little dangerous." The stories we tell shape how we see ourselves and how we want others to see us. All writers are storytellers as well — even if they write nonfiction. They weave words into patterns that call to the heart.

Whether we write our stories and family sayings down or not, we all have our autobiographies firmly lodged in our heads. Retelling stories with others helps us remember even more stories. "Do you remember when..." or "Tell me again about that time..." My cousin Maxine and I grew up together in central Wisconsin and we even went to the same grade school for a while. How could we not share stories? If one of us mentions hot dogs, we start laughing, as we see in our mind's eye a particular birthday party when we definitely overindulged. Or, "Remember when Mom slipped under the car on the ice and I couldn't get her out because she was laughing so hard?" Or, "Remember when Uncle Albert called our teacher Mrs. Farner 'Little Red Riding Hood' at the Christmas program when she wore that red dress? Boy, did she get mad!" "Remember how we used to lie on the lawn and see cloud pictures?" "Remember when Aunt Gilma would take us hiking along the creek with the promise we might find some shells with pearls? Did we ever find any?"

I reread my old weekly newspaper columns recently. Measuring the Marigolds *reminded me that all the little stories I wrote of our sons growing up would have been lost if I hadn't written about them. Our children grew up with the music from* "Inchworm." "Inchworm, inchworm, measuring the marigolds. Seems to me you'd stop and see how beautiful they are."

John and I laugh every time we remember being at Aunt Bertha's antique-filled home. When our son Joel was two, he called her cuckoo clock a "mustn't miss it" because that's what we said every time the clock chimed.

I enjoy looking at family picture albums. I page through my journals — and my mother's diaries. . . especially the final little green gold-edged book with its "secure" metal clasp.

John O'Donohue said, "Memory is the place where our vanished days secretly gather." My vanishing days are peppered, now, with stories I tell and the stories people tell me. Every story helps me remember and will sustain me, and them, through what is and what is coming.

ℵ   ℔

The two practices in the title of this chapter are different and similar. The memories come from the stories we tell. Telling stories not only creates memory; it provides an opportunity to revise a memory embellished over time.

We Tell Stories in Order to Live

Our lives are knit together by stories. We introduce ourselves by means of stories — some of which are true and some of which are mostly true. We pass stories on from our families, from our cultural heritage, and religious traditions. We make sense of disconnected experiences in our lives by fashioning a larger story or narrative. We reveal ourselves to others and we conceal ourselves from others through the stories we make up about ourselves. So stories, we might say, hold us together as well as keep us apart. Because we tell stories in order to live, we become our stories.

Memories are often stitched and beribboned into family stories and in the retelling, traditions are acknowledged and held fast. Karen tells the story of how, after her maternal grandmother, the mother of eleven children, gave birth to her first set of twins, she sewed two little christening gowns out of her wedding dress. Then, when Karen's mother and her twin sister arrived later, the soft white chambray gowns appeared again for their baptisms. Karen was baptized in one of them, as were her two sons, and most recently, her granddaughter Josie. The christening gown is now wrapped in paper and stored in Nathan's home for a time when, if she so chooses, Josie can carry on the tradition. And tell its story… the story of how three generations of grandmothers loved a little girl enough to give her this little gown and its story.

Mitch Albom says in *The Five People You Meet in Heaven* that no story ever sits by itself. "Sometimes stories meet at corners and sometimes they cover one another completely, like stones beneath a river." Each story we tell affects the other stories that have been told or that will be told. Albom says that the world is full of stories, but the stories are all one. If all stories are one, telling stories diminishes isolation as it certainly did for Tom McIntyre in the following story.

Every Story, Another Good-bye
Herbert's friend

Tom McIntyre did not live easily after Susan, his wife of forty-five years, died in a hospital two weeks after suffering a stroke. After she died, Tom said he would take a year to sort out his memories of Susan.

Unfortunately, six months after Susan died Tom was diagnosed with lung cancer. One lung was removed and radiation treatment followed. About the time that Tom was beginning to regain his strength, he experienced diabetes-related medical difficulties, and finally was told that the cancer had metastasized to his brain. He responded to the diagnosis of imminent death much as he had responded to other challenges in his life: it was something that needed to be accomplished.

Once everyone agreed that his time of dying had begun, he began to tell stories of his life. Tom was fortunate to have grandchildren nearby who prompted his storytelling with questions and attentive listening. One of his daughters described the process this way: "He simply wanted to empty himself of those memories and adventures because he wanted us to know all about his life, even as he anticipated his death. It was as if he was determined to be known fully before he died." It was clear to everyone that Tom felt better when he told his stories. So did the family. Every story was also an occasion to say good-bye once again. After he died, telling the stories of their parents was made easier for the children and grandchildren because they knew Tom's version of his story.

The story of Tom's dying is remarkable for two reasons. First of all, he was never isolated from his family and friends. After the experience of his wife Susan's death, Tom insisted that he wanted to die at home. "Pain's a lot easier to deal with in the comfort of your own home," Tom told his doctor. Tom was fortunate to have a loving family to care for him. Secondly, he had people who listened to his stories and his grandchildren were his best audience. When stories are told and heard, a bond of mutuality is also created with a dying person that transforms the dread of abandonment into communities of hope.

Honest Storytelling at Life's End

Frederick Buechner's novel, *Godric*, is about an earthy twelfth-century English hermit saint. Reginald has been appointed to write the biography of Godric and the novel is about this earthy saint's determination to tell the truth about his life and correct Reginald's "impulse to blessedness" where there is none. At one point, Godric observes that Reginald seems determined to "make saints out of flesh and blood." Making saints out of flesh and blood is a griever's temptation that can be contained by honest storytelling by the one dying.

Storytelling at the end of a life not only creates memories, it also validates our existence. Stories told by the dying are privileged acts of self-interpretation that contribute to the way the person will be remembered. In other words, it allows the storyteller a chance to conclude his or her own story. Caregivers, family, and friends may help the dying person rehearse a life so that the formulation of his or her story has some correspondence to the community's version of the narrative, but finally the dying person tells the authoritative version. If the review of a life is honest and complete, it will be easier for survivors to construct an authentic memory after death that facilitates mourning. They will make additions in the retelling, but the autobiography belongs to the dying person alone.

When dying individuals are disappointed with their lives or embarrassed by failure or unrealized expectations, storytelling is painful. Feelings of shame or fear of disclosure keep us from recounting a life. But stories are important because they can sometimes be a way to make amends for old hurts, to laugh at what we thought was so very important once, and to allow us to let go of disappointments. Storytelling can even be a way to acknowledge unresolved relationships and to say thanks and good-bye to forgotten friends. Gratitude makes storytelling easier.

Leo Tolstoy's astounding portrayal of dying in *The Death of Ivan Ilych* captures the pain of an unfinished or failed life with this question: "What if my whole life has been wrong?" As his life passes in review, Ivan Illych concludes that every aspect of his life had been false and it is too late to rectify it. When Ivan's family and friends visit, the falseness of his life is mirrored. "In them he saw himself — all that for which he had lived — and saw clearly that it was not real at all, but a terrible and huge deception which had hidden both life and death. This conscious-ness intensified his physical suffering tenfold." When people feel that their lives are incomplete or full of empty memories, it is important to help them tell what they can to die well. If, however, the pain of a life story intensifies suffering at the end of a life or the dying person has always been a reluctant storyteller, then the respectful, silent presence of those who care becomes another instance of unexpected grace.

When a Story Is Told, Someone Must Listen

Dying people remember a life in order to let it go. That is the work of telling stories. The task of those in caregiving roles is to listen. Lis-ten deeply. And bear witness to those stories accurately. It is both a promise and an obligation.

Henryk Mandelbrot, a Polish Jew and survivor of Auschwitz-Birkenau in Elliot Perlman's novel *The Street Sweeper*, is testing the willingness and ability of Lamont Williams, the street sweeper, to listen before telling his story.

"Listen and remember. When was I born?"

"Nineteen twenty-two."

"What day, what month? Remember me. There is no one else like me, and your Dr. Washington thinks I

have cancer so you have to remember. I will test you.
I was born December fifteenth, 1922 in the town of
Olkusz. Say it!"
"December fifteenth, 1922."
"Where?"
"I don't remember."
"No, you have to remember, Mr. Lamont. Otherwise,
  why are we talking?"

We may remember times when we wanted to test, as Henryk did, whether someone was hearing the story we needed to tell. "Otherwise, why are we talking?" In dying as in living, people are often reluctant to tell their stories because they are afraid no one is listening. As a result, too many people die without the opportunity to tell their life story. If storytelling is an essential dimension of dying, at least one person needs to listen and respond in a way that lets the dying person know he or she has been heard and understood and will be remembered.

Ira Byock puts this promise most clearly: "We will bear witness to your pain and your sorrow, your disappointments and your triumphs. We will listen to the stories of your life and will remember the story of your passing." By hearing, we bear witness. And often, when we listen deeply, we hear a larger story that gives meaning and purpose not only to the dying person but also to those who listen.

Faithful care begins with bearing witness to the dying person's story. The Lutheran pastor Bill White, a college friend of Karen's, believes the purpose of the funeral sermon is to tell two stories: the story of the deceased and the story of God and how the two overlap and intertwine.

Storytelling and Our Last Days
Bill, Karen's friend

Don Hunt was tall, athletic, extremely outgoing, and an artist. Normally full of vigor he suddenly looked tired and his speech began to slur. An MRI was ordered and the diagnosis was a malignant brain tumor. He underwent surgery, chemotherapy, and radiation, which slowed the tumor, but did not eliminate it. The cancer was, unfortunately, very advanced.

On one pastoral visit, I brought with me a TV technician with his camera. With Don's permission we set up a tripod in his living room. I asked questions and Don answered. He told of his boyhood, his attendance at a Christian college, and his life as a teacher. He spoke glowingly of his three daughters and the love he had for his wife.

I told Don that I planned to edit the film the following week. Don became the preacher at his own funeral. The hundreds of people who came to say good-bye to Don were delighted and surprised to see his face on a large screen telling the story of his life and giving a testimony to his faith. The film was no eulogy, but rather a tribute to God and his friends, the people of God. Don's filmed stories were testimony to his life and his faith and a gift to all who mourned his death.

Our lives are stories. If we are fortunate, if we are given time, the end of life becomes a time of reflection, a time to tell and listen to stories. When I invite people who are dying to tell me the stories of their lives, they often tell how God has accompanied them through every step of their illness. "I never feel alone," one man said. "This is a new experience for me and it is very comforting." My task is to listen and ask questions that will help them tell the stories. Some of these memories will make their way into the sermon after they have died.

At one funeral-planning conversation, I became aware of why people do not always tell or listen for stories while someone is dying. "Can we be frank, pastor?" one son began. "My father was an asshole. He died friendless. No one trusted him. Though I suppose my siblings and I loved him, none of us liked him. He was a terrible father. There will be few tears shed at his funeral." They proceeded to tell story after story of their father's misdeeds. In one case it was clear that the entire family had talked about these things for years. It was probably the first time they "told the truth about Dad." I believe that the experience provided a kind of catharsis. At last they had shared what they had carried for decades.

If the end of life is a time for summing up, then what is needed are opportunities to tell our stories. For that to happen we need to give the one who is dying an invitation to talk, and become good story-listeners. All it takes to be a good story-listener is a little practice and a lot of desire.

Bearing witness happens in many ways at the end of life: a hospice program's commitment to tell stories about a person who just died; the determination of a physician not to abandon someone who is dying; a nurse's quiet sharing of the nighttime terror of a dying patient; a volunteer who will hold a hand; the chaplain or minister's presence that transforms the loneliness of dying with communities of meaning and care; a hospice volunteer who listens carefully and records the story of a life; and the steadfast presence of families who bear witness to their love by giving consistent, dignified care and companionship.

Making a Memory: A Child's Perspective

Family and friends of the one dying will make their own memories from walking with someone they love, right up to the time of their loved one's death. Sometimes those remembrances will be clouded by unsettling images that accompany dying: body parts leaking, strong odors, temporary loss of mental functioning, upsetting outbursts, and a prolonged departure from life. Even though the goal of hospice is to make death more humanized than medicalized, there may be fleeting moments when the aesthetics of dying complicates memory. For the most part, however, the memories that family and friends will take away from the journey to death will be positive. They will also be personal. And therefore unique to the particular relationship with the one dying.

Even if children are kept from the dying person, they will have memories of being excluded. Herbert's granddaughter Julia was not excluded. She was six when her grandmother came to live with her family. She died when Julia was eight after a lengthy illness that Julia experienced fully. Julia was fourteen when she wrote this story about how she remembers the death of her paternal grandmother, her *abuela*, Emma Febos.

Our Divine Human Virtue

WISDOM

Stories and memories carry much wisdom. All we need do is listen. The Greek word for wisdom is *Sophia* — the one at the heart of all our creative acts. The one with us at birth and at death. Pierre Teilhard de Chardin calls her "the Essential Feminine." She is the living and dying process that fills our journey and enlivens every moment. How do we become wiser about our dying? Perhaps the answer is through our Sophia stories.

My *Abuela*
Julia, Herbert's granddaughter

I didn't understand it at first. Who could blame me? I was only five at the time she got sick. I can't remember exactly what my parents told me, but what I do remember is Dobby. Dobby, the house elf that keeps Harry Potter from going to Hogwarts in *Harry Potter and the Chamber of Secrets.* That is my memory — Harry Potter and tears for my abuela's liver cancer. This started the chain reaction of events that led me to be the person I am now.

Sometimes I forget that it even happened to me, but reflection reminds me that these events made me stronger and weaker. My house was where my *abuela* stayed. She never did treatment. She wanted to live life to the fullest, right up to the end. That was my *abuela*, my one-eyed, beautiful *abuela*. She is one of the strongest women I have ever met.

I remember that she lived in the same town, very close to my school. I wanted to walk to her house so bad after school, but my parents said I was too young. I never got to walk to her house to have a sleepover with her. I remember hating the lotion she made me put on... I would give anything for that lotion now.

Her death stays with me to this day. I realize now how selfish I was, but that didn't stop me then. I craved attention. I used to act childish to get the full attention of my parents. Now, I need attention from everyone, but it just boosts me to do better in school and have my teachers recognize that I am noteworthy. Heck, I'm "article-worthy; get-started-on-my-full-length-novel-biography-worthy." But, this full-blown cocky attitude has its roots in the pesky cancer in my *abuela's* liver. My parents' full attention was always on her. It was the push that I would later use to motivate me to do well. My *abuela* gave me exactly what I needed even when I didn't recognize it: she never stopped loving me no matter how sick she was.

Then, the end came. I remember I had invented a game with my cousin. My eight-year-old self had found great joy in spinning her around on a spinning footrest. We called it "Carnival." My mother came into the living room with tears in her eyes, and I had an idea of what was about to happen. When I was told she was dead, I remember feeling numb. I tried to cry to match my mother's actions. That's how she was reacting, so I thought it must be how I should react as well. I did cry, though, when I learned that I would have to leave my cousins early and miss part of the summer camp I was enrolled in for the duration of that week.

The funeral was on a Saturday, and the only thing I remember about that was kissing my best friend on the cheek. Other than that, I draw blanks. There are a lot of blanks for that period of my life. What I remember are lots of tears, lots of visits from a nurse, lots of embarrassing moments, but there were also a lot of accomplishments at that point in my life. As I see it now, her dying taught me how to live. Intensely. All because of a woman with liver cancer who was determined to kept her hair to the end. My *abuela*.

The candid memory of her courageous *abuela* will be part of Julia's life story and a significant memory of her childhood. More than we know, children listen carefully and remember clearly experiences of death, even when they do not yet understand that death is final.

When dying people can do little else, they still can rehearse a life. For family and friends, the task is to listen carefully and respond empathically without judging or correcting. It is the privilege of the one who is dying to tell his or her story his or her own way. Later, caregivers will also be able to tell the stories of the person's dying, which then become part of their personal memories as well as the family legacy.

FROM THE CAREGIVER'S GUIDEBOOK

Caregivers should expect to be changed by the stories they hear. Walking closely with someone on the journey to death deepens our understanding of being human. Fragility and death, because it comes with the finiteness of creation, is both a gift and a challenge. Just as ambiguity, paradoxically, leads to clarity, so too does vulnerability lead to strength from the struggle.

1. People who care for the dying need not rely on understanding various "dying stages." Instead, they can listen to and for stories. And try to understand what those stories are really saying. We die by stories rather than stages.

2. If the dying person is invited to tell his or her story, we are morally obligated to listen. It is about bearing witness to a life by listening to their stories. Some end-of-life caregivers write the stories told by the dying for those who survive. Being a story-hearer is a sacred vocation.

3. You can hear best when you respond in ways the dying person knows you heard them. Nod. Smile. Repeat portions to show the dying one you've heard. Add your questions to further the person's telling.

4. Tell stories when you are asked, but remember that listening can be exhausting and frustrating for the one dying. The stories you tell should be aimed at eliciting the stories he or she needs to tell.

5. If the dying one tells you a secret story, ask if it can be shared with others after he or she has died.

LETTING GO

"To die gracefully is to live fully;
to cling too tightly to life is to kill it prematurely."

Clyde Reid, *Celebrate the Temporary*

ℵ *from* Karen's Hospice Journal ℟

When my hospice nurse Sherri asked me the other day if we have a shower stool, I blinked and said, "Well, no. I haven't thought I'd need one." She just smiled and said, "We can get you one any time. If you're preferring to sit now in church, you may prefer to be sitting in your shower as well. It's just a way of conserving energy." It suddenly dawned on me that shower grab bars might not be enough for me to handle showering by myself when my energy is even more depleted.

There will come a time when I will have to let go of my former ways of many things, besides bathing, and accept a new normal. I've already given up walking any distance. With the exception of a little weeding, I've let go of gardening. Cleaning. Cooking. I will probably not cook again. I am no longer able to sit for any length of time at my computer but it is almost impossible for me to imagine giving up writing.

Looking through the latest tour catalogue that found its way into our mailbox, I think, "My bucket list has really shrunk." I had thought Machu Picchu was on it, but now I know it's not. I've let that go. It wasn't so hard. I've seen friends' pictures and I don't like high altitudes. I'll not get to Egypt. Or Petra. Let that go!

Letting go means making room for something else. But it also means that I need to practice letting go of controlling outcomes. I can't predict how long I'll be here, how I'll feel, if I'll have energy for something I've been planning on. As my husband said the other day, when we discussed our upcoming granddaughter's visit and my desire to still have energy for it, "You can make plans, but don't be disappointed if they don't turn out that way." I cannot let go of planning, however, because that's how I continue living. And I keep meeting new people and making new friends. It's who I am. And deep down, I think it's who I will be until I am no longer "this me."

People have written whole books on attachment, and how, in the end, the rope-like tethers to this life and this planet that we thought were so sturdy, are not. A Hindi teacher once observed, "This world is like a flower in bloom; as you watch it, it wilts right before your eyes. So, why are you attached to it?" Good question. Why am I so attached to anything? Anyone? Why am I still grabbing onto things I no longer need and no longer have a purpose for where I'm going?

My friend, the "Presencing" and "Theory U" business leader, Otto Scharmer, puts it this way: "To die is this: letting go and letting come. Letting go of one world and letting come of another world even if we don't know where that's really existing. But we'll only be able to find out when we have the courage to let go and to put our foot into the territory of the unknown."

So, I'm having fun letting go of things that I have enjoyed and treasured. I've squirreled away certain things for years, believing they've held some mystical meaning for me, but now I realize they're just material things. Take Sharon's beautiful gourd, for example. It was part of a ritual she created for me to mark my turning fifty-six. We called it my "croning ceremony." But I no longer need it on my shelf, so I returned it to her.

I read recently that we bring only five things into this world from that other place. Art, music, creativity, love, and a longing for home. Everything else we see around us, we've created here. So, why is it so hard to leave it all behind?

In speaking of the courage to "let go," Peter Matthiessen quoted Rainer Maria Rilke in The Snow Leopard. *The only courage, he said, that is demanded of us is to have "courage for the most strange, the most singular and the most inexplicable that we may encounter." Well, that pretty much sums up what I'm facing right now. Strange. Singular. Inexplicable. I'm climbing "Mt. Hospice" searching for my own snow leopard and the oxygen grows thinner. Matthiessen writes of how in mountain climbing, he has learned to walk lighter and stumble less. What a life-lesson! He kept his center of gravity deep in his belly and let that center of himself do the seeing. I try moving toward death by walking more slowly and with lighter footprints hoping I won't stumble. I know that climbers are apt to run into trouble when they "clutch." I practice unclutching.*

We watched the movie The Life of Pi *the other night and I was struck by the line "The whole [act] of life is letting go." Pi had to let go of the tiger, Richard Parker, who, when they parted, didn't even give him a backward glance. He had to let go of his family, his home country, and even the woman he loved. So, I ask myself, "Will I be able to graciously let go of the people I so love?" Or can I approach them, as I have with Sharon's gourd, knowing they were a gift to me, that they are beautiful, but now I just need to say "Thank you" and move on? To let go and let come.*

ℵ ℤ

Making Room for Something New

Karen uses the phrase "to let go of former ways." For the dying, that practice begins slowly — almost imperceptibly — and increases noticeably as strength diminishes. Letting go requires ongoing monitoring as changes occur. "Yesterday this was important. I couldn't possibly let it go! And today? Not so much." This process of letting go is an act of handing over or relinquishing ourselves to a process we cannot control. For some, it may seem like giving up on living, especially if possessing has been a central dimension of their lives. Others may experience letting go as a positive experience of unburdening or unfettering or being released or set free from too much stuff. Several maxims from Herbert's family embody this perspective. "There are no pockets in shrouds." And, "Have you ever seen a hearse with a U-haul trailer?"

"A current of loss flows through your life like the tide that returns eternally to rinse away another wafer of stone from the shoreline... The beauty of loss is the room it makes for something new," John O'Donohue said in *Eternal Echoes*.

Letting go comes in two phases. First, we identify those possessions, activities, or relationships that we treasure in order to let them go. Attachment is a normal component of being human. So naturally, the awareness that we are losing or getting rid of what we are attached to is difficult. But impending death inspires clarity about what we value and with that awareness comes grief. There is little that can be done to soften the discontinuity at life's end. Dying people are in the process of letting go of everything they have loved. It's how they get ready to die. Letting go of what might have been or what should have been also brings feelings of disappointment and grief. "I had always thought I might have..." So we even have to let go of our future plans and our dreams.

Second, letting go may be an act of generosity. We give over to someone else what we can no longer hold on to for ourselves. When Herbert left a teaching position some years ago, many of his colleagues gave gifts that were their own treasured possessions. To receive such a gift is a wonderful honor because it comes with a story from their lives about how much these "treasures" mean to them.

The result of letting go and handing over means we have room for something else. Doug Smith has put it his way in *The Tao of Dying*:

> In letting go
> There is gain.
> In giving up,
> There is advancement.

Letting go of control makes room for the gift of interdependence. Letting go of dreams makes room for ordinary moments of grace. Letting go of replicating past experiences makes room for tomorrow's surprises. Letting go of self-sufficiency makes room for discovering vulnerabilities previously unknown. Ira Byock says he's learned through his patients' dying stories "that people can become stronger and more whole as physical weakness becomes overwhelming and life itself wanes." Letting go makes room for something new.

Letting Go: Sadness and Surprise

Even though letting go may lead to something new, it still can be the occasion for sadness. Even the promise of some form of immortality cannot eliminate the pain of relinquishing or letting go of this life. Everyone and everything one has loved passes in review. We review life in order to let it go. And this is not easy.

Morrie Schwartz's book *Letting Go* chronicles his dying from ALS. He mourned all the people and places he left behind. As for all of us, Morrie's grief was an unavoidable dimension of letting go. He allowed himself to experience all the emotions of the grief: sadness, despair, anger, regret, and "the sense of finishing before my time." "After you have wept and grieved for your physical losses," Schwartz says, "cherish the functions and the life you have left."

With grief comes gratitude. From her grandmother and from Karen, Shelie Richardson has learned both the sadness and the surprise of letting go.

Our Divine Human Virtue

DETACHMENT

"I need to have empty hands to approach the unknown," said Jeanne De Salzmann, author of *The Reality of Being*. When we are willing to let go and empty ourselves, who knows what might rush in to fill the void. It might be hope. Or peace. Certainly it will be love, for that is always available once we recognize it in its various forms. We will face a time when we even need to let go of worrying about things. Or trying to control outcomes. Then we can rest.

Dying Versus Clinging
Shelie, Karen's friend

My grandmother died, living alone and still cooking for herself, at the age of ninety-seven. She was still of clear mind and sound body. She had voluntarily given up driving at age ninety-two when she stated, "I just can't see very well anymore." But that didn't keep her from her kitchen. She had been a professional cook and was cooking chipped beef and gravy on fresh-baked biscuits when her hip broke. The first couple of days after her hip surgery, they took her to physical therapy. On day three, she requested to speak with the doctor. "What are we doing this for?" she asked. "You and I both know that I will never go home again. I have lived a good life. I have children, grandchildren, and great-grandchildren. There is nothing left for me to do. I am all done here."

And so it was. She refused further food and asked to be made comfortable. We all came to say our good-byes. My father (the oldest son) was the last to arrive as he had to come from halfway across the country. He and my mother visited with her and kissed her and told her that everyone had been there and it was okay to go now. My grandmother died one hour later. Dying is not always easy. People are fearful of the unknown. Others do not want to let go of what they possess or those they love. Once her firstborn son arrived, my grandmother was free to die.

Now, for the second time in my life, I am watching someone I care about let go. I told my son last night, "For years Karen has been showing me how to live well and now she is showing me how to die well, too." I met Karen at our church prior to her diagnosis and have been watching her live and die for over ten years now. We both identify as Christians and we also embrace a broader spirituality that includes a variety of wisdom traditions. Watching Karen for this past decade has shown me that faith can be like a muscle strengthened by increased use. My own faith and trust in God has been strengthened by watching her exercise hers in the face of adversity. Living with a constant awareness of the fragility of life strengthens one's faith and makes it easier to let go. I pray that I can go forward having assimilated about living and dying from Karen and allow my own life to be transformed by these insights.

People sometimes ask Karen, "You seem to be so at ease with dying. How do you do that?" And she may respond by saying that at her age, seventy-three, she has many life memories and has whittled down her bucket list to almost nothing, so perhaps it's easier for her than for others. "If I were thirty-five, I'd have a different 'take' on this, I'm sure." Letting go, even at seventy-three, is not easy for anyone — even for those who feel they have prepared for death. We rarely know how much we value all the people and places and possessions we have until we have to leave them behind.

Letting Go Is Never Simple

When we let go of valued objects or old hostilities or unfinished projects and say good-bye to people we love or wished we loved, we experience pain. But some people hold on to everything they can, not just because the pain of letting go is too great but because the worth of their lives is defined by what they possess. In a recent article in *The Lutheran* magazine, Peter Marty has called the fear of getting rid of stuff *disposo-phobia*. It is a spiritual ache we experience when we equate letting go with deprivation. However, our attachment to stuff is not the only instance of disposopobia in life. How do you shape a conversation, Marty asks, with your aging mother who is reluctant to give up the family home, displaying contempt for your suggestion that she move into assisted living? Or how do you let go of old hurts or slights that you have harbored for years? Or how do you let go of worry that your adult son will not be able to manage his life after your death?

Marty suggests a strategy for letting go of stuff that we have modified for this discussion:

I) Tell the truth. Worrying about losing something is a silly way to live until you die. Hanging on tightly to stuff or resentments is a spiritual problem that takes energy that could otherwise be focused on living fully.

2)   It does not help to deny the anguish associated with letting go. Feel free to grieve the losses that are never easy or simple.

3)   Letting go can be a positive choice that affirms something more important than clutching the present. It is more than resignation.

4)   When you can clean out your closets and your calendar of clutter, there is much more room to be surprised.

5)   Be the kind of person you long to be by loosening your grip on unhealthy attachments.

St. Augustine once said that "God is always trying to give things to us, but our hands are too full to receive them."

Cluttering our lives with possessions is never simply the consequence of impulse buying or competing with our neighbors for the most tools in the most tidy garage. Nor is collecting or hoarding necessarily about being greedy. If we live by possessing ourselves, by holding on to ourselves, by garnering possessions as a buffer against helplessness and dependency, then we live in terror of death because life and all we possess will be taken from us. If, however, we start with the presumption that all life is a gift, then gratitude is not an occasional moment when we remember to say thank you to a spouse or to a service provider. Instead, it creates a way of living that acknowledges human neediness and dependency as unavoidable. Gratitude, then, becomes as normal as breathing.

If our life review is dominated by sadness for what did not happen and disappointment for what we did not receive or achieve, it is more difficult to let go of what we do have. In a culture dominated by pervasive expectations of entitlement, the spiritual task of letting go may be the most difficult of all. And yet, the practice of letting go generates freedom to live fully and freely until we die.

In *The Four Things That Matter Most*, Ira Byock says it is not only important to express gratitude — we need to be able to receive it as well. "When we are truly able to accept that kind of thanksgiving, a wonderful sense of resolution can occur. We feel recognized and accepted, and we complete the emotional transaction that began when we were thoughtful, considerate, or generous." Letting go and living gratefully are companions from the beginning of life to its end.

From the Caregiver's Guidebook

Assuring dying persons that everyone and everything will be taken care of, that their responsibilities will be cared for by others, gives them permission to die.

1. You will provide continuity for the dying one's living even while he or she is letting go of so much. If someone who is dying is accustomed to sherry at four in the afternoon or the *New York Times* with a cup of coffee in the morning, making those routines happen for as long as possible is a gift of care.

2. Encourage grieving by being present and carefully listening to their pain without discounting their sadness. Remember, they are giving up everything.

3. To help the person let go, talk about how you will be okay and what things are in place for that. The person may have problems letting go if he or she is concerned about you socially, spiritually, or financially. Also, telling the dying one verbally it is okay to die gives him or her permission to do so.

4. You are now also letting go. Caring for this person has been nearly a full-time job. Your life will now be quite different after this person dies. Consider looking into a bereavement support group to help in adjusting to the new rhythm your life will now assume.

The Joy of Gift-Giving

"There is only one deprivation... and that is not to be
able to give one's gift to those one loves most.
The gift turned inward, unable to be given, becomes a
heavy burden, even sometimes a kind of poison.
It is as though the flow of life were backed up."

May Sarton

⚮ *from* Karen's Hospice Journal ⚮

You look down and there is hair all over your shower drain. It falls into whatever you're cooking. Buzz cut time. And now that you're bald, your choices are alfresco, hats, scarves, or wigs.

The first time I lost my hair, I thought, "There must be other women like me who might like to cover their heads with a beautiful designer hat." So I decided to spend my "sitting-around time" hand sewing one-of-a-kind hats made from recycled wool sweaters. Over the course of three years, I made hundreds of Kelsey Mountain hats — sold some, gave most away. Each hat started with a circle. A circle holds deep meaning for me and I'd bless it and say to myself, "Someone will wear this and it will make her happy." Every time I sold or gave a hat away, I remembered to add, "Wear it in good health." It was one of my most creative pursuits and now that I no longer need to make any more hats, I gave all the hats I had left, along with bags of unused wool, to my friend Wanda. It fills me with joy to know she will continue using the wool for her beautiful recycled wool crafts.

The steroids that always accompanied my chemo treatments left me wired. Sleepless, I'd get up very early to write. And write. And write. Counting this book, I coauthored or solo-wrote eight books since my diagnosis ten years ago. It's as if the cancer cells demanded creativity. My hope is that these books will be a gift to the people who read them.

After my initial chemo treatments, I decided to return to painting. I turned our little basement studio into a space to transform used furniture into "Goddess

Furniture." I painted onto chairs and tables, for the most part, symbols that recall ancient mother-figures. Venus of Willendorf. Birds. Water. I gave all the furniture away to either fund-raising projects or to friends.

When our older son's two massive pipe-organ projects came to fruition, I painted faux-carving onto wooden pipe-shades. It was my gift to their Swedish University and to him. What an incredible honor to be able to give my time and meager talents to further ongoing music! And to have the fun of doing it with him and his colleagues. I remember what Dorothy Day said once: "Give only if you have something to give; give only if you are someone for whom giving is its own reward."

I guess I learned about giving from my Norwegian Lutheran parents who taught me that if we've been given much, much will be expected of us. I'm not a great artist, but everything I've painted, I've given away, so my art wasn't so much what I created, or even how well, but how it flowed through me to someone else. I've noticed that sometimes gifts become re-gifted. It happened with an oil painting I did of Banff's mountains and a lake in British Colombia for a family in the small Wisconsin town in which we lived. Decades later, their son, believing that art should be returned, if at all possible, to the person who created it, sent it back to me. What a gift! We hung it at the head of our stairs when I entered hospice and I am blessed by it every time I see it.

I relish looking through clothes, jewelry, books, special rocks, thinking, "I wonder who might like this." It also allows me to help those who will have to do a massive clean-out after I'm gone. Not that they couldn't. It's just that I'm having so much fun finding various treasures and deciding who to give them to. I've read that my (truly old) Scandinavian ancestors used to have what they called "giving circles" at which they shared their stuff. Nothing got clogged. Or hoarded. They kept it all moving. My friend Michael Cecil tells me that in Ashland, Oregon, he and Barbara belong to a potluck dinner giving circle where, once a month, people first speak to their needs, and then they go around the circle again, and each one says what he or she has to give to those needs. What a gift-giving community!

And why shouldn't we give? After all, everything we have was once given to us. I no longer have a need to hang on to or buy new things. How freeing is that!

N K

The Attitude of Gratitude

A soul filled with gratitude gives gifts freely. To be grateful is a spiritual attitude formed by the recognition that our entire life is a gift. Some call it grace. Everything we have and are comes to us as a gift. We don't own it; we just have it "on loan." If we truly believe that, we are free to give it away. If we don't practice giving, we lock ourselves up. Or if we believe it's our right to possess and regard our life as an entitlement, we may view death with terror because it takes everything away. So we presume to stockpile against helplessness and dependency and even death. We may find ourselves bargaining for more and more and we might feel resentment because we didn't get what we expected or deserved out of life. As a result, we do everything within our power to prolong life so we can get more. Death then becomes a robber... something to fear, something outside us, something to fight against.

But when we live as if all life is a gift, gratitude becomes as natural as breathing. Being grateful and giving thanks are borne out of an acceptance of one's own limitations in living and in dying. Every life ends unfinished or incomplete because we are finite creatures. No matter how long a life might be prolonged, there always can be something more to experience. When Jonna told Karen about a surgical procedure that might extend her life a short while, Karen pondered this option and then said, "But because death will come, does it really matter exactly when? I'll always have one more person to talk to, one more email to write." Jonna laughed and said, "Or one more book to get published!" To which Karen added, "Death will come when death will come and it will always be too soon. My hope is that it will come gently."

For most of us, death comes too soon, or in instances of agonizing suffering and personal decline, too late. We may worry or be sad about an unfinished life but we can rest easy that our failures are also incomplete and finite.

The spiritual core of gratitude allows us to recognize that we are connected to one another in mysterious and sometimes miraculous ways. True gratefulness rejoices in the other. Then we can reflect back the goodness we have received by looking for opportunities to give.

Most everyone will agree that gratitude is a virtue with no downside. It is both the most pleasant of all virtues and the most virtuous of the pleasures. And yet, because people typically consider gratitude a virtue and not simply a pleasure, it does not always come naturally or easily. The loss of rootedness in place, increasing secularism, and a diminishing appreciation of the past all contribute to the erosion of gratitude in modern cultures. As a result, life-review at life's end takes imagination and courage. Nonetheless, it can be a healing process. And when done with humor, it can even be playful. The dying person may suddenly realize that now the accounts are closed. The books have been audited. Nothing more needs to be done.

Our Divine Human Virtue

GENEROSITY

Beliefs in abundance and scarcity are just that: beliefs. What is *enough*? And is there more where that came from? Falsely believing that if someone gets a bigger piece of the pie, our piece will be smaller negates the possibility that the pie is much more generous than we may have thought at first. Mathematical cosmologist Brian Swimme says "we are the Generosity of Being evolved into human form." If we truly are made of generous stuff then we cannot but help give generously to others.

The Variety of Gifts from Dying Persons

When Nora was dying, her biggest worry and frequent contention with her son was the set of fine china she had owned since he was born. She wanted to be sure it would be cared for properly.

Sam's deathbed concern was about his tools and the basement full of woodworking benches and saws. None of his children had any interest in tools and Sam was worried that they would rust away.

While he was dying, Marcus was determined to talk by phone with old friends (including two old girlfriends) to hear their voice once more and thank them for the gift of their friendship. Near the end, when he did not have the energy to talk anymore, he listened to the recording of their voices and imagined being surrounded by love.

Ellen was to have received a list of all her sister's antiques, which she had carefully numbered and coordinated as gifts to her relatives. But her sister died before Ellen got the list — and no one in the family received what was intended. Everything went to a more distant branch of the family. Death was tinged with loss on several levels.

Katy Butler had just talked to her mother, Valerie, who had rejected heart surgery that might have kept her alive. Giving up hope is hard, Valerie had told her daughter as she struggled with pain. Four hours later her mother called her daughter back, as Katy Butler wrote in her book *Knocking on Heaven's Door: The Path to a Better Way of Death*, to say "I want you to give my sewing machine to a woman who really sews. It's a Bernina. They don't make them like this anymore. It's all metal, no plastic parts."

To determine a meaningful gift, we need to give it time, thought, intentionality, and energy. There is, however, always the risk that a gift may not be received in the spirit in which it's given. Receiving gifts from the dying requires a special graciousness. Even if the paintings or furniture or dishes or tools do not fit the lifestyle of the chosen recipients, rather than say no, they should feel free to accept them and then, later, offer those gifts to others. The act of giving then may become a blessing for the giver and the receiver.

The Gift of Stories

Storytelling at the end of life is a gift and as we have discussed, telling stories also helps us to let go. Even when physical constraints restrict our personal freedom, when medical procedures may isolate us from community or when survivors are tempted to close our story prematurely, we can still fashion a life-narrative. Telling our story may be our

last intentional act. Desmond Tutu puts it this way: "I have a dream...
that my children will know that they are members of one family, the
human family, God's family, my family." Stories are all one because the
human family is one. When we add our stories to the whole, we help to
create a foundation from which future generations will dream.

The Gift of Blessing

In his book *Leading Causes of Life*, Gary Gunderson identified blessing
as one of the five life-giving causes. Blessings are received from others
and given to others. To be blessed and to be a blessing are deeply embedded in the connections with those who have gone before and not
yet come. It is difficult to imagine our lives without receiving blessings
that have the power to change how we think about ourselves and others.
Because we cannot count on the privilege of blessing the next generation at life's end, we need to do it when we are able.

We bless our beloved partners and children who live after our death
by telling them how they have been a gift to us and how grateful we are
to have been a part of their lives.

We bless the next generation when we invite them to awaken their
spirit of adventure, holding nothing back, as they follow their deep
desires.

We bless our colleagues when we affirm their gifts, acknowledge
what we have learned from them, and encourage them to continue to
give to others as they have given to us.

We bless our friends whenever we tell them what they have meant to
us and thank them for their presence in our life.

The Gift of Wisdom

"Death," theologian Marcus Borg has said, is the "teacher of wisdom." There is a particular wisdom about life that comes to those who
are consciously dying. Or perhaps it's simply a more profound perspective on living. Borg says death teaches us that time "is too precious to

be spent being morbid." Death liberates us from all of our culturally-induced trivia; it promotes authenticity, and makes it possible to love life without holding back. We give objects, ourselves, our stories, our love, last conversations, and our wisdom harvested from the nearness of death to those we love and sometimes to strangers who will listen.

It is likely that the gift of wisdom from those who are dying may be the most difficult to receive. Wisdom is not so much handed on to others; rather it is a personal thing that each discovers in his or her own way. Some last words carry special weight and their significance and influence may linger over generations. For example, Karen's grandmother's last words were "Jesus, I see you. I'm coming." That has profoundly affected Karen from the time she was old enough to understand what those words meant. One of Karen's childhood friends died after he said, "Am I still here? Oh, they make this so easy!" Others make comic exits. Oscar Wilde, for instance, in a seedy hotel room in France remarked: "This wallpaper and I are fighting a duel to the death. Either it goes or I do." Many people, however, go privately and silently. They may consider it a gift to their loved ones to wait to die until everyone has left the room.

Gifting the Dying

If they have the opportunity, family and friends will naturally want to say thank you to the one who is dying, and to let them know what they have meant to them. Karen has received countless emails and letters from friends and colleagues expressing just that. And she has had many conversations about who she is, who they are, and how their lives have intertwined — often quite miraculously. "They will never truly know how wonderful their words are, and how much they have meant to me," she explained. "Being 'touched' hardly covers it. They reached out to not only briefly touch me but seriously to hold and caress me. They pray for me and hold me in their hearts. Who could ask for anything more?"

Herbert, too, has told Karen numerous times, "Thank you for helping me, early on, work with my writing, as you have helped so many others over the years."

Bob knew that his very special friend David was near death but it was only after Bob's pastor encouraged him that he wrote an email thanking David for their friendship. Sadly, David died the exact time that Bob was writing to thank him. Following our intuition and acting on our best intentions is important at any time, but particularly important when your friend won't be around much longer to hear your words. Err on the side of just putting your words out there. Don't worry about it being the right time or the right words. Just express them, in whatever way you feel most comfortable.

Perhaps the most important gift that family and friends can give to those who are dying is permission to die. Let them know "we will be fine." "It's okay to go." "You can do this!" Kathryn Beck, a hospice nurse for twenty-five years, puts it this way: "To help someone let go, the dying person needs to hear that you will be okay and what concrete things are in place to make that happen. Dying persons may be reluctant to let go unless they hear that you will be okay socially, spiritually, or financially. It is also important for family and friends to be very explicit about giving permission to die."

The Gift of Music for the Dying

In *The Mozart Effect*, Don Campbell says that for many people music is the bridge between life and death. Campbell reminds us of how Mozart died at thirty-five on November 20, 1781. Imagine the scene in Vienna as his friends gathered around his fevered body to sing portions of Mozart's unfinished "Requiem." He had finished only seven stanzas of "Lacrimosa." Before he died, he sang with his friends; he puffed out his cheeks, pretending to be trumpets. "Here is my death song. Didn't I tell you I was writing a requiem for myself?" Campbell says, "Music and sound weave a magic carpet for the soul's journey home."

Hospice singers. Hospice harpists. However the music enters those "last spaces," music will bless families and friends in countless ways. Therese Schroeder-Sheker developed end-of-life music-midwifery to a fine art. She spent long hours resurrecting the music from the medieval monastery of Cluny in southern France and used it in her Chalice of Repose palliative care and hospice program in Missoula, Montana. She calls what she and her volunteers do "music-thanatology."

Music can communicate beyond words. Islene Runningdeer, a therapist in Karen's hometown, says, "Sound is just vibration of matter. Music is powerful energy. That's why I call music therapy energy medicine." Jonna Goulding says, "When patients are unable to communicate what they are going through, music and the arts are a way to crack open the doors so that they can be supported in their journeys… it can change the entire feeling in the room when people are scared or angry or suffering." Runningdeer explains that that process of end of life and dying can be a really rich time to finish things, to have an accounting of what we've done and accepting things we weren't able to do. "And being able to forgive ourselves and others. Music can help."

John Hartman, the volunteer coordinator for VITAS Innovative Hospice Care in Florida, told Karen about how they use music.

Bob Marley Comes to Hospice
John, Karen's friend

One of our technicians at a central Florida hospice in-patient unit looked at me and said, "Watch this. It will amaze you!" Bob Marley took out his cell phone and started to play some music for a patient named Donald. In about three seconds, Donald, who had been diagnosed with Stage IV brain cancer, who couldn't tell us what he'd just eaten for dinner or the name of his wife of thirty-plus years, said "Bob Marley," and began singing along. Marley's work with music demonstrates how a positive change in mood or behavior can be brought about in the listener. Music has been used since time immemorial to comfort one another, and, who hasn't been comforted by hearing a lullaby?

In hospice and hospital facilities that provide musical support, John Hartman explained, families can arrange for bedside vigils by typically one to two specially trained musicians who will sing or play live music for someone who is dying. The purpose of such a vigil is to provide comfort and support both to the patient and loved ones. Music vigils can take place anytime during hospice care, but can be particularly beneficial during critical times, such as the days immediately prior to death, during times that hard decisions have to be made, or when artificial life-support equipment is being removed.

Musicians differ in the details regarding how they would like to conduct a music vigil. Some prefer that those in the room remain silent, while others encourage participants to talk quietly with one another and the dying person as the music plays in a supportive manner, honoring and reinforcing the importance of the family gathering. Musicians are trained to observe body processes and mental states, adjusting their playing in ways that are appropriate to what the patient is feeling at that time. The music is improvised or modified at the moment it is created to adjust to the immediate needs of the patient. For this reason recorded music is not used in formal music vigils.

Karen's harpist friend, Margaret, brought her small strumming harp with her when she visited one day. She gently strummed it on Karen's back and its vibrations vibrated "calm throughout my body," Karen said.

Where They're Ready to Meet Me
Karen and her friend Margaret

Margaret Stephens has been sending the gentle, lilting chords of her Celtic harp around the rooms of the Dartmouth-Hitchcock Medical Center since 2005.

For years Margaret wore a pin given to her by the palliative care people: "No One Alone." With tears in her eyes, Margaret said, "That's so important. No one should be alone with their pain and fears. The thought that people might be by themselves is horrible to me. Music helps."

Indeed it does. Over the years, people have expressed a range of emotions following Margaret's harp music. "It gave me an emotional purge, which I obviously needed." "It's so peaceful and soothing — it calms me down before my doctor's appointment." "I learned that there are notes and chords which help the bowels relax and remove cramps. I wish I had more time with Margaret." "Margaret's music helps my mind, body, and soul escape from the drill of pain." Another said, "The music reached a part of me untouched by medication. In a way, it freed my soul."

One nurse said, "I was dashing out of Radiation to try to get a list of jobs done amidst 'tiredness' and a weary feeling from twenty-plus treatments. Strains of the harp stopped me in my tracks. A calm came over me!"

Another told of her husband's pulmonary artery pressure lowering when Margaret was in the room — and remained steady at that range for more than twelve hours after Margaret left.

Healing harp music takes people to what they describe as a "wonderful place." Some feel as if they're floating on a cloud. Perhaps that's why many who hear Margaret's harp think of her as an angel.

One day, Karen asked Margaret how this has informed her own views of dying. She thought about that for a while and then she said, "I like the phrase Richard Mcquellon and Michael Cowan used in *The Art of Conversation through Serious Illness: Lessons for Caregivers.* They said, we're in 'mortal time.' I guess that's what I'm learning. These people I meet remind me how precious every day is and I try to live in the present moment. I meditate. I center. I go into the stillness and become a part, for a brief time, of the nonmaterial world. Then I'm able to be with people where they're ready to meet me."

Music *is* powerful. It may not be curative, but is can be a healing gift in living and in dying. The old Celts believed that the whole world was sound. When we forget that sound, we feel lost. But when music fills our souls, we are found.

FROM THE CAREGIVER'S GUIDEBOOK

The motivation for gift-giving comes from the grateful appreciation that one has lived by the grace of others. Giving gifts at the end of a life also makes it easier for survivors to grieve without having to decide later *who should* get Grandma's china or Dad's toolbox. The spirituality of gratitude throughout life is knowing that one lives and dies by the gifts of others.

1. Caregivers are greatly helpful when they tell visitors who want to bring something that small single servings of "easy to eat" foods are always welcomed.

2. Being able to receive the gifts that the dying want to give, even if you don't want or need them, is an act of charity rather than dishonesty.

3. Ask questions and help the dying one to decide "who gets what." Especially if his or her mind is the least bit clouded, he or she will appreciate the help because the dying person really does want to give. All too often, people may dismiss plans for giving things away as a kind of denial. As a caregiver, however, you can help the dying one do this when he or she has the clarity, interest, and energy to give the gifts away.

4. The primary caregivers also need gifts of care that will sustain them. They often do not feel free to ask for help. Take the initiative to offer help to caregivers. Volunteer to sit for a while so the primary caregiver can take a walk. Or visit a friend. Or nap.

How Are You Feeling?

"Feelings are for the soul what food is for the body."
Rudolf Steiner, *The Way of Initiation*

ℵ *from* Karen's Hospice Journal ℥

The famous Woody Allen quote pops into my head whenever anyone asks me how I'm feeling. I want to say, "Well, I'm not feeling afraid, if that's what you're asking. I'm not afraid to die. I just don't want to be there when it happens."

But my truth right now is that I'm happy to be feeling anything. And I do want to be there. If I didn't feel I wouldn't be alive. I recently heard about an octogenarian actress who told her friend, "If I didn't hurt when I wake up in the morning, it would mean I was dead." I even thank my feet for their neuropathy because even if sometimes they feel like little loaves of dead bread, I know they're there and that I'm still alive. And I readily acknowledge them so I don't trip.

Thank goodness, I'm not a robot. Or a computer. Or some off-planet big-eyed being who can't feel emotions. Feeling makes me human. And my feelings are mine. Mine alone. You can't argue with how I feel. My feelings are real. For me. And recognizing my feelings can be the first step toward my own healing, and the healing of others. I read someplace recently that healing begins with listening — and then these nine words: I can understand how you might feel that way.

I'm on a roller coaster now. Like big waves, my feelings rush in so fast and so disordered that I feel pummeled by sand and water and wind all at once. And then the calm comes and I'm almost numb. Sometimes I call that stage peace. *Feelings can be affected by the moon; like tides, they ebb and flow. I am moonstruck with hope.*

The Japanese, I understand, have a word for holding very strong but different emotions at the same time: wabi-sabi. *Beauty and sadness. Grief and happiness. Attraction and repulsion. Yin and yang. Thoughts and emotions. Heart and head. Living and dying.*

I live, now, bookended by wabi-sabi. *I am united by both ends of the emotional spectrum. I shed tears of grief and tears of laughter at the same time. Both are salty. Both are me. Both are real. And yet, I realize at some deep level, it's likely that neither are real.*

When people ask me, "How are you feeling? Really?" I suspect they're actually asking, "How are you dealing with your feelings? And how can you help me deal with mine?" And "Do you want to talk about how you're feeling?"

I continue to search for language to respond in some honest fashion to "How are you?" I try to put it in a current perspective. "Today is a good day." "Do you mean right now? Right now, I'm very good." For me, this implies that I'm not always this way. But in this hour, in this "now," I am at peace.

Then we have a conversation about how we can be sad and at peace at the same time and both are valid feelings.

Wow. At peace. Others have asked me what I mean by being "at peace" and I mull it over again and again. What do I mean by peace? Not numbness. I'm more alive than that. Not nervous or anxious. Certainly not fearful. I come back to Julian of Norwich, holding that little hazelnut in her hand and seeing the world and realizing that "all will be well." Being at peace means that all is well with my soul. All is well. That's my mantra, now. I can hold cancer and wellness at the same time. I'm dying, but I'm living. Wabi-sabi.

❧   ❦

Those who are leaning into death need what everyone needs: accurate empathy that confirms what they feel and thereby validates their being. When someone is dying, Sherwin Nuland has observed, "the walls of the room enclose a chapel, and it is right to enter it in hushed reverence." Karen's reflections invite us to embrace all the feelings that accompany one who is consciously dying. To keep hoping while facing the ignominies of dying, people need permission to feel negative feelings as well as the positive ones.

The Heart Knows

James Stephens in *The Crock of Gold* said, "The head does not hear anything until the heart has listened... what the heart knows today the head will understand tomorrow." The heart is often regarded metaphorically as the seat of emotions. Our heads may be very confused about death and dying, but our hearts know that we can accept what is happening or will happen to us. Or the opposite may be true. The head has a kind of intellectual clarity that is often overwhelmed by intensely chaotic and conflicting emotions about impending death and dying. A host of feelings converge. Love. Anxiety. Terror. Stress. Fear. Anger. Powerlessness. Loneliness. These emotions are linked to what is happening physically as an individual is dying.

The wise Lakota Sioux, Black Elk, said that the "eye of the heart sees everything." The Maya have a word for "my heart is your heart" and it is *Lak'ech*. People from Kenya might say, "Because we are, I am." Or if you're from Zimbabwe, you might phrase it: "I am well because you are well." We would be well served to come up with an English word or phrase that shows this kind of compassion and love stemming from the heart-place within us. The heart pumps not only blood and oxygen but creates an electromagnetic field that radiates up to ten feet around the outside of our bodies. Love is palpable. And real. It's regenerative and it keeps spiraling out. Scientists tell us this field is about 5,000 times more powerful than the field created by our brains. Research from the HeartMath group has discovered that the heart can transform stress, better regulate emotional responses, and harness the power of heart/brain communication.

So, it's our emotions that pump out an electromagnetic field that sensitive people (and certainly animals) can pick up. Besides fear and anger, we also pump out love and compassion. When people are caught up in a disaster or group tragedy, they feel the emotions of those around them. Time and time again people will rush in to help, forgetting their own safety. Our feelings are contagious and our thoughts and feelings are powerful energies for action. After experiencing intense connection with others after a group disaster, people often comment, "Why can't we feel this way all the time? Why does it take a tragedy to make us realize that we have hearts?"

The dying often come to a new understanding of heart. They are cracked open in ways that seem to allow them to be able to contain much more than at other times of their lives.

All the D's are Normal

You may feel that you're the only one feeling all these various things right now, but you're pretty normal if you slip from one right into another. And you don't know which "D" is going to raise its head next. So remember, it's normal to feel all these "D's": dark, doom, despair, depressed, doubtful, down, drab, drained, defeated, defensive, driftless, droopy, deteriorated, denied, dejected, deprived, desperate, desolate, detached, destabilized, disoriented, dazed, defensive, degraded, demanding, dependent, deserted, despondent, despair, delicate, different, diminished, disabled, disadvantaged, discomfited, disconsolate, discriminated against, depreciated, disgusted, disinterested, disturbed, disloyal, dismayed, dismal, dispossessed, drugged, drained, disregarded, distant, distressed, divided... and sometimes, you just wish you had your "druthers." I'd "druther" be someone else. I'd "druther" be somewhere else.

Our Divine Human Virtue

GENTLENESS

Karen once wrote a poem called "Gentle me, Jesus" in which she prayed, "smooth me into sphere-shape, perfect like your own; round me when I turn rigid; bend me when I am boxed." When we respond with gentleness instead of harshness, when we react with circles instead of right angles, with quiet instead of anger, we can change the energy of the room. We can speak gentle truths; we can hear gentle responses. Tenderness can replace strain and quiet can calm.

You may not feel all of these "D" words or you may feel some of these emotions at various times. But you're also capable of feeling a whole lot of the "other D's" at the same time, including: *determined, discerning, devoted, diligent, dynamic, defiant, desirable,* and, don't forget — *divine.*

The eighteenth-century scientist and Swedish mystic Emanual Swedenborg called us "Divine Humans." That's why we decided to include a sidebar virtue in each chapter of this book called "Divine Human Virtues." He said we each bear the "divine mystery" because we can combine (like *wabi-sabi*) complete opposites. Dying, if we are awake and willing, can enable us to become soul-alchemists so we are able to transform the "lead" of our prior negative emotions into the "gold" of something so much more. At death, Swedenborg claimed, the social masks worn on earth dissolve and the true self is revealed. In our expanded awareness, he pointed out, we are able to experience and feel so much, much more.

Feeling restless at this time is also very common. It's as if our unease is trying to tell us something. Karen has expressed to her husband John, "I don't know why I'm feeling so antsy today. Did I have too much caffeine? Or am I just reacting to the steroids my doctor wants me to take to reduce swelling and maybe give me a bit more energy?" Carl Jung said in his essay on "The Soul and Death," that "restlessness begets meaninglessness, and the lack of meaning in life is a soul-sickness whose full extent and full import our age has not as yet begun to comprehend."

So to counteract "soul-sickness" let us feel — to the greatest extent possible — every emotion at hand. And be grateful for each of them. And we need to remember that we can hold more than one or two emotions at a time. In the following poem written near the end of her own journey, Karen captures the experience of intensity and immediacy in her dying "menu" and the inevitable *wabi-sabi* nature of the process.

Today's Feast

Sticky sweetness spills the rim of the tiny
golden waffle square within square within square.
Sacred geometry waits on my simple breakfast plate.

I love the closeness, the intimacy,
The immediacy of it all.
No longer craving the long-view, my eyes focus
on the here not there, the now not then, the why not when.

World commentators hold no sway.
Their voices no longer cling to the corners of my brain.
Lists are tomorrow's nerve ends, not these fingertips. Not today's.

Today, all is sweet. Or tart. Or salty. A white grain
suspended between my lips. My tongue. My menu.
I no longer anticipate the next fry, another burger,
some other Sunday's sundae.
No. It's today's feast. Now's guest. This very moment's quest.

I adore the urgency of it all.

Karen Speerstra

In *The Etiquette of Illness*, Susan P. Halpern, a cancer survivor, points out how people might not dare to ask "how you are feeling?" because they're not sure if the dying one wants to be asked. And they risk the possibility of using such a stock question when the answer coming back might be more forthright and honest than they're prepared to receive. Halpern points out that the unwritten question looming there might be: "Do you want to talk about your death?" If they are as transparent as Karen, the answer will likely be "Yes. Let's talk." And because time is short, let's talk NOW.

We all hope for the death the poet Rilke described: "Oh Lord, give each of us his own death, the dying, that issues forth out of the life in which he had love, meaning and despair." Love and despair. Meaning and emptiness. Delight and disappointment. We have identified ambiguity as a constant companion for the dying. Feeling contradictory emotions like relief and rage simultaneously is common. However, holding together two intense and appropriate feelings is not an accomplished art for human ones. We prefer that things are this OR that. Not so for the dying or for the living. Ambiguity reigns.

Emotional Contradictions

The loneliness of dying surrounded by friends.

It's a fact that everyone dies alone, even if we are surrounded by close friends and family. This is the ultimate loneliness of having to die. No one can do it for us. There are no deathbed surrogates. The theologian Paul Tillich wrote this about loneliness in a sermon: "No communication with others can remedy it, as no other's presence in the actual hour of our dying can conceal the fact that it is our death and our death alone." Who can endure such loneliness?, Tillich asks. The process of dying includes holding on to those we love while we watch all significant human relationships slowly unravel.

The ordinary and inevitable loneliness of dying is often complicated by medical technology that isolates people from ordinary social interaction for the sake of better treatment. In many and subtle ways, the medicalizing of death keeps the dying from family and friends. Offering choices to someone who is dying is critical. Would you rather have an oxygen mask over your face or be able to kiss your wife?

Social isolation exaggerates loneliness in painfully subtle ways. While it's not pleasant to admit, hospital staff tend to ignore the cranky patients. Family and friends might ignore the dying because a) they believe that death is contagious; b) they don't like unpleasant odors; or c) they don't know what to say. Charles, a friend of Herbert, prepared a special bed for his wife to sleep in when she came home from the hospital. There was only room for one in the bed. Later, after his wife died, Charles struggled with the awareness that his fear of death had intensified his wife's loneliness while she was dying.

The dread of abandonment even when caregivers stay present.
The fear of dying echoes the infant's terror of separation and one's approaching death may evoke a primal dread of abandonment. It should not be surprising then that dying persons rage out of fear, frustration, and helplessness that they might be abandoned by those they love. Expressions of rage are often a desperate cry for presence as if to say "don't give up on me, don't leave me, I'm still here." Unfortunately, these protests often have the opposite response of the intended effect: they drive away the people they most wish to be present.

When Anger Prevails, Living Does Not
Herbert's student, David Altshuler

Larry, recently retired at the age of sixty-five, was a successful businessman who lived in the San Mateo hills with his wife, Sandra, and his mother-in-law, Louise. He and Sandra were high school sweethearts and had been together nearly fifty years. "He's a man of few words," Sandra told me one day. "But when he says something he really means it from the heart," she added.

Larry had been diagnosed with a rare malignant tumor on his brain, which the oncologist described as rarely treatable, but he was planning a number of chemotherapies that "could" work. Larry was already grieving. His energy was angry, however, and during later admissions to the hospital he would express his anger by talking about the "injustices" in his life and in the world. Sandra kept saying, "I can't believe it, David, Larry just retired and now he's got to go through this!" Larry was usually sarcastic and frequently responded with comments like, "Yah, I could think of better things to do today."

The family refused comfort care. They said that putting Larry on comfort care meant resigning him to death and they were not ready to consider that possibility despite Larry's rapid decline and increasing pain levels. Sandra finally admitted that she did not know how to live without Larry and she did not know how to let go. Sandra seemed greatly relieved once she finally admitted her fear and anxiety. But in the weeks, days, and hours before that moment, Larry suffered immensely. It was only in Larry's last hours that the hospital could help him find some peace in his dying process.

Sadly, Larry's dying story is all too common. The inability of family and friends and medical professionals to acknowledge that death is near and unavoidable adds to the anguish that so many dying people experience. Larry did not have to die angry.

Fears come in many and surprising ways even for those who are consciously dying.
Fear of the unknown is intensified at death because of our general discomfort with uncertainty. The level of pain, the loss of body control, diminished mobility, incontinence, the response of loved ones to the ignominies of dying, and fear of medical treatments that might make our situation worse all contribute to generalized fear for the one dying. Even the strongest and bravest person may say to someone he or

she loves, "Don't leave me alone. I'm afraid of dying." Bargaining for more time, as we have already said, is often prompted by a fear of incompleteness. People who believe their worth is determined by what they do and accomplish may be fearful of failing and being judged incomplete.

Dying is a journey into the unknown. It evokes a range of contradictory feelings in the one dying and in his or her family and friends. A "good death" is a relative thing, Nuland observes. "There isn't much you can manage beyond trying to keep things neat and keep things painless — keeping someone from being alone."

The Bible tells us that "love casts out fear." Love is the one bond that is unbreakable in death. Love promises spiritual companionship that gives hope and enables the dying to live with emotional contradictions and finally discover their own way to die.

Suffering and Hope Together

We are most divine and most human when we face our own mortality. It's then that we learn that suffering and hope are linked together. It is, as Erik Erikson once observed, the indispensable factor for the possibility of human wholeness. Hope does not try to avoid the fears and pains of finite existence; nor is it naïve about suffering as part of living. If we divorce hope from suffering, we risk becoming victims of illusions and create images of false hope at the end of life. If we divorce suffering from hope, then we are likely to become victims of cynicism or despair and surrender hope altogether.

Paul Tillich has said it very well: "One must accept suffering with courage as an element of finitude and affirm finitude in spite of the suffering that accompanies it."

What Do We Hope For?

Herbert's friend Marty

Marty and Bill had been married for only ten years. They had known one another in graduate school when Bill was a Jesuit priest. Their relationship was said to have been made in heaven. Bill died from an inoperable brain tumor. After his death, Marty wrote:

When Bill was dying, I said exactly that to a friend: "In the darkest moments, we don't know what to hope for at all." Should I hope for him to beat this infection, but continue living in a world without language? Should I hope for death to intervene quickly, mercifully? Outside of a miracle, I couldn't imagine an outcome that would restore any shred of the Old Life, the life we thought we'd signed up for together.

I could literally not imagine what to hope for, but a deep and abiding hope held me. In dark uncertainty, where desire refuses to focus, you discover hope *in* someone or something. You don't so much have this hope, the product of fierce focus or creative imagination or even deep faith. Rather, this kind of hope has you. All you have to do is fall into it, like a trapeze artist falls into a net.

It takes courage to let go of everything, including our goodness, in order to believe that we will continue on in ways we cannot know. We do not *have* hope: rather, *hope has us.* Marty dared to let go of everything because she knew the safety net was there. In the end, that is the most friends, family, hospice caregivers, and medical professionals can do: be a safety net to catch people should they fall in the midst of pain and suffering.

The reciprocity between suffering and hoping was a critical factor in Karen's decision to suspend further treatment. "I have decided," she wrote in the first hospice journal, "to consciously trade treatment not only for more physical stamina, but also for what I hope would be a more wide-awake brain. I want to participate fully in my living until I die."

When we embrace all our feelings, all our emotions including suffering, hope will endure and sustain us. We can then truly *live* and face our last moments with integrity and wholeness.

From the Caregiver's Guidebook

Because dying individuals are more "raw" than they normally would be, their feelings are more apt to get hurt easily by what people say or don't do. Caregivers need to assure dying persons and themselves that everybody is doing the best they can. Don't impose your personal ideas and philosophy onto the dying. Let them discover for themselves what is "real" and "important." Hold their understandings and their unpredictable emotions without criticism or contradiction. Fears are not always easy to share. It is incumbent on caregivers to take fear seriously and respond graciously.

1. Instead of asking, "How are you?" or "How are you feeling?" consider other ways of phrasing that such as "How has this week been for you?"

2. The emotions of the dying will vacillate from silly to sad, from feeling depressed to feeling "up." And that's normal.

3. It is normal to feel exhausted and that the dying process seems to be taking a long time. When you have thoughts like "I wish this were over," remember that is normal as well. You need to find ways to "keep up" a normal life and do the thing you enjoy doing. Get away — if even for just a short time.

4. Everybody — caregivers and the dying alike — needs to be gracious and forgiving, especially with themselves and with one another because emotions are unpredictable and very real for every person experiencing them.

⸱ On Gratitude ⸱

We may not think much these days about virtues. But they're real. And we have them, nevertheless. They are our soulfulness. Our way to be both Divine and human. They are the essence of paradox because they're in us, and yet beyond us.

Christians call the three main virtues faith, hope, and love. Early on, the church fathers added four others (borrowed from Greek philosophy) that form the classic seven: prudence, justice, temperance, and courage.

Every religious path calls out various virtues. Jewish tradition holds on to loving God and obeying his laws. Islam claims about thirty-six, including gratitude. Cicero called gratitude the parent of all other virtues. It's our heart-memory, as an old French proverb puts it.

Gratitude is the emotion we feel when we are thankful and when we stop to count our blessings. An "ungrateful wretch" can't feel it and instead is resentful, hostile, and indifferent. People who are rarely thankful for anything forget the great beauty all around us. They miss the goodness.

When people in various studies conducted on gratitude are asked to record, over a period of weeks, instances of feeling thankful or grateful, the thankful groups invariably become more optimistic about life and look forward to the future. They even have fewer physical complaints. So feeling thankful for anything — big or small — is a healthy endeavor. "I'm grateful for the bagel I had for breakfast because I really like cream cheese." "I'm grateful for finding a parking space when I was short of time." "I'm grateful for having X in my life." And people who regularly record their thankfulness moments are more likely to reach more of their goals, thus feeling positive about life in general. We might call gratitude our spiritual intelligence.

James A. Autry, in *Choosing Gratitude*, said, "When you have a life-threatening illness, the days no longer pass like dry leaves in a gale, uncounted and unheeded. Instead they are individual glasses of rare wines, to be sipped and savored."

Savoring our gifts and passing them on breaks down barriers and embraces life.

The one who is dying may be surrounded by the gratitude others express toward him or her — their last chance to say "thank you for…" And when the person who faces his or her last days is able to keep saying thank you, everyone is doubly blessed by the giving and the receiving. Thank you for laughing with me. Thank you for your story. Thank you for taking the time to come over. Thank you for bringing the casserole. Thank you for noticing that I could use that. Thank you for loving me, even when I may not be the most lovable. Thank you for having patience. Thank you for gracing this day. Thank you for being in my life. Thank you for just being you!

PART FOUR

DYING *into* LIFE

The Goodness of Grieving

"No one ever told me that grief felt so like fear.
The same fluttering in the stomach,
the same restlessness, the yawning. I keep on swallowing."

C. S. Lewis, from his journal after his wife's death

❧ *from* Karen's Hospice Journal ❧

I know everyone grieves in her own way. Both my parents died so quickly —
Dad in his lawn chair, Mom in her bed — that I was unable to separate out what
was grief and what was just sheer shock.

But now that I'm feeling my own grief at leaving so much behind, I'm trying
to pull my mind around it all. I break into tears at the most unexpected times. I
realize that leaving John will be the hardest. Ever since he sent a love letter to me
from his little apartment as a new Lutheran parish minister, saying he would love
me until his last dying breath, I knew I'd found "the" partner for me. Our friends
tease us because we're such a strange statistic — the same two people together for
forty-nine years?

Then of course, I'm grieving leaving behind our two sons, our daughter-in-law,
and our granddaughter. Saying good-bye to that little six-year-old as she stepped
onto the shuttle bus to whisk her away to Boston and a plane to Colorado after a
fun-filled five-day visit was the hardest work I've done yet. Her precious hugs, her
smiles, her long eyelashes, her perfect brows, her big blue eyes, her sense of humor, her
striking intelligence. How can I leave all that behind? Tears splash in counterpoint
onto my keyboard as I write these words. I think about the very real possibility now
of not seeing her again, except on Skype, which is wonderful in itself but Skype
doesn't give hugs. What, I wonder, will she remember of me and of my dying? Or
of my life? And in the end, will it really matter?

I'm grateful, though, that Josie will remember a fairly energetic and vital grandma
who could still play with her. Both of my grandmothers were named Julia. The last

memory I have of my maternal grandmother was when I was nine and I was brushing her long hair as she sat in her kitchen one night. It had only specks of gray in it. My paternal grandmother died when I was two. She had knit me a pair of mittens and my parents quietly held my hand as I approached a mound of covers in a tall metal bedstead. She was so far up, I couldn't see her very well, but I knew this was an important moment. Her eyes were big and I smelled something very strange. I didn't like that smell. I later learned she had breast cancer. Wrinkling my nose, I reached up to receive her gift. I didn't know her, but I knew from that moment that she loved me.

During Josie's last visit, she asked me to read Charlotte's Web. Wilbur's plea, "Don't let me die!" caught in my throat. But since I was getting into all the different character voices, I hoped she thought it was just the piglet speaking, not Grandma revealing more of herself than might be just and appropriate even for a sensitive kindergartner. But children, I believe, have their own built-in protection barriers steeled against seeing more than they are able to absorb or bear. I trust she'll remember me as her living grandmother who in fact was already dying when she spent her last week with me.

And, of course, I grieve at the prospect of leaving all my friends. Along with our supportive neighbors. And my dear little church and the folks I've worked with around Vermont. And my books. And my sophiaserve blog readers, and my gardens and my woods and Jon Stewart and my favorite Kokopeli coat and Downton Abbey's fourth season, and...

Enough, already! I remind myself to reread this book's chapter "Letting Go!" But it's so hard to say good-bye to everything I've cherished for over seven decades. Eventually I start thinking about all the things I've already said good-bye to. Houses I've loved. Parents. Grandparents. Best friends. Communities I was an integral part of. Students I'll never see again. Colleagues I've cherished. My uterus. Pottery I've broken. Cars I've totaled. So I've had practice!

It's difficult, maybe even impossible, to grieve alone. Even Pi on the lifeboat had a tiger to share his grief with. I remember how my aunts gathered in my mom's kitchen after she died, to support me, an only child, and to support each other as *they mourned their beloved sister. We made ham sandwiches. We washed up the dishes together. We laughed. We told stories. We cried together. And somehow we got through it.*

When I think about what I'm leaving, great sadness nearly overwhelms me. But I remember that Tantric discipline the sherpas were well aware of. Lung-gom. It's the ability to glide along with uncanny swiftness and certainty. Even at night. It can be translated as "wind-concentration." Prana. Vital energy. Breath. I call "Her" Wisdom-Sophia.

Snow leopards are usually found above 5,000 feet. Some as high as 18,000. They approach you with pale blue eyes and frosty gray coats. Siberian priestesses were often buried with snow leopard images around them. Even in death, they were lionhearted and strong. They can bring down creatures three times their size.

Bring on the skull drums and the "kangling" trumpets. I'm following leopard tracks.

꿩 꿩

The task of leaving behind everything and everyone we have loved in order to get ready to die is a richly rewarding and a regularly overwhelming dimension of dying. It evokes great sadness. In a strange and oxymoronic way, grief becomes Karen's friend and healer. Grieving can be a midwife that births new possibilities, even while we are dying. Karen views her hospice team as her midwives whose respectful presence honors the spirit of new birth in her.

Remembering What Is Important

Death has a way of bringing clarity to what we value and are attached to. When grieving is part of the divine art of dying, we remember what is important, mourn what is lost, and cherish the memories we can. Grief is the price we pay for loving.

In *All Our Losses, All Our Griefs*, Herbert and his coauthor, Kenneth Mitchell, said that our attachments to friends, children, objects, projects, and dreams are never forever. Attachment is a human necessity and loss is unavoidable because we are finite. It's how we build and live within human communities: loving and losing and loving again. But our attachments are uniquely our own. So is our grief. Because losing what we love is painful, we often avoid grieving, perhaps especially when we grieve the loss of everyone and everything we value.

Grief includes expressing the ordinary emotions that accompany loss like sadness, disappointment, anger, guilt, emptiness, fear, even despair. The intensity and range of grief evoked by remembering and letting go will be unpredictable and often surprising. Ira Byock has rightly observed that "grief is neither a disorder nor a healing process; it is a sign of health itself, a whole and natural gesture of love. Nor must we see grief as a step toward something better. No matter how much it hurts — and it may be the greatest pain in life — grief can be an end in itself, a pure expression of love."

For the dying, the anticipation of losing people we love provides a unique opportunity to share that love directly. Their grief is immediate and pervasive and not easily ignored. They grieve in order to prepare to die. While survivors will grieve with the dying loved person, they will feel the loss most deeply after a death. Then they will need to grieve the death of someone they love in order to live again. That grief is forever and keeps alive the bonds that were shared even at the cost of pain. For both the living and dying, however, grief is a good friend because it helps us remember and conserve the past.

The decision to live consciously and freely toward the end means that the dying are awash in grief — letting go of everyone and everything they have loved. Although it is impossible for family and friends not to grieve along with the dying person as he or she lets go of everything, it is important to remember how necessary it is for dying people to be able to express their grief. That grief takes many forms. The dying person's response to these losses is seldom smooth.

Many Kinds of Losses

We are almost always surprised by what evokes grief. Sometimes we don't know how intensely we value something until it is lost or about to be lost. In her hospice journal, Karen identified a wonderful variety of people, activities, TV shows, foods, and patterns of living that she is anticipating losing. Being free to grieve all our losses without judgment makes it possible for life's end to be rich with remembering and memory-making and, of course, sadness.

Loss of Things

Handing over of material things may be the easiest kind of loss for the dying. That is, unless, he or she has been defined by those possessions. That makes it harder. While there is often an unexpected freedom from having fewer things to worry about, watching treasured possessions walk out the door is an occasion for sadness.

Functional Loss

The loss of energy, strength, mobility, concentration, control, and predictable bodily functioning is more difficult. Even the loss of dependable routines can bring on great sadness and impatience because they are all signs of decline and intimations of approaching death. Someone who wanted to do Karen's portrait asked if she could sit for two hours. "Sitting is no problem," she said, "but I've noticed that standing grows more and more difficult."

The Loss of Dreams

The loss of one's dreams and of not meeting expectations or deadlines can conjure up grief for the dying person. Deep, enduring sadness that a life did not turn out as he or she thought it should may be difficult to share except in limited ways. The loss of dreams is a very private sadness sometimes laced with shame or disappointment that may be mourned privately.

The Loss of New Possibilities

When we live until we die, it's natural to form new friendships, meet new people, and have new opportunities. Suddenly, all this potential for future happiness and fulfillment also goes away. That's more cause for grieving. Karen experienced this when she was asked to talk to a group of chaplaincy and hospice volunteers at the local hospital. Her first inclination was to say, "I appreciate the invitation but I'm not sure I have the energy for it." But her husband and son encouraged her to go. They had watched her "come alive" when she meets and speaks to other people so they knew it would be more helpful than harmful. She went and later said, "This was an unexpected gift for me. I met so many wonderful people — some of whom want to stay in contact with me. They even helped contribute ideas to this book!"

One new friend of Karen's at a particularly lively lunch conversation one day said, "Where have you been? I've wanted this conversation forever!" The dying need to continue loving and giving and, ultimately, deeply grieving for their new attachments as well.

The Litany of Lasts

When she visited the Yucatan, Karen thought, "Well, this is the last time I'll be here!" She pushes the shopping cart around her local supermarket wondering if this will be the last time she'll get groceries. Since, like all dying folks, she doesn't know, she thinks, "Maybe not. Maybe I'll push a cart down one more aisle and have one more visit with that person, or I'll read one more book by this favorite author." Nevertheless, she compiles her "litany of lasts" in her head — and goes on. When both of her sons visited at the same time, the four of them roasted a turkey and cooked a Thanksgiving dinner together, knowing they may not have a chance to do that again. Then they prepared a birthday celebration for husband John's eightieth birthday — laughing, screaming, trying out new cooking and coping skills.

Eventually, as one moves closer to death, it's natural that families and friends begin to give special attention to the last time something might happen. Hospice nurse Sherri told Karen about one of her clients who was no longer eating, but several days before she died, said she wanted one last piece of pizza. She loved it. Then she went back to not eating again.

We think of a last dinner out, our last lovemaking, the last time a person can leave the bedroom or the bed and so on. An esteemed religious leader is reported to have told an orderly shortly before his death: "Put me on the bedpan straight; it may be my last shit." While the "litany of lasts" may seem excessively morbid, each moment provides time for recollection and an invitation to mourn. It also keeps the dying person connected to family and friends. This ordinary desire to ritualize one last trip to the summer cabin or one final baseball game or dinner at a favorite restaurant may become complicated if it puts the dying person at medical risk. But it's usually a risk worth taking.

Once More to the Lake House
Shirley, Herbert's friend

Sam loved our lake house. We had purchased the land with a shack on it when we were newly married. Over the years, the lake property was a prized getaway. In the beginning, we would camp there. When the children were born, we bought a trailer for Sam and me and the children slept in a tent. Eventually we built a simple A-frame that became "the lake house." We planned to live there after retirement.

Just two years before Sam could retire, he was diagnosed with lung cancer. We did many "lasts" at the lake including a spectacular Fourth of July picnic with all our family and some friends. By mid-August Sam was confined to bed in our home. Somehow he convinced his doctor and me and all the children to make one last visit to the lake house over Labor Day weekend. Sunday evening, he remained in his lawn chair watching the stars and listening to the crickets while I cleaned up the kitchen. When I came to take him to bed, Sam was dead. Despite the comments of several well-meaning friends, I never regretted the last trip to the lake house.

Our Divine Human Virtue

COMPASSION

The Dalai Lama says that on every level of human life, "compassion is the key thing." Most particularly, then at the end of life, we reach for this key to unlock what has been bound, to release what has been held, to free ourselves from our self-imposed prisons. Compassion is a loving correction that can unleash a fire within us that burns away our regrets and our past pain. Compassion can turn our lives upside down, Matthew Fox says, "and that is not necessarily a bad thing."

In the process of bringing closure to a life in order to let it go, grieving is a constant companion for the dying as well as their caregivers.

Grieving does not end with one good cry. Because the loss is ongoing, it is also accumulative. In *Letting Go*, Morrie Schwartz observes that grieving contributed to his emotional composure, making it easier for him to embrace whatever came each day. "I let myself experience the grief, the sadness, the bitterness, the anger, the dread, the regret, and the sense of finishing before my time. I let the tears flow until they dry up…. Crying has helped me gradually come to accept the end — the fact that all living things die." The freedom to grieve and the freedom to love are inextricably linked for living and dying alike.

Saying Good-bye to Those We Love

Letting go of stuff and memories is necessary and ultimately not that difficult. But saying good-bye to those we love is different. William M. Lamers, Jr., a hospice physician, has observed that dying people usually do not separate themselves emotionally from their loved ones as death approaches. Many dying people tell of increased closeness to their spouses and loved ones as life comes to an end. The grief for everyone is palpable as death draws near.

Karen's cousin Maxine expressed her deep anticipatory grief by saying, "How will I ever get along without you?" Karen's own grief at saying good-bye to her was lessened a bit when she was able to say, "But you're strong — physically now, after your liver transplant, mentally, and certainly spiritually. You and I both will be fine." During her transplant experience, Maxine had relayed to Karen how her donor had said, "When I die, I want to donate my organs to help others who need them for life. This body on earth is just a rental unit." But saying good-bye, even to "our rental units," is difficult work.

When we mourn, Cythnia Bourgeault says in *The Wisdom Jesus*, "we are in a state of freefall... To mourn means to live between the realms." But she points out a need to enter this brutal form of emptiness because if we can remain open to it, we will be "become intertwined in a greater love that holds all things together. To mourn is to touch directly the substance of divine compassion. And just as ice must melt before it can begin to flow, we, too, must become liquid before we can flow into the larger mind. Tears have been a classic spiritual way to doing this."

As the dying one "lets go," the great challenge for caregivers is to stay present. Because dying cannot be fixed or reversed or stopped, it naturally evokes feelings of helplessness. The natural impulse is "do" something about it. Fix it. Stop it. Change it. The hardest thing of all is just to show up, to be present even when we feel so helpless and wait and keep watch with someone we love who is near death. When we flee from suffering, we abandon the one who suffers. Grieving as family and friends while continuing to be present with the dying loved person requires a delicate balance among the mutually conflicting demands of holding on to, letting go of, and drawing closer to the dying patient.

Ira Byock calls staying as long as is necessary or appropriate "active loving care." Doctors and other members of our medical communities often feel helpless, impotent, unable to imagine what else might be done for a dying patient when they have exhausted all the tests and treatments they know of. But building loving communities of care is a sign that we are not powerless in the face of grieving and suffering.

Hope is renewed when we can wait in helplessness while someone we love dies. We can still tell stories and sing songs or listen to songs sung. We can express regrets and make anxieties known. We can give. Above all, we can lament. Medication may manage physical pain but sometimes one's emotional suffering also needs venting. Like the psalms of lament found in the Bible, both the dying person and caregivers can protest against God and love God at the same time. When our grief is a lament, the dying admit they feel abandoned and admit they're in the dark. We know what hurts and we know it will not go away quickly. But implicit in the lament is also the keen understanding that the hope that endures is born in an honest acknowledgment of the situation. Pain isn't mute. It can be shared So is hope. It begins in helplessness and hopelessness.

Hopeful Grieving

Martin Luther was asked what he would do if he knew the world was coming to an end. He said he would plant a tree. After being in hospice care for a month, Karen spent a whole morning with her young granddaughter, Josie, planting moss roses, impatiens, and colorful begonias. Hope bloomed. Flowers remind us to continue to grow and transcend both joy and anguish.

Good grieving makes it possible to love freely even to the end of a life. As dying people become more at peace with their impending death and if their pain is well managed, they are likely to become less preoccupied with themselves and more concerned for the well-being of others. They become more involved in living, even as they are resigned to their dying.

From the Caregiver's Guidebook

Grief is a good friend for living and dying because it helps us remember and conserve the past, rather than denying that we once had meaningful things but that we now no longer have them. With each loss, there is lament as the losses mount. Grieving continues to be necessary so that grief does not accumulate.

1. Remember that the person you are caring for is wounded. He or she is suffering. So are you. Recognizing that will make you a better caregiver because you *feel*.

2. Let the person talk about what he or she is afraid of. Your job is to listen and to not be afraid yourself.

3. Try reading one of the psalms of lament, if that is in the culture of the person dying.

4. Do a life review with the person to help him or her recognize his or her losses.

5. Remember that you, too, are grieving, even though it may be anticipatory grief. Try not to feel guilty if you sense you're getting back to normal too quickly. All of your feelings are valid.

RITUALS FOR THE JOURNEY

"You should have a ritual for life.
All a ritual does is concentrate your mind
on the implications of what you are doing...
The ritual enables you to make the transit.
Ritual introduces you to the meaning of what's going on."

Joseph Campbell, *A Joseph Campbell Companion*

⸙ *from* Karen's Hospice Journal ⸙

I invited a couple of my musician friends over for lunch and to play some music for me — music they may (or may not) play at my funeral. It's up to them. I don't think too much about what will happen at my funeral because my family will do a great job planning that later ritual. But I did mention to these two good friends that it would be wonderful if their music could grace our service. So I asked them over so I could hear them rehearse.

Our son Joel joined them on the piano as they shared Telemann and Mozart in this little ad-hoc concert while joined by the cooing mourning doves outside our window. My whole body absorbed the vibrations of their bassoon and flute right there in our music room where the grand piano holds court. Together, we created a morning ritual. Music is usually an integral part of any liturgy or ritual, whether it's drumming, singing, or sending one's breath across a hole or a reed to create sound. This morning was no exception.

After they left, I asked myself why this had been so meaningful for me. I guess it was because ritual creates a space that's held open. Time stands still. Listening to and watching my friends, I could feel their music taking me to another place.

Then I remembered reading somewhere that the word ritual actually means "to fit together." My friends' bassoon and flute and piano fit together perfectly. Whenever I invite people into our home, hospitality creates a ritual, of sorts. We eat together. We talk — often about important things. We fit.

I have noticed an almost ritualistic aura around some of the conversations I've been having lately. They come by phone, by email, by mail (often accompanied by gifts people have carefully made or chosen just for me). Or in person. By deciding to die transparently, as I have chosen to do, I've offered the invitation to people for these conversations to take place. It gives others the opportunity to approach this complex "dying chaos" more safely. Because I have had some recent publicity around a national book award, my name and face and story have appeared in local media. So, from the guy at the hardware store to my dentist, to my neighbors on our little mountain, my community seems to know what's happening to me right now. It gives license for them to talk to me in ways I've not experienced before. Nor, perhaps, have they. A friend told me yesterday that because she now thinks of me every morning, her morning coffee ritual has taken on new meaning. She thinks about what's truly important to her, as she asks herself, "I wonder how Karen is organizing her day today."

Yesterday the FedEx truck brought me a shower chair. It's a tangible white plastic symbol that marks another step in my passage from strong legs to weaker legs. I thought when it arrived I'd shed a tear or two. But I didn't. Instead, it's a little secure and welcomed addition to our bathroom.

Jonna explained how her hospice team often marks the passage of someone in their care by intentionally placing salt in water — salt for tears. Salt for life. Salt for passage. How appropriate. We're born in salty amniotic fluids. Surely salt can usher us into another new existence. I'm also anticipating wonderfully scented oils on my body during those precious exit moments. And music! Don't forget the music!

ℵ ℵ

Rituals come in many forms with many meanings for many purposes. Karen has described meaningful moments around music and conversation that became for her transforming ritual actions. Rituals provide time, space, symbols, and bodily enactment for engaging significant life situations that give shape and meaning to our lives. A ritual may be as simple as coffee with a friend or prayer with a trusted spiritual companion or listening to music that touches the body and as complex as a funeral liturgy or the election of a pope.

Because rituals express what cannot be captured in words, they are particularly necessary to framing the transitions and illuminating experience at life's end. Just as we use playful and poetic language to speak about mystery, we use symbols and gestures and song to point to speak the unspeakable in human pain and make public what cannot be seen. Rituals like Karen's musical moment often invent us as much as we invent them.

Predictable, Practiced, and Purposeful

Many creatures engage in patterned shared behavior for the purpose of survival, order, and even comfort. Crows, for instance, will engage in what seems like ceremony around another dead crow. They may even cover the body with grass. Elephants rock their huge bodies and grieve over a loved one for weeks. Dogs will exhibit listlessness and loss of appetite when they are sad.

While animals may grieve in their own ways, they certainly don't practice rituals as we humans understand them. We engage in them because we expect certain things will happen. We'll get an insight we hadn't had before. We'll establish more ties with our community. Or in the case of end-of-life rituals, we simply find them comforting.

Rituals are imaginative and shared. They are often filled with storytelling or acted out. They are what Flannery O'Connor called very large, simple caricatures for the nearly blind. Rituals weave our human fabric into divine stuff. Together, we relive our legends. We sing common songs. We light and blow out candles. We hang wreaths, inaugurate presidents, and crown monarchs. We cherish our traditions and teach them to our children. Cultural anthropologist Mary Catherine Bateson calls ritual "metaphysical housework." Rituals tidy up our edges and make neat the things that feed our souls.

Rituals depend on cultural traditions. Tibetan Buddhists, for instance, speak of the necessity to be awake at the time of death. They regard life as eternal, requiring constant preparation, remembrance, and release. From *The Tibetan Book of the Dead*, monks and nuns memorize and rehearse chants during life so that, at the moment of death, they will not fall into the illusion of nonexistence. Chants, drums, and gongs form special end-of-life music for many people.

Because they're anchored to tradition, ritual acts are usually predictable, practiced, and purposeful. They're predictable because people have experienced them before, and they know, at least roughly, what to expect. Rituals are practiced because they have roots, either to family or cultural traditions and you're committed to stay with certain rituals throughout the proscribed time. And, ideally, you've already practiced them. It is easier to meditate in a crisis if you have already done it before in times of calm. When ritual practices are repeated often enough, prayer and meditation may become like breathing.

Prayer: Rich and Powerful

Praying together, silently or out loud, is perhaps the most common human ritual. It offers us a way to be truly present. Sometimes when Karen prays, she holds an object — a special stone, a shell, or a little sculpture. When we pray, we often use proscribed and written words. Other times, words simply come to us. Anne Lamott says there are really only two prayers: "Help me! Help me!" and "Thank you, thank you." Both are appropriate for a family's last days together. Ritual and prayer language can be rich and powerful, or as empty as an abandoned chrysalis.

It is appropriate to pray at any time when the dying person welcomes it. American Zen Buddhist roshi Joan Halifax said, "May my body be a prayerstick for the world." Karen prays, "May my dying be a beacon of light to show that each of us is a light-filled being, every minute of every day."

Many of us pray what people have consistently called "The Jesus Prayer" which is: "Lord Jesus Christ, have mercy on me, a sinner." Sociologist Kyriacos Markides says this prayer is like moving around in a polluted city wearing an oxygen mask over your nose. Nothing can touch you. But prayer can also be like shooting shafts into the dark, according to Frederick Buechner in *Godric*. "It's reaching for a hand you cannot touch." Yet Godric prays "the way he breathes, for else his heart would wither in his breast. Prayer is the wind that fills his sail."

Karen often uses the Prayer of St. Francis as she meditates. That's the one that begins, "Lord, make me an instrument of your peace." The last line provides her with special comfort now: "In my dying I am born into eternal life." Some find St. Ignatius helpful. "Take, Lord, receive all my liberty, my memory, my undertaking, and my entire will. You have given all to me. Now I return it. Give me only your grace and your love. That is enough for me." Those words may help the one who prays distinguish between surrender and resignation. Surrender doesn't mean giving up, but rather handing over in trust.

Wendell Berry in *Jayber Crow* says "prayer is like lying awake at night, afraid, with your head under the cover, hearing only the beating of your own heart. It is like a bird that has blundered down the flue and is caught indoors and flutters at the window panes."

When we pray, we need not be "logical." We can turn off the rational mind. After all, as the poet Kazim Ali says, "Prayer is speaking to someone you know is not going to be able to speak back, so you're allowed to be the most honest that you can be. In prayer you're allowed to be as purely selfish as you like. You can ask for something completely irrational."

When Mohammed went on his "night journeys," he is said to have ascended to the seven spheres of heaven. During that journey, we are told that he met Moses who helped him negotiate with Allah about how many times a day one should pray. The answer was "fifty." But, thanks to Moses's help, Mohammed negotiated Allah down to five.

No matter how many times a day we pray, prayer invites us to speak from our intuitive hearts rather than our linear brains. Sometimes, prayer may become an intimate conversation where previously unspoken words like pain or death or fear can be spoken and heard. However we define it, ultimately, prayer is trusting that someone is listening to what our hearts are saying. And we are not alone.

Rituals at the Time of Death

In the fifteenth century, a little self-help book was published called *Ars Moriendi* (The Art of Dying) giving instructions about dying well in the face of the macabre agony of the Black Death. The dying person was vulnerable to being snatched away by evil powers. Most of us do not picture a cosmic struggle at the time of death. Dying today presents new challenges. Nowadays, we're more apt to struggle against tubes and medical procedures than demons. To even admit we're dying is a betrayal against the confidence we claim to have in medicine and technology, but we do have alternatives. This book on the divine art of dying is a modern *ars moriendi* that seeks to provide a positive alternative for living toward death.

Rituals at the time of death may take many forms. There was a time in Christian history when people feared eternal judgment so intensely that the ritual act was reconciliation or baptism or both to insure they would be safe after death. Some people will want to be sure that they are reconciled with God and the ones they love at life's end.

Traditional rituals that "commend the dying to God" may be particularly helpful in marking the decision to discontinue treatment and take the turn toward death. It invokes prayers for a Divine sustaining presence as an individual continues a journey toward death. It often includes a prayer "to support us all the day long until the shadows lengthen and the evening comes and the busy world is hushed, the fever of life is over and our work is done." The ritual of commendation is intended to be a comfort for family and friends as well as the dying person, who is "handed over to Holy One" for sustaining care when healing is no longer possible.

If the dying person is conscious, he or she may choose to share songs and other expressions of communion with family and friends. The use of hymns when death is near is a common practice among many religious traditions. Buddhists near death may invite a monk to chant passages of sacred writing. Whatever form it may take, this last act may give a person permission to die because the people he or she loves have commended him or her to God or the source of life and all is well with their world.

Our Divine Human Virtue

REVERENCE

When we revere something, we can see beyond borders into that which is essential and very meaningful. We can say, "I revere, I honor, I acknowledge, I appreciate" what is important. Albert Schweitzer understood this reverent way of being. He said we live with reverence "in order to raise life to its true value. To affirm life is to deepen, to make more inward, and to exalt the will to live." We live until we die and by paying attention to what's important, every moment, we deepen ourselves and those around us.

A Peaceful Death
Herbert

My mother-in-law, Alice, died at ninety-three in our home in the arms of her daughter. On the day she died, Alice had just come to us from a rehabilitation hospital recovering from a broken hip. She napped in the afternoon. After a hearty meatloaf dinner, she watched us play *Spite and Malice*, a card game she had taught us. Then she watched *Judge Judy*, one of her regular routines. Then, on the way to the toilet, she suddenly felt very sick. Moments after we laid her on the bed, her eyes were fixed someplace far away and she died. We sang and prayed and gave thanks for her life before calling 911. [Note: if you wait, be sure to have the necessary documentation *readily available* regarding Do Not Resuscitate!] After the rescue squad and policeman had left, Alice's son and granddaughters and great-granddaughter had arrived. We told stories for a couple of hours before calling her designated crematorium. With great dignity, they wrapped her body and put it on the gurney. Our little company of mourners formed a candlelight procession to accompany Alice to the van that would take her body to be cremated. Alice died the way she lived — with quiet dignity.

Care of the Body

After Karen's friend Jan died, her daughter Carrie and Jan's good friend, a hospice nurse, washed her body before the funeral director took her away. While there may be common psychological and physical aspects to dying, there is considerable ritual diversity about the care of the body at the moment of death. In general, the care of the body has spiritual, physical, and social importance. Herbert had a student from Korea who was the oldest son in his family. The family waited until he returned from Chicago so that he might prepare his father's body for burial. By contrast, the northern European societies that have been dominant in the U.S. regard death as a private event that can be handled by qualified professionals. No special attending is required.

In many cultures, however, preparation of the body for burial is a carefully organized and ritually orchestrated social act that sustains family structures. In religious traditions where the soul of an individual may inhabit another body, proper purification is necessary so as not to infect the next body. In his book *Beyond the Good Death*, James W. Green makes this observation: "Jewish washings and Hindu cremations are about purification and spiritual transformation, enacted through observance of sacred traditions with rites that direct attention to worlds imagined but not seen."

In this life, we are known through our bodies. Washing the body at death is a way of honoring our human nature. Washing a body caresses it. Mary Magdalene washed Jesus's feet prior to his death. Our mother's birth waters wash us into the world; why shouldn't water usher us out? And for Christians who believe that the waters of baptism initiate a new life in God, washing at the end of a life is a ritual action that continues that relationship with God at death.

Anointing the Body

Karen has mentioned her desire for aromatic oils to be applied to her body at death. Lavender perhaps. Her friend Sharon, a flower-essence aroma therapist, gave her a little vial of Angel's trumpet to, as she put it, "ease your passage between the worlds." It came with these affirmations: "From Spirit World, I was born on Earth. From the Earth, I will be born again into Spirit World. My Spirit Self will illumine the Portal of Death. I surrender my will to Divine Will. I am this Radiant Self."

It's common in some Christian traditions to anoint someone who is seriously ill with blessed and holy oils. Anointing the sick with oil follows practices recorded in the New Testament as part of the healing ministry of Jesus. Some Christian traditions will not use oil but will nonetheless pray with the sick for healing. When someone is dying or near death, anointing may still be used but the focus shifts from healing to commendation of an individual to God. In the Roman Catholic tradition, what was once popularly referred to as "last rites" is the sacrament intended to provide food for the soul on its journey to God.

In addition to offering traveling mercies for the dying person, these ritual practices have a common experiential purpose for family and friends — namely, to let him or her die feeling blessed.

Anointing Susan

Herbert

Susan had been dying for some time and was finally near death. Her husband, all her children, and two close friends were around her bed. There was no visible sign she was conscious but everyone believed she was listening. She always did. Herbert invited each person to anoint Susan and offer their own prayer of blessing after which she was toasted with single malt scotch. When her husband woke in the night, Susan's body was cold. He went back to sleep, and called their children in the morning to tell them their mother had died in the night. Blessed and at peace.

Creating New Rituals

Many of us depend on traditional rituals to help us make our way through a crisis like dying and death. Sometimes, however, it's necessary to create new rituals when we can't find any existing ones to fit our situation. Using music and familiar objects and ordinary material such as the salt and oils, people devise very meaningful rituals to make sense of their lives and effect healing. Herbert and his coauthor Edward Foley, OFM, have written about creating new rituals in *Mighty Stories, Dangerous Rituals.* Here are their five simple rules to follow:

I) Respect the chronology of the human story. Let the whole story be heard.

2) Allow a significant role for nonverbal symbols. There are times when words fail and only symbolic gestures convey the depth of pain.

3) Resist the impulse to explain. Learn to live in the ambiguity of both story and ritual. We do not always have to know what it means and sometimes it is enough for the significance of the dying experience to be held in the mystery of ritual.

4) Attend to the particularity of the moment. While a variety of ritual patterns can be employed across a variety of situations, it is also important to improvise in response to the specific human need.

5) Beware of overcomplicating the ritual. Less is more. A single act of blessing, laying of flowers, cleaning a closet, giving shoes to the Salvation Army, burning a document, or handing over a gift may be far more effective than piling a number of ritual gestures together.

Medical technology has created the need for new rituals around the withdrawing of life-support systems from those who are unconscious and dying or turning off mechanical ventilators for those who are already brain dead. Constance wanted a minister to anoint Fred but she wanted to be alone with him when she turned off his ventilator. By contrast, the Benson family that had gathered around Grandpa Anchor wanted a medical professional to turn off the ventilator as they sang. Families need to know that the decision to take such action is separate from the action itself. Whatever feelings family members might have about a decision to discontinue life support, the ritual action provides an occasion to support one another in a complex time. Because there are no prescribed rituals from any religious tradition for many of the present circumstances of dying, this is an occasion for imagination and improvisation.

Mourning Rituals

Rituals at death occur in three distinct ways. First, as with Karen's music ritual, they occur on the journey to death. Then other rituals occur at the moment of death when the body must be prepared. Finally, we as humans create various mourning rituals after death has occurred. Both the purpose and the nature of mourning rituals have changed and continue to change, partly in response to altered views of death and grief and partly because the old patterns of burial cannot be sustained in modern society.

Karen and Herbert both grew up in rural Scandinavian communities. Karen's Wisconsin hometown had 150 people; Herbert's Minnesota town had a population of 95. Their cemeteries were next to their churches. It was easier to accompany those who had died to their graves in that context than in modern urbanized societies in which people might live, work, play, and worship in distinct communities without any clarity about where they wish to have their remains reside after death. Moreover, the purpose of mourning rituals has shifted. Rituals after a death are now more likely to celebrate a life than prepare a proper send-off or mourn a death.

Although much has changed about rituals of dying and after death, we crave "something" that pulls at our collective memories in ways that we never fully understand. It connects us with inner bonds we can't see, but we can feel. And we long to participate. Remembrance is at the heart of all liturgy and ritual. We remember human events and at some level we are connected to the entire cosmos — past, present, and future. Ritual is that powerful.

Grief demands ritual. Sooner rather than later. The window opportunity for a grieving ritual after the death of a loved person does not remain open indefinitely. Postponing a memorial ritual keeps grief private and does not foster communities that sustain mourners when the emotions that follow a death are most intense. William Purdy has described an interfaith memorial service sponsored by Continuum Hospice Care in New York City. The service includes a moment when people are invited to bring a memento of their loved ones to place on a remembrance table with live music but no speaking. It is a ritual that transcends all difference of religious and cultural perspectives. It works, according to Purdy, "like the Navajo medicine man's powerful point of the spear."

Authentic rituals provide the occasion, the language, and the gestures for people to encounter realities and truths that, if left to ourselves, most of us would choose to avoid. Rituals enable us to tell, hear, and act out the truth about ourselves and our world. Words are balanced with silence, stories with song, light with darkness, individual pain with communal suffering, despair with hope, symbolic action with personal reflection, in order to create an environment in which suffering is validated and hope is restored.

FROM THE CAREGIVER'S GUIDEBOOK

Rituals are an important resource for dying persons making their last journey because they order an often chaotic process. Rituals are also helpful for family and friends because they regulate accessibility, as well as make and keep connections within communities of significance. Because people are emotionally and spiritually vulnerable as they are dying, old habits and traditions add security and dependability at life's end. As the caregiver, you may or may not be comfortable with every aspect of any particular ritual, but if it is important to the person and his or her family, then it's worth supporting.

1. Honor all the rituals. Find out which ones are important to the dying person long before they are actually enacted.

2. Be bold and imaginative in adapting traditional rituals for unique moments on the death journey.

3. Whenever possible, promote the connection between rituals and storytelling.

4. Consider doing what one hospice volunteer does. She pauses before entering the room to pray for help in leaving her ego at the door. "Empty me of 'me' so I can be your ears and your voice." Discover what prayer means to the dying person.

5. A benediction from family and friends is a word of gratitude and connection at life's end that brings peace and closure.

When Death Draws Near

> "Death may be an ordinary, everyday affair,
> but it is not a statistic. It is something that happens to
> people.... If we practice dying enough during our
> lives we will hardly notice the moment of transition
> when the actual time comes."
>
> Madeleine L'Engle, *The Summer of the Great-Grandmother*

ℵ *from* Karen's Hospice Journal ℣

When I ask people what they think about death, they'll invariably say, "Well, everyone will do it." "Nobody gets out of this world alive." But then if I press them about their own dying, they're not so forthcoming. "I haven't really thought about it," is the usual response. Or "I can't really imagine myself dying." Acknowledging one's own death pulls all kinds of sticky thoughts from deep places about what your own dying might be like.

I've read lots of books on near-death experiences, including the neurosurgeon Eban Alexander's Proof of Heaven, and I've watched videos of interviews with people who tell of their "coming back." I find them interesting and comforting, but my actual process still remains unknown. And since they've only been "near" death, they don't really know either.

Somebody once said dying is like taking off a tight shoe. Or stepping over a threshold into another room. Others liken it to the sleep that comes before you're dreaming. It's that release of everything physical; you let yourself go into the void. It's at that moment when our physical senses no longer function. I guess we just let gravity pull us into that peaceful space. There's no pain. No attachment. Nothing holding us back. We just surrender to that sleep-space knowing we're safe. We'll wake up again. We do this every night. So why am I fearful of dying? Dying must be like that "giving up" feeling when my body and mind just turns off and I surrender to sleep every single night. I am not my thoughts — they too just disappear when I go to sleep. I'm guessing I won't be aware of any physical discomfort. And then, I believe I'll "wake up" to a new "radio frequency," a new dimension, a new way of being.

Van Gogh, who loved to paint them, thought the stars would be accessible after death. "Just as we take a train to get to Tarascon or Rouen," he said, "we take death to reach a star. We cannot get to a star while we are alive any more than we can take the train when we are dead. So to me it seems possible that cholera, tuberculosis, and cancer are the celestial means of locomotion. Just as steamboats, buses, and railways are the terrestrial means. To die quietly of old age would be to go there on foot."

Well I'm not going on foot. And I think I hear the "star-train" chugging down the track.

❧   ❧

Metaphors about the moment of dying are varied and very personal. Karen watches the Milky Way and is waiting, with Van Gogh, for something more cosmic. Others hope to simply fall asleep. The phenomenon of near-death experiences provides people who have NDE with personal awareness that the mystery of living is more than dying. People who believe they have died and gone over to the other side find the experience assuring. The fearful unknown is less unknown. Dying becomes a peaceful moment when one can move with less anxiety into a level of stillness, into the thin places of even deeper stillness.

The Dying Moment

Death, we have said, gets our attention. The awareness of death reminds everyone that human beings are finite, limited, and vulnerable creatures sustained by significant relationships and communities. When death is near, vulnerability increases, relationships matter more, and questions about the dying moment frequently occur.

People fear the dying moments more than the actual death itself for good reason. The dreaded image of dying in a hospital bed hooked up to machinery and consumed with discomfort still happens too often. There is an alternative, however. P. M. H. Atwater describes what it feels like to die in *Beyond the Light*: "Your body goes limp. Your heart stops. No more air flows in or out. You lose sight, feeling, and movement — although the ability to hear goes last. Identity ceases. The 'you' that you once were becomes only a memory. There is no pain at the moment of death. Only peaceful silence... calm... quiet. It is easy to breathe. In fact, it is easier, more comfortable and infinitely more natural not to breathe than to breathe... you are still alive."

The decision Karen and many others have made allows them to begin an intentional process of living fully and finally dying consciously. There is still widespread resistance to choosing a more humane dying rather than a frantic end-of-life assault crammed with desperate measures. Bill Keller's account of the death of his father-in-law Anthony Gilbey, published by the *New York Times* on October 7, 2012, provides this positive alternative picture of the dying moment: "Unfettered by tubes and unpestered by hovering medics, he reminisced and made some amends, exchanged jokes and assurances of love with his family, received Catholic rites and managed to swallow a communion wafer that was probably his last meal. Then he fell into a coma. He died gently, loved and knowing it, dignified and ready." We should all die so well.

What the dying discover as they near the dying moment is the gift of surrender and the peace of not fighting. If one has fought death for a long time, there is both beauty and relief in surrendering consciously to dying. There is no reason to fear. Even so, there will be days when the agony of leaving everything behind is almost unbearable. Margaret, a friend of Herbert we introduced on page 57, wrote this as she came near death: "As I sink into soft acceptance of my current situation, it is a wonderful place to be. It's not frightening; it's just peaceful and beautiful and brings me into great gratitude." Margaret died resting in stillness. We don't learn to surrender at the moment of death: it is, rather, the result of a lifelong practice of loving and letting go. For people whose lives have been governed by possessing and holding on, letting go at life's end will be challenging. Letting go is an "art" best learned while living before dying.

Realistic Hoping

Living fully toward death is unavoidably an experience of unpredictability, instability, and vulnerability. Being vulnerable means simply being susceptible to physical or emotional wounds. The dying person's awareness of vulnerability makes trusting necessary. And when trust is present, both the dying person and his or her family will be able to hope honestly and realistically to life's end. The promise of the caring presence creates an environment for the dying in which they are held, in which their pain is heard, in which the lifelong need for attachment is nourished. At the same time, a dying person may want to be alone with friends and family not far away. Or he or she may choose one particular person to be with him or her on the last leg of the journey. The circle of people with whom to interact often becomes smaller over time as death nears.

As death nears, hoping still matters even though the options are fewer. "My only hope is for a peaceful ending," someone might say. Or "I hope she can make the fortieth wedding anniversary party." When it is no longer realistic to hope for a cure or for a little more time, anticipating an accommodation to familiar routines or a visit from someone we love makes hoping real and immediate. The

Our Divine Human Virtue

KINDNESS

It's the small drink of water. The smile at the checkout line. The pat on the back. The congratulatory phone call. Small acts of kindness create big changes in our own hearts and the hearts of others. Mother Teresa, the embodiment of kindness, encouraged us to "be the living expression of God's kindness; kindness in your face, kindness in your eyes, kindness in your smile, kindness in your warm greeting." At the end of life, we can all engage in kind speaking and kind listening.

ultra-marathon runner and author Bernd Heinrich notes that hope is like the aboriginal long-distance hunter who succeeds by "keeping in mind what is not before the eye." Dying is like that: seeing clearly what is not before the eye. Joel's reflections on his mother Karen's dying bring to our awareness the present reality of hoping.

It's Still Now
Karen's son Joel

The first time I almost died, it was over so quickly that it all seemed more like an adventure than a near disaster. It was January of 1990 and I was visiting the Greek Orthodox monasteries in Metéora. I wandered into a blast site because I thought the warning was just Greek folk singing, and a construction worker remembered the English word "boom" in time to keep me from being blown off a bridge two hundred feet above the Plain of Thessaly.

The second time I almost died was in January of 2001 and actually involved a hospital, and some languages I could speak, so it seemed a lot more real. I was in the cathedral in Lübeck, Germany, for a conference, and on the last evening, listening to a wonderful Baroque performance, I got a sudden pain in my left side that didn't go away. The next day, on the ferry back to Gothenburg, the pain spread to my left shoulder and by the time I got to my apartment I was coughing up a little blood, something that is really impossible to ignore.

Off to the hospital, where a doctor correctly diagnosed a pulmonary embolism. But now it was too painful to lie down on my back in the CAT scan machine in order to make sure. I was taken up to a ward and the pain was now so intense that I was barely conscious. While I was standing in a tall walker with padded arms as the nurses drew blood, my right hand started making shapes. Three fingers straight up and splayed, two pointing left, a fist, thumb slips in between the second and third finger, and then the third and fourth, circle with thumb and fingers... and on and on. I had learned the American deaf sign alphabet in high school and now my hand was talking in a language I barely knew. The three words repeated "What now? Only... "What's the next word? I'm waiting?! I thought I was about to get an answer from my subconscious or God or somewhere to clue me in about what to do next.

The nurses figured out that the position I could sleep in with the least pain was to park my wheelchair close to the edge of the bed, lock the wheels, and just let me face-plant my head into a pillow on the bed. Lying there, working on this puzzle, the idea suddenly came to me that the message was complete after all, it was just the punctuation that was screwed up: "What? Now only." Nothing comes next. There is no next. There is now only. This pain is my now, right now. I can accept it because this now will change like all the other nows have changed and this is the now in which I get to experience this blinding pain. Either the next now will be my death or it will be a now with less pain, and either way I have no control.

For the last ten years my mother has been living with (not fighting, not warring against, but living with) cancer, and I have been very careful in that time not to talk about her condition much with friends and colleagues because everyone's reaction to cancer is always a "what next" reaction, never a "now only" reaction. In my current "now" she has entered hospice and I am surprised at how few of my friends knew she was this sick. Through remissions and surgeries and chemotherapy sessions I have been kept in the now, dragged back into the now, sometimes face-planted back into the now by her journey with this cancer, by the impossibility of being able to control "what next," and the infinite joy of occasionally being able to experience "now only." Sometimes consciously, sometimes unconsciously, my right hand spells out this simple koan I was given, or that I gave myself. I can do it so fast now that it's a single gesture, and when it happens I look up again, and it's still now.

Now Only

"Now only" provides a wonderful mantra for living near death. The worry about what will be next is past. Living fully while dying is sustained by the promise that tomorrow will be a new day with new gifts and surprises as we celebrate the ordinary. The capacity to envision possibilities that are not readily apparent today creates hopefulness about tomorrow and the willingness to wait. As one lives near death, however, the future narrows and the present increases in importance. The present is filled with possibility by "keeping in mind what is not before the eye."

As death nears, our awareness of time changes. *Chronos* time, from which we get "chronology," no longer stretches endlessly. Instead, there is *kairos* time from the Greek word that describes the time that you can't measure by clocks or calendars. It is the "now only" time. Karen often loses track of whether it is morning or afternoon. Or even what day it is. She says: "I find myself losing myself in writing and I look at the corner of my screen and lo and behold, three hours have gone by. Sometimes I wonder if that's because I'm growing more used to eternity with each passing hour."

Einstein taught us that time doesn't flow in one direction. It spirals. The future and the past exist simultaneously. One of the things people who are dying think about is what they are afraid of when they face — rather up close and personal — their own death. Pain? That can be controlled. Abandonment? Perhaps. But the larger fear may be that we're most afraid of being free of time. Outside time. When you're outside of time, you're no longer in control. That can be very S-C-A-R-Y!

It is a constant challenge for caregivers of the dying to stay in the moment — in kairos time — with a focus of living toward death even though the rest of their lives is governed by ticking clocks and paging calendars.

Honest Dying

What makes it possible for people near death to live fully in the "now only" without too much worry about "what next?" What sustains caregivers and those dying in their determination to live honestly and consciously toward death? What makes honest dying possible? We propose it is hope. Hope drives us to belong to something more than ourselves and offers a deeper purpose and a wider vision. It is hope that enables us to live *toward* our end and *with* our end, casting a light on the darkness that ultimately engulfs us. Hope is a verb. It's an action, not a possession. It's something we do rather than something we possess. And it is a present and future reality sustained by imagination, acceptance, and trust, all of which are available to us in our dying as well as our living.

Joan Halifax described her decades of caring for the dying in *Being with Dying* with these words: "'Death with dignity' is another concept that can become an obstacle to what is really happening. Dying can be very undignified. Often, it's not dignified at all, with soiled bedclothes and sheets, bodily fluids and flailing, nudity and strange sexuality, confusion and rough language — all common enough in the course of dying. The stories we tell ourselves — good death, death with dignity — can be unfortunate fabrications that we use to try to protect ourselves against the sometimes raw and sometimes wondrous truth of dying."

It is difficult to imagine losing bodily functions at the time of death and still retaining dignity. We chafe at being physically dependent and intimately cared for at the end. Or, like Karen's father, we speculate where we will be at the time of our death. In talking with her sons about dying, Karen learned something new about her father. She laughed with her sons as they recalled how their grandfather Juel told them that his greatest fear was actually not dying in a hospital, as Karen had heard him say, but dying on the toilet! He knew of someone who had died in his bathroom and he confessed to them, "That would be the worst!"

Still Deciding at the End of Life

Vermont, where Karen lives, recently enacted a law that allows doctors to write what they estimate might be ten to twenty lethal prescriptions annually. It's loosely based on Oregon's 1997 ruling, which was followed by Washington and Montana. Opponents of these laws argue that the law could be abused and vulnerable people, especially the elderly, could be coerced by family members into ending their lives. But others argue that this enables people to make informed choices in a carefully regulated way. The truth is that people inevitably make choices at the end of living that affect when and how they die. Even so, the dying moment is unpredictable. It will come when it will come.

One could argue that putting such life-and-death matters in the hands of politicians is not the best route, regardless of how careful the regulations are. But we can also argue that physicians should be free to provide patient-directed dying as much as they provide direction for living. If termination of suffering is the goal, then it behooves us to figure out how best to accomplish this. The old argument no longer works: it is not "playing God" to make decisions that affect the dying of someone terminally ill. It is being a responsible steward of a life given and graciously received.

Karen's friend Judy Brown, a poet, wrote of her father's decision to die in *The Choice*. He was Dr. Kevorkian's tenth assisted suicide. The book is her account of how her father chose to die by his own hand, in his own house, in his own way, and how she rebuilt her life after his death. "Life makes its way," she says at the end with these hopeful, poetic words, "meandering, unfolding, petals bending with the dew drops... tendrils seeking places to take hold where once nothing would grow." Brown believes that life unfolds into death and growth is then still possible because in some very mysterious manner, "life makes its way."

Some people, as did Brown's father, plan their exits. But even when a "normal" death is anticipated, the exact moment of death occurs unpredictably. When the "your time left" topic arises, and it often does, Karen simply says, "I just don't know. I'm living a mystery." She says that even to the people who comment, when they hear she is in hospice care, "Oh, I suppose you have six months, then?"

But she explains to her family what her medical information leads her to believe. "Once my intestines are blocked (which they will be at some point) I won't be eating or drinking anymore. Who knows? That may give us another three weeks — or less. That's all I know. For sure." But she also knows that her family will give her permission to die. They won't cling. Nor will she.

We know we will all die sooner or later. Still, we continue to question how or when and why. In his novel *Moloka'I*, Alan Brennert wrote a story about an eight-year-old girl who contracts leprosy and is sent to live in the leper colony for the rest of her life. She grows up in a school for girls and is befriended by a Catholic nun who remains her friend. Near the end of the girl's life, Sister Catherine, the nun, says, "I've come to believe that how we choose to live with pain, or injustice, or death is the true measure of the Divine within us.... I used to wonder, why did God give children leprosy? Now I believe: God doesn't give anyone leprosy. He gives us, if we choose to use it, the spirit to live with leprosy, and with the imminence of death." It is in living honestly with our mortality that we are most divine.

Living fully until we die is both active and passive, both something that happens to us and something we do. We are deciding as long as we can what to eat for lunch or not eat, whether to eat lunch in bed or in a chair, the color of the blanket, the presence or absence of friends, the location of the bed. We can choose how to live until we die and in that choosing, we may also influence when or how we die. And yet death happens to us. It happens to *me*. Yet it is something I *do*. On that we have no choice.

FROM THE CAREGIVER'S GUIDEBOOK

People tend to think that a person who is irreversibly ill will give up hope and stop living if he or she knows how serious his or her condition is. So family and friends sometimes fabricate stories. And paint rosy scenarios. But there is nothing more crushing for a dying person than to feel lied to, abandoned and isolated emotionally by dishonesty. The experience of mutuality and trusted presence transforms the dread of abandonment and our terrors of isolation into communities of hope.

1. Be honest. True dialogue can happen when you don't have to be concerned about remembering which lies have been told. This is healthy both for you and for the dying one.

2. Your task is to walk with those who suffer so they will know they are still loved — and will continue to be loved, no matter what. Deal with their bodily needs in smart, easy ways. Make the bed comfortable. Provide clothing they are comfortable in. Use all the hospice tricks in the book to ease their passage.

3. Try to accurately assess the person's strength and coping skills. Don't assume anything. Help them to envision realistic possibilities. And help them to be patient.

4. Volunteers, friends, and family members provide a safety net for catching each other. Be as compassionate to yourself as you are to others. Get plenty of sleep. Eat properly. Remind yourself of your true worth — for you are providing so much!

LIVING IN THE MYSTERY

"Do not fear your death. For when that moment arrives,
I will draw my breath and your soul
will come to Me like a needle to a magnet."

Mechtild of Magdeburg

✑ *from* Karen's Hospice Journal ✑

Every Sunday I join other voices in my church to proclaim the Nicene Creed: "I believe in things seen and unseen." I rest easy with that. Even though I'm quite curious, I don't have a burning desire to explain all mysteries. I do know that everything, including me, has its origins in the Divine. And I don't have to see that to believe it.

I also know that the "I" the mystic Mechtild of Magdeburg refers to is the "I" beyond the "me" that this tired body still clings to. It will "draw my breath. . . like a needle to a magnet." So why should I worry? Why should I struggle? There's nothing to fear. A friend has told me, "Be in the joy of death. Being released from suffering is worthwhile. It's like turning off a TV set. Bingo! The illusion stops. It stops very, very quickly. In an instant."

Is eternity an illusion as well? Am I really already living an "eternal life" right now? Like the Bhagavad-Gita says, "Never was there a time when I did not exist, nor you, nor all the kings; nor in the future shall any of us cease to be." I don't closely follow Hindu teachings, but that totally makes sense to my Christian ears. I know some people don't buy into this idea of "us" existing "before." A "we" together in eternity. But that's not been a stumbling block for me. I will, I believe, rejoin that cloud of witnesses, the ones who have "gone on before." And the ones who will come "after."

Before and after. These linear time-words tend to trip me up if I'm not careful and then I so easily slip into the old "then" and "now" dualities, when there really is only now.

Sometimes I also find myself wondering about things like how (or if) what I am going through and writing about might affect other people. Carl Jung said in one of his letters, "When something happens here at point A which touches upon or affects the collective unconscious, then it has happened everywhere." Or as Edgar Allan Poe wrote in an 1885 dialogue between two angels: "The track of every canoe remains somewhere in the oceans."

Is my dying, then, somehow touching others? And aren't all of those other deaths now also touching mine? In some entangled, quantum way, we are all dying at the very same time since in the eternal now there is no time. My mind boggles and bobbles.

I am now living in between times. I am both living and dying in such a real way that I feel suspended like a big pendulum over some mysterious middle ground. It sounds strange for me to even write this, but I feel that I have become more human *in this liminal time. I use the word* liminal *to mean this gauzy threshold I now straddle. The time in between. I've been reading* The Lace Reader *by Brunonia Barry, a novel that uses the metaphor of making Ipswich lace, or bobbin lace, and tells a story about the women who could "read" the patterns. "Sometimes," Barry says, "when you look back, you can point to a time when your world shifts and heads in another direction. In lace reading this is called the 'still point.' The point around which everything pivots and real patterns start to emerge." I, too, seem to have found my "still point."*

N K

Our Sacred Quest for Eternity

A friend of Karen's put a bumper sticker on her car that says: I BELIEVE IN LIFE BEFORE DEATH. She knows eternity isn't off somewhere in the ether, beyond us in some never-never land, but right here and right now in the ordinariness of everyday living. The poet Blake got it. He saw eternity in a grain of sand, in a wildflower. We hold, he said, "infinity in our hand and eternity in an hour." We belong here. And yet, we're forever. And what connects the now with the forever? Thornton Wilder put it this way: "There is a land of the living and a land of the dead and the bridge is love; the only survival, the only meaning." Love connects us. Love both tethers and releases us.

We have different words for how we visualize eternity. The Muslims call it *moksha* — "total release." The Buddhists, *nirvana* — "to extinguish." Tao names it "The Mother of All Things." Christians simply say *heaven* — a resurrection. Most Christians believe that nothing — not even death — can separate them from the love of God in Christ Jesus.

Some express eternity as a void, an eternal resting place. That is a bit unsettling for Karen. She finds the old Victorian hymns that seek rest in Jesus the opposite of what she's hoping for. "I want activity, not passivity. New horizons, not limited views. I look forward to the 'next chapters,'" she says. Different and even more challenging work to do. "Potential, not lazy stasis," she once explained. But "bliss" can hold many meanings, including "rest." And this state may not necessarily be "lazy" as much as it might be restful and restorative. And for many, it's likely to be a "deep peace" as the Lutheran pastor Joe Hauser expresses it.

A Deep Peace
Karen's friend Joe

I have thought a lot about my dying. That doesn't mean that I like to dwell on morbid things. After all, I have congestive heart failure, prostate cancer, and on top of that, I am seventy-eight years old.

I have done all the things — or at least most of the things that the experts advise one to do when dying is on the near horizon. I have made out the advanced directives and given them to my wife, Penny, who posted them on the refrigerator; I have written my will. I have told my three adult kids that I'm not getting any younger and that "the time" is rapidly approaching. The message is "think about when your dad will no longer be with you."

I had the gift of being with my older sister when, after months of dying with malignant melanoma, she died at the age of fifty-eight. Prior to her death, every night she would have her husband drive her to the ocean where she would sit in silence and reflect on her dying. She said it gave her deep peace.

I don't live near the beach. I live in Las Vegas — a big city — but I experience a peace — a deep, enduring peace. I don't fear dying. Granted, I don't want it to be painful but my physicians assure me there are protocols to minimize any pain.

What enables me to approach my dying with confidence is the resurrection of Jesus Christ. I live into his promise. "Because I live, you also will live." I agree with my friend Karen, who said that dying will be a mystical experience. I believe that; I believe that when my dying is over I will pass over into the joy of Christ's presence. I believe that because, and only because, of his grace. He will take me by the hand and welcome me home — his prodigal son-and-daughter — and invite me to his homecoming party.

Whatever we decide to call this place with no place and this space with no space, it is home. And we're going there for our homecoming party, as Joe clearly sees it.

It wasn't that clear for the poet Rilke, however. He called death the side of life that is turned away from us. It's the side we deny and keep in shadows most of the time. Karen was coming out of those shadows that December evening as she trudged uphill through her blessed recognition moment, and clearly saw the porch light burning.

Making the Leap

People who are getting ready to make that leap, that dance, that stroll into the mystery of death, do it in various ways. Karen readies herself by writing, for in the forming of her words she better understands her thoughts. She reads what others have said. She meditates. She immerses herself in psalms and other biblical works. She engages in deep and very rich conversations with her family and friends. We are convinced that it is through our loving relationships that we begin to know more of the Divine. It is through our community and our friends that we begin to sense what Christians have long called "the communion of saints... the cloud of witnesses." We are not alone.

Others, in the face of death, become very silent and spend most of their waiting time in a quiet space, choosing to be alone. Buddha said death is the temporary end of a temporary phenomenon. People spend time near their end wondering about what has been real and what has been only this "temporary phenomenon" we call life. And they ponder how, or if, what awaits them just over that next threshold might be even "more real." What is "real" and what is "illusion" is debatable.

Anyone thinking deeply about these last moments may discover the insight the journalist Eleanor Clift came to as she wrote about the "good" death of her husband. As she learned more about hospice, she remarked, "Why don't we know more about death since we've been doing it since time began?" Why, indeed?

Sometimes the term "good death" is used to describe an easy passage from one way of living to another way of being. As a hospice doctor, Ira Byock has observed that some people experience tremendous suffering while others meet the end with a sense of peace. Medication is not the only difference. Like many others, he came to believe good deaths aren't random events, but they can be fostered. But he rejects the term "good death" because it seems too formulaic and prescriptive. Also, it seems to further divide the living from the nonliving when, as Karen is discovering, it's *all* about living. She prefers "dying well," the phrase Byock uses, just as she has chosen to concentrate on living well.

And dying well for Karen means no denial. After all, why deny death when we know that 100% of us will do it? It's certain. Esther Dyson, the Swiss journalist who normally writes about digital technology, said, "I personally like the certainty of death. It is amazingly relaxing to realize that one can't do everything. If I knew I were going to live forever, I would feel obligated to fix all my imperfections. I would have to learn many languages; I would worry about my teeth...."

No more earthly worries. That's what death frees us from.

All our lives, we poke at death, trying to figure out how we feel about it. As children, we watch how our parents and other adults deal with death. We wonder if we'll cry. We wonder how the dead can be living again if we fill their graves with dirt. We wonder what they'll eat. As we grow older we watch fake deaths on video and movie screens and we ride scary roller coasters and jump from high places, just to test the idea of dying. We brush against it in art and songs. We use humor to disguise our unease, and tell jokes about dying and death to relieve our unease. Yet when someone we love dies, there is no doubt about it. Death is permanent for us. They're gone. Period. And it hurts for a very long time. It's like when your house burns down, Mark Twain once said. You don't realize the extent of your loss for years.

Secular or Sacred?

Facing the moment, for the one dying as well as the ones remaining, makes us pause and reflect on what about our lives has been sacred and lasting. Madeleine L'Engle said, in *Walking on Water*, "There is nothing so secular that it cannot be sacred." Hebrew scholar Abraham Heschel agreed. In fact he said the road to the sacred leads through the secular. To get to what's sacred, all we need do is look down and notice that what's under our feet is already sacred space.

The new common use of *spiritual* as a more inclusive term than *religious* means you don't spend a lot of time trying to figure out who is worthy of your love-investment because the bottom line is: everyone is. Karen has had several conversations over the years with physicians about what *spiritual* means. Her oncologist who knows she's writing this book has told her, "I'm not spiritual. I don't get that stuff. I'm more of a mechanic." But Karen is familiar enough with him to know better. He is a skilled "mechanic," that's true. But he also deeply, deeply cares. He just doesn't choose to use the language others might choose because for him, it's far too loaded. But for Karen, caring deeply also means *spiritual*.

On the other hand, Jonna, her hospice doctor, has chosen to use the title "Palliative Care and Spiritual Director" to define her professional self. She's pretty clear about how we don't separate our physical, mental, and spiritual lives, but live them wholly and completely as one.

Our bodies are sacred. That's why we honor them with special practices as we die and after death. And places on our earth are also sacred. Chaco Canyon in New Mexico, for instance, is "where heaven and earth meet." Cathedrals, pyramids. Delphi, the Black Hills, Stonehenge, Mecca, Machu Picchu, Lourdes, Fatima, Palenque, Cozumel, Fuji, Ayers Rock... people visit these places just because they seem to drip holiness directly into our hearts, bypassing the logic of our brains. A hospice room can also be one of those very sacred places, as can an ICU or a nursing-home room. What makes it sacred are the people filled with love who surround the dying one.

Trying to define *sacred* is a bit like trying to define a kiss. A kiss is so much more than faces brushing and skin touching. It's intention. It's a mysterious union. And this union defies words. But since feeble words, incomplete symbols, and partial images are all the tools we have, we depend on them to express this "crossing over" mystery.

From "Crossing Over"
By Karen Speerstra

... you have taught us "crossing over" is not without peril.
We step, oh so gingerly, onto unknown paths
While you brave uncharted waters:
    Here be Dragons.
For our journey you offer sailing-seeds,
Packets of life-yielding scents of tomorrow.
And we begin to grasp what you already know:
    It's safe to cross.
For Hope is copper-wrapped, carefully crafted;
Joy, deeply rooted, holding fast;
And Love, our very Heartwood, stretches limbs to embrace
Those who cross
    and those who pause.

When we ponder "mystery" we might ask: Where did we come from? Where are we going? What made us as we are? The Dagara people who live in West Africa call mystery the thing knowledge "can't eat." We can't *think* our way to understanding mystery. Nor can we rely on our senses. Mystery, they say, is to shut one's eyes and ears. Mystery is silent and dark.

In his book *Perelandra*, C. S. Lewis explained mystery this way: "There seems to be no center because it's all center." All is sacred. "Within the sacred," Ira Byock says, "the mystery of life is miraculous. There is no terror, only awe. All paradox and conflict are resolved, or more precisely, dissolve." Then we get, as Joanna Gillespie puts it, "a benedicted glimpse." During Karen's earlier diagnosis, Joanna sent Karen a gift from Tucson. It was a little silver medal — a *milagro*. A "miracle." She wrote: "I couldn't find one with ovaries, so I'm sending you this one with breasts. The lovely thing about Mexican religiosity is that it gets quickly from the soul into the body... every time you touch a *milagro*, it's a prayer. And when the healing occurs, you pin it on the shirt of a saint to show your blessing and gratitude."

Our Divine Human Virtue

LOVE

Katharine Hepburn said: "Love has nothing to do with what you are expecting to get — only what you are expecting to give — which is everything." Love is heart-power and it can't be defined by the brain. It showers us with magic, as Thomas Moore put it, "and even in the midst of pain it can offer moments of rapture." Love at the end of life is a force that cannot be denied. Nor can it be rationed, for love overflows and cannot be contained. True love is unconditional. We need do nothing. Love just is!

My "Benedicted" Glimpse of Heaven
Karen's friend Joanna Gillespie

For whatever it means, I want to add my glimpse into heaven, something that was a comforting assurance of God's-in-her-heaven, all's-right-with-the-world, for me. It was two years ago now, after I'd fallen and broken my femur and after the surgery that knit it all back together. I woke early the morning after the surgery, having slept deeply, despite the pain and anxiety underlying every conscious thought. I was aware of being alone, shivering on a huge white fluffy cloud, surrounded by deepest darkness, blackness, no peep of light from anywhere. Was I meant to feel fear? And gradually, light entered from the edges all around, and our recently dead son was there, smiling, floating on the cloud with me, assuring me there was nothing to fear. I could reach out and take his hand;

light was breaking all around. It was like being rescued from my cloud of aloneness, my isolation, my sadness and dismay... a great awakening! I was warm through and through, "benedicted" in the broadest sense. It was a blessing come to vibrant life, showering me with brilliance and cleansing! I was filled with assurance and joy. That's the vision — the awareness — the near-end-of-life glimpse into the future that I've been given so far. I'm deeply grateful for it, with all its contradictions and fuzziness.

The Ground of Our Being

Some mystics, such as Meister Eckhart, described the nameless void we've talked about throughout this book as the "Ground of our Being." While some may view the "void" as negative, it is, as all paradoxical things are, also positive. The architect Christopher Alexander, in *Our Luminous Ground*, says ground is not distant. It's immediate and authentic. "It is the 'ground' beneath our feet, the ultimate ground of substance on which all things stand. The fact that this ground is nameless, without substance, without form, and yet intensely personal, is one of life's great mysteries." This "void," Alexander insists, contains all that is in us. "We are charged, for a time, with finding a new form of God, a new way of understanding the deepest origins of our experience, of the matter in the universe so that we, too, when lucky, with devotion might find it possible to reveal this 'something' and its blinding light."

Alexander speaks of how people are composed of living centers, living fields profoundly linked to fields of intensity and wholeness of other centers. Therefore, we feel healed and whole and very alive when we are with others who are focused on creating living structures of various kinds. We are, he says, united by joy, happiness, and laughter as well as by tears, loss, death, and betrayal. "Unity comes from the fact that the various centers are harmoniously connected and that every center helps every other center." In his various books, he uses words such as "deep interlock" and "mutual embedding." "Inner calm" and "Nonseparateness." "This is, perhaps, the central mystery of the universe: that as things become more unified, less separate, so also they become more individual and most precious."

We are, it seems, each a unique individual, centered and grounded in this life. Yet we are intricately connected. Karen likes to say we are all mystics in the making. We sense at times, especially in moments of crisis — floods, tornados, hurricanes, terror attacks — that we were meant to be together. To truly live together. To help each other. To hug and support one another. We grow, then, into an awareness of our spiritual wisdom. We are aware of love as the core of our being. We experience how to give to others, from the very ground of our being. It is this centering and grounding that enables us to leap into the unknown at the moment of death, assured that we are loved and safely held and we will go on and on and on....

The End and the Beginning of Our Journey

Karen's friend Barbara recently walked the 450 miles of the *el camino*, as a *pelegrino*, a pilgrim, staying in hostels open to travelers who have their credentials — their passports — issued by the Confraternity of St. James. As she walked along the 1200-year-old trail, she thought of how we are all pilgrims journeying through life. "We start off, not always knowing where it is we want to go or the way. We may change course, we may get lost or set off in new directions. But we don't go alone. Although our lives are singular and personal, we have companions sharing the journey giving comfort and joy, influencing our decisions and affecting our lives in many ways... Some of our companions will be with us to the end. Some will have left us before our trip is completed. But all of these special people have affected and enriched our lives in uncountable ways." Barbara described to Karen how she put the names of all these people into an imaginary drawstring bag in her pocket and carried them with her into the cathedral in Santiago. "I found a quiet pew and then I took everyone, name by name, and thanked them all."

Through our life's journey, we collect names of those who care for us, who sustain and protect us. When we "draw their names out of our pockets," we are filled, as Barbara was, with gratitude.

When an artist, such as Laura Baring-Gould (see p. 64), begins a work — whether of hanging boats or sculpting giant bronzed pears — there is only an idea. A dream. Then mystery begins to work itself out of nothing into something. The Eternal Dancer dances in all things. The Eternal Painter brushes all canvas. The Eternal Singer's voice is heard in all things.

D. H. Lawrence suggested that all we can do is "build the ship of death to carry the soul on the longest journey." It's a fragile ship of courage, an ark of faith. Yet, just as Laura's ships carry an inner light, each of us sails into the unknown with the promise of that radiant and mysterious light to come. Martin Buber, the Jewish philosopher and religious thinker of the early twentieth century said, "All journeys have secret destinations of which the traveler is unaware."

Coriolanus, in the Shakespeare play of the same name, says to his mother, Volumnia, in Act IV, "... when the sea was calm all boats alike showed mastership in floating. Only in a storm were they obliged to cope." Facing death may feel, for many, like stormy seas. Boats, however, can become for us a living metaphor for not only our fears, but also our consolation. The Old Norse people used the same word for "boat" as they used for "cradle" and "coffin." Early Scandinavian graves were often marked with stones arranged into the image of a large boat, symbolically carrying souls to the afterlife. Or they used actual boats, usually on fire, to float the remains of their loved one off to Valhalla. In Sweden, even today, large wooden boats often hang from the naves of every village church. It's as if they silently pray: Bring them home, safely.

Many cultures, including the Egyptians, used the boat as a symbol of one's journey to the afterlife. And we may use nautical terms to describe the journey we're engaged in right here. We are both "captain" and "crew." We chart the course. We steer by the stars. We run aground or avoid treacherous rocks. As sailors across life's waters, we constantly make choices. And we dream about the outcomes of our decisions.

Each of us can make our choices and approach those rocks knowing it is our divine right and our divine art to figure out *how* best to safely journey. And *when*.

The *why*, we already sense. It's to sail home.

> "Serene light shining in the ground of my being,
>   draw me to yourself.
> Draw me past the snares of the senses,
> Out of the mazes of the mind,
> Free me from symbols, from words
> That I may discover the signified:
> The word unspoken in the darkness
> That veils the ground of my being."
>   *Byzantine Hymn*

⚘ *from* Karen's Hospice Journal ⚘

My job now is to recognize new patterns and to die well. No, not well. Extravagantly. My purpose, as expressed by Stephen Jenkinson, the Canadian Algonquin healer who helps people get over their deathophobia, is to love the end. Not just accept my ending, but to love it! With great gratitude. After I have said everything I have left to say, I will remember that the only thing left to say is "I love you."

As I view my planet now from my upstairs hospice room, sharper colors outline the mountains in the distance. Two words come to mind: intensity and perfection. I look up and notice more magnificently tinged clouds. Stars pepper the night sky, and the labyrinthine Milky Way that will undergird my passage becomes a scarf of light. This same sky has been hanging over my head for seventy-three years but now I can finally see it. Everything is mystery! It's all so much more than I thought. All this is not easy, but it is, at some mysterious level, perfect.

A Final Story

by John Speerstra, Karen's Husband

Karen said, "I want to go." My band was to play on the last Sunday in October for our director's ninetieth birthday. We went. I found a parking spot right by the door. By this time Karen was walking very slowly with a cane in her right hand and hanging on to my arm with the other. She sat with Shelie, our pastoral care minister, and ate a little chocolate cake. Karen was vibrant and happy. After two hours we returned home. I lifted each of her legs in succession to the next stair tread in order for her to get back up to our bedroom.

A walker soon replaced Karen's cane, followed closely by a hospital bed brought in by the hospice people. But not before her legs refused to support her one evening and she sat down on the floor behind the walker. We could have called for EMT help. I called Sue and Maureen instead. Two semiretired operating-room nurses from a little way down our hill, they came quickly and with all the right moves put Karen safely and lovingly into her bed. Good neighbors, a solid community: priceless.

Our son Nathan arrived from Colorado on the second Sunday in November. Jonna, Karen's good friend and palliative care doctor, called our older son, Joel, in Sweden and told him to come as soon as possible, and not to wait until Wednesday as planned. He came the next day. Very weak by now, Karen looked up and said, "Hi, sweetie." Shelie came that evening and performed the ritual for Commendation of the Dying with scented oils. Just before we started, one of Karen's last clear words was "Music?" with an imperceptibly arched eyebrow, as if to say "Come on guys, haven't you read that chapter?" After a frantic and frankly comical few moments of our diving for CD players and juggling CDs in the air, Hildegard of Bingen filled the room and Karen's collection of her music continued to play until she passed.

The three Speerstra men took over Karen's care. We did all the tasks through the night that a home health aide would have done. Karen's systems had begun to shut down and she died the next afternoon while we held her hands and talked to her. For the last thirty minutes of her life, every exhaled breath was a vocalization, a last song in a life full of singing. Jonna arrived five minutes before Karen took her last breath.

In the next steps, we were all sustained by the framework of ritual. Sherri, our hospice nurse, along with Jonna and Joel, washed and dressed Karen's body. Karen already had made a mock-up of the Order of Service program for her funeral. Nathan and I prepared the place in the cemetery where the container for her ashes would be buried. Joel and our church organist, Kathy Hartman, rehearsed the musicians: a choir, flutes, recorder, a vocal duet, piano, organ, and not least of all a trumpet for the last verse of the final hymn. The Reverend Angela Emerson gave the best funeral sermon, some said, that they had ever heard. Herbert's daughter Joy gave a reading about boats and a passage from the end of this book, and Laura Baring-Gould, whose small bronze boat sculpture had ridden on the covers of Karen's bed, passed that boat to everyone at the service, inviting all to breathe a word into it before we placed it in the box with her. One friend wrote later: "It was Laura who, in a few elegant words, rescued the boat from being a symbol of individual journey to becoming an icon of shared life in the spirit. By the time we had all finished breathing into the boat, I suspect that no one there doubted that we are all in it together, in the business of living and dying, and that our own life and death are linked together with Karen's in love."

We gathered for the committal at the cemetery out in the country at Old Christ Church in warm, golden sunshine. It proved to be the last perfect day of autumn in Vermont. Karen's friend Sharon, along with our granddaughter, Josie, sprinkled flower petals into the grave. People left reluctantly.

Joel and Nathan filled in their mom's grave and then joined the rest of us for good food and reminiscences of a life well lived and a grace-filled death. That was Karen.

FROM THE PUBLISHER

I met Karen Speerstra many decades ago when I was just starting out as a publisher. Now I see how her presence "book-ended" and informed my adult life.

In the early '80s she managed a large publishing house. We competed for the same market but she never saw it that way. Instead, she shared information and suggested ways we could work together. This was one of the most important things I would learn from her and became the hallmark of how we operate today.

She was full of ideas and knew how to listen in such a way that it made my ideas bigger and more relevant. There would be a spark in her eye and the hint of a smile. This was her way of empowering everyone around her.

A few years later, she sat captivated when I told her about the film I was making on dolphin communication and it was then that we discovered we shared many spiritual interests. So it was natural, when my wife Geraldine and I were launching Divine Arts, that Karen would be our first stop.

How right we were! She guided manuscripts our way, evaluated submissions, copyedited, wrote a blog for the website, and penned three books for us (*Sophia: The Feminine Face of God, Color: The Language of Light,* and *The Divine Art of Dying*). She was the heart of Divine Arts.

It seems like just a few days ago that she pitched us on *The Divine Art of Dying*. She said she didn't know if she would live to finish it but trusted that her writing partner, Herbert Anderson, would carry on. But she surprised us all. In a very few months, despite her failing condition, she delivered the full manuscript! We joked about how fast she wrote. Perhaps she could still deliver another book?

Not long before she died, she appeared to me in a dream. "Karen, what are you doing here?" She said, "Testing." It seemed as if she were testing to see if we could communicate in dreams after she passed over. It gave me comfort knowing that her great light, held in the hearts of her family and friends, would never be extinguished. Her humor, her nonstop giving, her love and generosity is too big to get your arms around.

Here's to Karen — the Feminine Face of Light!

Michael Wiese, Publisher
Divine Arts

SELECTED BIBLIOGRAPHY

Albom, Mitch. *The Five People You Meet in Heaven*. New York: Hyperion, 2003.

Alexander, Eban. *Proof of Heaven*. New York: Simon & Schuster, 2012.

Anderson, Herbert, and Foley, Edward. *Mighty Stories, Dangerous Rituals*. San Francisco: Jossey-Bass Publishers, 1998.

Assante, Julia. *The Last Frontier: Exploring the Afterlife and Transforming Our Fear of Death*. Novato, CA: New World Library, 2012.

Atwater, P. M. H. *Beyond the Light*. Carol Publishing, 1994.

Autry, James A. *Choosing Gratitude*. Macon, GA: Smyth & Helwys, 2012.

Avram, Wes. *Discerning God in Everyday Life*. Grand Rapids, MI: Brazos Press, 2005.

Bateson, Catherine. *Peripheral Visions*. New York: HarperCollins, 1994.

Becker, Ernest. *The Denial of Death*. New York: The Free Press, 1973.

Berry, Wendell. *Jayber Crow*. Washington, DC: Counterpoint, 2000.

Bourgeault, Cynthia. *The Wisdom Jesus*. Boston: Shambhala, 2008.

Brauer-Rieke, Gretchen. *In Advance: A practical guide to making your own end-of-life health care decisions*. Oregon Edition, Second Edition, 2012.

Brennert, Alan. *Molok 'I*. New York: St. Martin's, 2003.

Brody, Jane. "When the Only Hope Is a Peaceful Ending." *New York Times*, March 10, 2010.

Brown, Judy. *The Choice: Seasons of Loss and Renewal After a Father's Decision to Die*. Conari Press, Berkeley, CA, 1995.

Brunonia, Barry. *The Lace Reader*. New York: HarperCollins, 2006.

Buechner, Frederick. *Godric*. New York: HarperCollins, 1980.

————. *Wishful Thinking: A Seeker's ABC*. New York: HarperOne, 1993.

Burt, Robert A. *Death Is That Man Taking Names.* Berkeley: University of California Press, 2002.

Butler, Katy. *Knocking On Heaven's Door: The Path to a Better Way of Death.* New York: Scribner, 2013.

Byock, Ira. *Dying Well: Peace and Possibilities at the End of Life.* New York: Riverhead Books, 1997.

———. *The Best Care Possible: A Physician's Quest to Transcend Care Through the End of Life.* New York: The Penguin Group, 2012.

———. *The Four Things That Matter Most: A Book About Living.* New York: The Free Press, 2004.

Campbell, Don. *The Mozart Effect.* New York: HarperCollins, 2001.

Casell, Eric J. *The Nature of Healing.* New York: Oxford, 2013.

de Saint Exupery, Antoine. *The Little Prince.* New York: Harcourt, 1968.

Elkins, David. *Beyond Religion.* Wheaton, IL: Quest Books, 1998.

Forster, E. M. *Howards End.* Mineola, NY: Dover, 2002.

Fox, Matthew and Sheldrake, Rupert. *Natural Grace.* New York: Doubleday, 1996.

Fuller, Robert C. *Wonder: From Emotion to Spirituality.* Chapel Hill, NC: University of North Carolina Press, 2006.

Gilman, Anne. *Doing Work You Love.* New York: McGraw Hill/ Contemporary, 1997.

Green, James W. *Beyond the Good Death: The Anthropology of Modern Dying.* Philadelphia: University of Pennsylvania Press, 2008.

Groopman, Jerome. *The Anatomy of Hope.* New York: Random House, 2005.

Gunderson, Gary, with Larry Pray. *The Leading Causes of Life.* Memphis: The Center of Excellence in Faith and Life, 2006.

Halifax, Joan. *Being With Dying.* Boston: Shambhala, 2008.

Hall, Douglas John. *Lighten Our Darkness: Toward an Indigenous Theology of the Cross.* Philadephia: The Westminster Press, 1976.

Halpern, Susan. *The Etiquette of Illness.* New York: Bloomsbury, 2004.

Keen, Sam. "Beyond Psychology: A Conversation with Ernest Becker," in *The Ernest Becker Reader*, ed. by Daniel Liechty, Seattle: The Ernest Becker Foundation, 2005.

L'Engle, Madeleine. *A Swiftly Tilting Planet.* New York: Square Fish, 1978.
————. *Walking on Water.* Wheaton, IL: Harold Shaw, 1980.

Lustbader, Wendy. *Counting on Kindness: The Dilemmas of Dependency.* New York: The Free Press, 1991.

MacEowen, Frank. *The Mist-Filled Path.* Novato, CA: New World Library, 2002.

Marty, Peter. "Letting Go." *The Lutheran.* July, 2013.

Matthiessen, Peter. *The Snow Leopard.* New York: Viking, 1978.

Mitchell, Kenneth R. & Anderson, Herbert. *All Our Losses, All Our Griefs.* Philadelphia: Westminster Press, 1983.

Moore, Thomas. *The Original Self.* New York: HarperCollins, 2000.

Nemerov, Howard. "Waiting Rooms," in *The Collected Poems of Howard Nemerov.* Chicago: University of Chicago Press, 1977.

Nouwen, Henri J. M. *Our Greatest Gift: A Meditation on Dying and Caring.* HarperSanFrancisco, 1994.

Nuland, Sherwin B. *How We Die: Reflections on Life's Final Chapter.* New York: Alfred A. Knopf, 1994.

O'Donohue, John. *Eternal Echoes.* New York: Harper Perennial, 2000.

Perlman, Eliot. *The Street Sweeper.* New York: Riverhead Books, 2012.

Rahner, Karl, trans. Charles H. Henkey, *On the Theology of Death*, New York: Herder and Herder, 1961.

Rauch, Jonathan. "How Not to Die." *The Atlantic*, April 24, 2013.

Rinpoche, Sogyal. *The Tibetan Book of Living and Dying.* New York: HarperOne, 2002.

Rosenthal, Ted. *How Could I Not Be Among You.* New York: George Braziller, 1973.

Rossetti, Stephen. *When the Lion Roars: A Primer for the Unsuspecting Mystic*. Notre Dame, IN: Ave Maria Press, 2003.

Schwalbe, Will. *The End of Your Life Book Club*. New York: Alfred A. Knopf, 2012.

Schwartz, Morrie. *Letting Go: Morrie's Reflections on Living While Dying*. New York: Walker and Company, 1996.

Sigmund, Barbara. *An Unfinished Life*. Princeton, NJ: Princeton Arts Council, 1990.

Smith, Doug. *The Tao of Dying*. Caring Publishing, 1998.

Stephans, James. *The Crock of Gold*. New York: Macmillan, 1956.

Stortz, Martha Ellen. "The School of Hope." *Santa Clara Magazine*, Winter 2006.

Tillich, Paul. "Loneliness and Solitude," in *The Eternal Now*. New York: Charles Scribner's Sons, 1963.

———. "Waiting," in *Shaking of the Foundations*. New York: Charles Scribner's Sons, 1948.

Tolstoy, Leo. *The Death of Ivan Ilych and Other Stories*. New York: Alfred A. Knopf, 2009.

Walker, Val. *The Art of Comforting*. New York: Penguin, 2012.

Walsch, Neal Donald. *Home with God: In a Life That Never Ends*. New York: Atria, 2006.

Wilbur, Ken. *Grace and Grit*. Boston: Shambhala, 2000.

About the Authors

After being diagnosed with ovarian cancer in 2003, KAREN SPEERSTRA published eight books, including *Color: The Language of Light* (Divine Arts), and *Sophia: The Feminine Face of God* (Divine Arts), which won the 2013 Nautilus Book Award Gold Medal in the Religion/Spirituality category. Previously, she worked as a freelance writer, writing numerous articles, children's religious curriculum, and poetry, spent ten years also writing weekly regional and national newspaper columns, and had been an executive in the college text and professional book publishing world. She and her husband, John, raised two sons, Joel and Nathan.

HERBERT ANDERSON is retired from a teaching career that began in Princeton and ended in Berkeley and spanned five decades. He lives in Sonoma, California. He is Professor Emeritus of Pastoral Theology at Catholic Theological Union in Chicago and was for three years Director of Pastoral Care at St. Mark's Episcopal Cathedral in Seattle, Washington. Anderson is a Lutheran pastor whose ecumenical spirit has been fostered by working in a variety of contexts. He is the author or coauthor of over ninety articles and thirteen books. *All Our Losses, All Our Griefs*, co-authored with Kenneth Mitchell, is generally regarded as a classic in grief literature.

DIVINE ARTS

Celebrating the sacred in everyday life

COLOR
The Language of Light

"Color is the language of light; it adorns the earth with beauty."
—John O'Donohue, *Beauty*

A unique look at all aspects of how color speaks to your soul, *Color* takes the reader through birth, darkness and light, auras, chakras, the rainbow, to the afterlife, exploring how artists use color, how we have "coded" colors for healing, and ultimately delves into the spirituality of color and mysticism.

Through illustrations and essays, this book explores how we can all read the marvelous language of light, heightening our awareness of the deep sense of beauty around us and within each living being, nurturing our imagination.

$18.95 · 270 PAGES · ORDER #COLOR · ISBN 9781611250183

SOPHIA — THE FEMININE FACE OF GOD
Nine Heart Paths to Healing and Abundance

WINNER
Nautilus
Gold Award
2013

Even as much of the world is increasingly challenged in the way of environmental disasters and a general lack of compassion, respect and love for the feminine is clearly growing. This book offers historical context, poetic meditations, and practical methods for integrating the power of "the Goddess" in your life at every level.

After centuries of "hiding," the Divine Feminine (a.k.a. Great Mother, Holy Spirit, Sophia) is showing herself again. She's aware of what we've been doing to our planet and to ourselves and offers her age-old but ever-new wisdom for spiritual growth and healing. Within the context of "spiritual memoir-essays," *Sophia —The Feminine Face of God* brings together the many faces of Sophia — historical, folklored, fairytaled — as well as stories of her mystical presence throughout different times and cultures. This book is about how Sophia enlightens, strengthens, and illuminates... how she calms and excites, befriends and nurtures.

$18.95 · 340 PAGES · ORDER #SOPHIA · ISBN 9781611250046

Divine Arts sprang to life fully formed as an intention to bring spiritual practice into daily life.

Human beings are far more than the one-dimensional creatures perceived by most of humanity and held static in consensus reality. There is a deep and vast body of knowledge — both ancient and emerging — that informs and gives us the understanding, through direct experience, that we are magnificent creatures occupying many dimensions with untold powers and connectedness to all that is.

Divine Arts books and films explore these realms, powers, and teachings through inspiring, informative, and empowering works by pioneers, artists, and great teachers from all the wisdom traditions. We invite your participation and look forward to learning how we may serve you.

Onward and upward,
Michael Wiese, Publisher